ANGER: THE WORM IN MY APPLE

ANGER: THE WORM IN MY APPLE

Destroying the Rotten Fruit of Anger; Harvesting the Tasty Fruit of the Spirit

With Small Group and Personal Study Guide

Dr. James M. Cecy

JARON
MINISTRIES
INTERNATIONAL

ISBN 978-0-9969556-6-9 PAPERBACK
ISBN 978-0-9969556-7-6 eBOOK
Library of Congress Control Number: 2017954585

Unless otherwise noted, Scriptures taken from the NEW AMERICAN STANDARD BIBLE (NASB), Copyright © 1960, 1962, 1963, 1968, 1971, 1972, 1973, 1975, 1977, 1995 by THE LOCKMAN FOUNDATION. A Corporation Not for Profit, LA HABRA, CA. All Rights Reserved. Used by permission. http://www.lockman.org.

Transliterations of all Greek and Hebrew words were taken from a variety of sources such as *The Exhaustive Concordance of the Bible* by James Strong, *An Expository Dictionary of New Testament Words* by W.E. Vine, *An Expository Dictionary of Old Testament Words* by F.F. Bruce, and the author's preferred transliterations to allow for ease of pronunciation.

Portions of this book are adapted from a variety of Dr. Cecy's audio, video, and written publications, including *The Emotions: God's Energizers* (1998), *Anger: The Worm in My Apple* (1998), *Connected to the Vine* (2006), *The Fruit of the Spirit-Filled Life* (2010) and *Wise Living in a Foolish Age: Studies in the Book of Proverbs* (1976, 1996, and 2010).

For further information about media and live seminars, contact:

JARON Ministries International, Inc.
4710 N Maple Ave, Fresno, CA. 93726   (559) 227-7997

JARON is a registered non-profit organization (501c3) in the State of California.

JARON Ministries website: www.jaron.org
Dr. Cecy's website: www.puritywar.com
Campus Bible Church website: www.campusbiblechurch.com

Published by JARON Ministries International, Inc.
Printed in the United States of America

DEDICATION

I owe my interest in a biblical understanding of the human emotions to Dr. Dennis Guernsey, one of my professors at Talbot Theological Seminary. He is now in heaven enjoying the full spectrum of emotions in the presence of Jesus. Sadly, I never got to thank him for providing me a framework for counseling others these past four decades. May this book, which contains some of what he taught me long ago, be a legacy to his ongoing influence in my life, personally and professionally.

My thanks also to the gardeners, farmers, ranchers, botanists and agronomists God has brought into my life, especially Jan Holcomb-Weddington. Their deep love for God's creative power helped this ill-equipped city boy attempt to write a book where the running analogy and primary metaphor is, surprisingly, agricultural.

I am blessed to have taught much of this material to congregations of people at home and around the globe. Throughout the years many of these precious folks have provided their Scriptural insights and life experiences that have given me the confidence to believe these principles work for all of my fellow inhabitants of *terra firma*.

Although thanks are due the many who reviewed this manuscript at various stages, I especially want to acknowledge the tireless hours my ministry associate, Don Neufeld, dedicated to battling computer glitches, format changes and my constant revisions. Throughout this project, he was truly an example to me of one who is walking in the Spirit and harvesting the sweet fruit—especially patience and self-control.

As always, I am grateful to my immediate and extended family. Their love and support have provided me the soil in which to grow from being an angry young teenager to, I trust, a more love-filled, joy-filled and peace-filled older man.

Finally, I dedicate this book to my Lord and Savior, Jesus Christ, who "redeemed my life from the pit" (Psalm 103:4). May He be pleased to use this book to bring spiritual, emotional and physical health to many generations.

CONTENTS

PART TWO:
HARVESTING THE TASTY FRUIT OF THE SPIRIT

APPENDIX

PREFACE

A PERSONAL WORD OF TESTIMONY

THE HARVEST OF GENERATIONAL CHAOS

When my father died of a sudden heart attack, I was just nineteen. I was angry. Angry at both of us for the cruel things we said to each other the night before. Angry at him for dying before we could get it resolved. Angry at God, who I felt had deserted our already fragmented family. I began running inwardly because I had no place to run outwardly. On the outside I was numb. Some, including myself, saw it as indifference. I simply went on with the rest of my life. Or so I thought.

As a young man I could see that, in many ways, I was truly like my angry father. I did not lash out physically, as he sometimes did, but I used many devices to get my own way. Small in stature, I soon learned to use my ungodly mouth as a tool of vengeance. I cussed at people like a sailor (By the way, I was one!). I lied, manipulated everyone within reach, and punished others from a distance. When angry, I simply got even and smiled while doing it. At one point, my abusive treatment of others resulted in a Navy shipmate putting a cheap contract out on my life. He paid to have me killed for $20 worth of Philippine pesos. (Obviously, he had anger issues, too!)

Where did my insidious forms of ungodly anger come from? My sin nature? Of course! The devil, the flesh and the world? Absolutely! But I have since learned that my "family of origin"— going back for generations—was the soil in which my own fleshly, devilish and worldly anger grew. Although my family history is sketchy, as most are, the more I discovered about my family, the more I recognized my childhood home was a reflection of the home in which my father, and his father before him, lived. It was clear; I came from a long line of angry people.

I have been told that in my family tree is an infamous gangster by the name of Alfonse Capone, my cousin through my great-grandmother on my father's side. I doubt if I need to elaborate on his life of crime. He was known to have said, "You get a lot more done with a kind word and a gun than a kind word." That was the code by which he lived and many suffered from his poisonous wrath.

Throughout his life his explosive anger was expressed in ways too cruel to mention. (He did not get the scar on his face at a Bible study!) His use of a baseball bat to crack skulls has become fodder for movies and crime novels.

One of the saddest moments of my ministry was when I was preaching at a leadership conference in the Chicago area and an older lady came to me and said, "Your cousin killed my uncle." Although I was not to blame, I felt disgusted that the blood of Capone ran through my veins. So did his anger, though certainly expressed quite differently.

Then there was my grandfather, Big Al's first cousin. As far as I understand, he was not known for his outbursts of anger. He was, however, remembered by some for his passive-aggression and tendency to withdraw from others, including his children, especially after his wife, my grandmother, died.

I have been able to piece together at least some of what may have formed the basis of my grandfather's repressed forms of anger. My grandfather's father died very soon after my grandfather was born. His mother married a man who was openly disappointed in my grandfather. This angry step-father eventually sent my grandfather to America with just $12 in his pocket. Some say my grandfather left by choice. What is known is that his family ties were severed. My grandfather was forever the outcast of the family in Italy. In fact, many in Italy denied his existence.

I am told that years later my step-great-grandfather attempted to contact his step-son, only to be spurned by my still angry and rejected grandfather. My grandfather had moved to Toronto, Canada, where he suffered the intense racial prejudice and physical attacks many Italian immigrants of his day experienced. In spite of the many obstacles, he grew a thriving and lucrative construction business, only to have it demolished during the Great Depression. These experiences became the soil in which my father and his siblings grew.

My father was a pre-teenager at the time his mother died and, along with his siblings, was raised by his older sister. In the midst of the ostracism he faced as a young Italian, my father also became the often-needed protector of his father and siblings, especially the two who were disabled. Street-fighting became a way of life for him. Sadly, that tendency toward physical violence was even directed toward one of his brothers, who passed away from a heart attack at the age of thirty-one, very soon after a fist-fight with my father.

In his later years, my father was able to keep his anger under some control. In fact, he was loved and respected by many for his intelligence and generosity to strangers. I witnessed, however, occasions where his childish anger got the best of him. His verbal and physical abuse was directed toward my mother, eventually my step-mother, and sometimes to me. Though he was often remorseful, he was also quite unpredictable. Of course, my propensity to unwisely speak my mind fueled the rage. I pushed his "anger button" often!

Until the day of his death at age forty-nine, my father's life was a barrage of unresolved hurts, frustrated expectations, failed pursuits and broken relationships. I rarely saw him happy. Although I know it to not be clinically correct, I have often expressed that my father died of anger. He was not alone in his rage.

One of my able-bodied uncles, my father's younger brother, was especially renowned for his anger and life of crime. Some family members suspect "Uncle Crook," who spent time in the penitentiary, was also involved in murder. No one knows for sure but few of us would be surprised if it were true. I was a witness to his volatility.

As a young teenager, I was in a car with my visiting uncle as he got in a minor altercation with another driver and his very large son. My uncle sent me running to my house to get his bodyguard, who strapped on a gun, just to help my uncle settle the argument. I wondered what kind of man would bring an armed bodyguard to a traffic dispute! He, too, died a miserable and angry man.

Moving on to my generation, the legacy of anger prevailed. One of my cousins, whose father had died after fighting with my father, grew to become widely known in the community as volatile, violent, and extremely dangerous. Just before he went to jail the last time, he was given a preliminary diagnosis as a sociopath. He was involved in a number of criminal activities and, at the age of thirty, died in a high-speed chase, running from the police.

Where did my cousin learn this? I suspect partly from his father, my uncle, whose anger was also well-known behind the closed doors of his life. Where did my uncle and my father learn this? From our grandfather. Where did our grandfather learn this? From his step-father, our step-great-grandfather. Now we are talking about four generations of chaos and conflict!

THE HARVEST OF GENERATIONAL PEACE

Folks, I was the angry little boy who lived in the shade of those angry people. And the generational anger showed up early in my life—in abusive speech, passive-aggressive attitudes and ungodly behaviors. But, by the grace and mercy of God, the little boy in the shadow emerged a very different young man—full of peace with God, himself and others. For this I have the indwelling Holy Spirit of God to thank. Jesus Christ truly transformed my heart and my behaviors. Trusting Him alone for my salvation at the age of twenty-one was the single most important event of my life, not only spiritually but emotionally.

Yes, my life changed. Not immediately, of course. But now at the age of sixty-seven, I can honestly say that if I were told I was going to die very soon, I know of no one with whom I am angry and in need of immediate reconciliation. To date, I know of no one who would want me dead—though I sometimes wonder if that fellow sailor, even after forty-five years, is still waiting for his twenty dollar contract to be finalized!

What about the fifth generation—my children? Or the sixth generation—my grandchildren? As troubling as my family history might be, I know I am not responsible for my ancestors. I can, however, influence my descendants. Yes, I still get angry, sometimes at my children and grandchildren, but mostly at the dog and cat. But those precious kids and those silly pets are so forgiving. Lately, I have even been reduced to pray, "Lord, help me to be the kind of person my wife's cat and dog think I am and my family needs me to be." It's all quite humbling.

In some parts of Italy, I'm told, there is a practice of throwing things out the window on New Year's Eve, especially those things that troubled you most in the last year. I suppose one could enjoy the tradition, even using the occasion to toss out the dog and the cat. But there are more substantive things I need to cast out of my life. I need to continue to throw out the rotten fruit of my anger and seek to harvest the tasty fruit of the indwelling Holy Spirit, the One who came into my life when I trusted in Jesus Christ as a young man. That is one of the reasons I wrote this book.

The content of this book is not primarily professional, though I pray the academic side will give you confidence in its biblical authority. This book is not mainly anecdotal, though I hope the agriculture analogies will give you some food for thought and a few laughs, even in the midst of the painful realities of the consequence of our sinful anger. This book is largely personal. Its message is for me. Hopefully, it will help others, as well.

One of my life goals is simply stated and deeply felt. Someday, when I am long gone, and someone says to my children and my grandchildren that they are just like me, I hope they will stick out their chest with pride and not their tongue in disgust. My greater goal is that the prayer of the apostle Paul would come true in the generations to follow:

> Now may the God of peace Himself sanctify you entirely; and may your spirit and soul and body be preserved complete, without blame at the coming of our Lord Jesus Christ (1 Thessalonians 5:23).

I do earnestly pray that the fruit of my life falls from a godly tree, and my family enjoys an amazing harvest of generational peace. May that be true in your family, as well—one day and one life at a time, Sweet Jesus!

Soli Deo Gloria! To God alone be all the glory!

Dr. Jim Cecy
Fresno, CA.

INTRODUCTION

ANGER: THE FRUIT- DESTROYER

Two thousand years ago, the apostle Paul described the ever-increasing rage we will witness on the world scene, as the end times unfold, prior to the return of Jesus Christ: "But realize this, that in the last days difficult ["violent," Greek: *chalepos*] times will come" (2 Timothy 3:1). He continues by describing these violent days in detail:

> For men will be lovers of self, lovers of money, boastful,
> arrogant, revilers, disobedient to parents, ungrateful, unholy,
> unloving, reconcilable, malicious gossips, without self-control,
> brutal, haters of good, treacherous, reckless, conceited, lovers of
> pleasure rather than lovers of God, holding to a form of
> godliness, although they have denied its power; Avoid such men
> as these (2 Timothy 3:2-5).

Much could be written about the ungodly fruit of each of these expressions of violence, played out one generation at a time. Unless we have been living in a bubble, we are all too familiar with the undeniable condition of our world:

- rampant violence in the workplace
- reckless road rage on our streets
- unreported domestic abuse in our homes
- cruel cyber-bullying among our youth
- wide-spread character assassination among our leaders
- senseless gang-related murders in our cities
- indiscriminate shootings and bombings around the world
- uncontrolled outbursts of anger in public places
- unimaginable treachery and brutality behind closed doors
- pointless arguments over anything and everything
- unrestrained anger in all of its many ungodly forms

We live in an angry world and, if he were alive today, the apostle Paul would be quick to add, "You haven't seen anything yet. It will get worse before it gets better."

But what about those everyday aggravations? Whereas, there are many books written for a certain segment of our society whose anger is completely out of control, this book is primarily focused on the everyday challenges of living in our anger-producing, wrath-inciting world. Living this side of heaven means we all need anger-management—even on the best of days.

Every November in America, we celebrate a holiday we dare to call *Thanksgiving*. But it is not always so pleasant. Picture this scene: We are seated at a large table. Before us lies a magnificently prepared feast of all our favorite holiday foods. We bow our heads to ask the Lord's blessing and to give sincere thanks for His abundant goodness. It's a photo moment.

We sense a commotion and open our eyes slightly to witness the children throwing food at one another. We lift our heads to find Grandmother with a glob of mashed potatoes, including brown gravy, hanging from her silver-gray hair! We are confronted with the obvious: "Where there is no peace, there is no feast."

Later in the day, we sit down to watch a football game. Our favorite team is playing against their greatest rival. The score is tied with only a few seconds left in the game. Our team has the ball and is on the move. Suddenly, one of our nephews grabs the remote control and switches the television channel. The dictionary is quite rich in words to describe how we might be feeling at both of these moments:

• annoyed	• antagonistic	• bitter	• burning
• cross	• dangerous	• deadly	• exasperated
• fed-up	• ferocious	• fired up	• frustrated
• furious	• griped	• hostile	• hurt
• indignant	• irked	• irritated	• livid
• mad	• peeved	• provoked	• savage
• sick	• seething	• sore	• troubled

And there went Thanksgiving! Following it went the fruit of the Holy Spirit in our lives: love, joy, peace, patience, kindness, goodness, faithfulness, gentleness and self-control (Galatians 5:22-23). Anger can truly be a fruit-destroying invader.

I once read the following dictionary definition: "Anger is a strong emotion of displeasure." That certainly seems to fall short, doesn't it? Somehow when we are ready to explode—to pound on a table or punch a wall, it hardly captures our feelings. When we are angry, our conscience doesn't whisper in our minds, *"I am experiencing a strong emotion of displeasure."* No! It is shouting in our heart of hearts, *"I am really angry, furious, livid and at the boiling point!"*

Don't minimize our feelings with definitions that lack pathos. Don't euphemize our anger with innocuous words. Call it what it is—an all-consuming, intense emotion. We get it. And sadly, those around us also get it. We need to understand, on a deeper level, what we are feeling and why. We need real-life solutions; not just shallow definitions and statements of the obvious. We need help and we need it today!

Part One, with its fourteen chapters, will provide us the tools to identify the positive aspects of anger as a God-given emotion and will provide a biblical strategy to seek and destroy the rotten fruit of anger in our lives. Part Two, with its eleven chapters, will present the ultimate solution—walking in the power of the indwelling Holy Spirit of God. In doing so, we not only deal with the deeds of the flesh, but we will harvest the cornucopia of the tasty fruit of the Spirit, one day at a time. Following each chapter is a section of questions titled *Inspecting the Fruit,* along with an assignment for additional study called *Further Advice from the Master Gardener.*

I present all of this not just to deal with our anger daily and to help heal our broken earthly relationships, but to bring true and lasting peace—a double serving of *shalom*—in our relationship to God, Our Heavenly Father. Where there is <u>His peace</u>, there is a <u>lasting feast</u>—a life of thanksgiving.

> Let the peace of Christ rule in your hearts, to which indeed you were called in one body; and be *thankful.* Let the word of Christ richly dwell within you, with all wisdom teaching and admonishing one another with psalms and hymns and spiritual songs, singing with *thankfulness* in your hearts to God. Whatever you do in word or deed, do all in the name of the Lord Jesus, giving *thanks* through Him to God the Father (Colossians 3:15-17, emphasis added).

PART ONE

DESTROYING THE
ROTTEN FRUIT OF ANGER

CHAPTER ONE

ROTTEN TO THE CORE

"But the things that proceed out of the mouth come from the heart, and those defile the man. For out of the heart come evil thoughts, murders, adulteries, fornications, thefts, false witness, slanders. These are the things which defile the man . . ." (The words of Jesus recorded in Matthew 15:18-20)

I was blessed to have an apartment-dwelling mother who knew nothing about growing fruit and everything about enjoying it. So, it was not unusual for me, a week after her death, to plant an apple tree in my backyard as a tribute to her fruitful life. In fact, to this day we call it the Nanny Tree. Like my mother, I also grew up in the city. I knew little about apple trees, other than enjoying their fruit, some of which I stole from neighbors' trees or the corner store. (But that's another story.)

My first harvest of the Nanny Tree proved disappointing. The fruit was substantial, but most of the apples were marked with little brown circles. My inexperience did not prepare me for that first disgusting bite, as I bit into a worm. I came to learn for myself what most fruit-growers know: The only thing worse than finding a worm in an apple is finding half a worm!

I asked a friend, who is an expert in field crop production, to tell me about my rotting apples. She quickly diagnosed the problem. "It's Codling Moth." At first I thought she said "Cuddling Moth," but there is nothing cuddly about this little critter. Its Latin name, she explained, is *Cydia pomonella*. Even that sounds like something you might name a pet. But this moth is evil to the core (pun intended). It is found almost worldwide and brutally attacks pears, walnuts and other fruit trees. Those Mama Moths had the gall to lay their tiny eggs on the surface of my apples—you know, the ones I dedicated to my deceased mother!

Their baby larvae burrowed their way from the surface to the core. Those little creatures ate away at my mother's apples until they grew to just shy of an inch in length. Then, like ungrateful teenagers, they decided to leave home and dig their way out. Like all spoiled children, they left a rotting mess behind. I also expect they left the nest and grew up to become pupae, entering the cocoon stage where they emerged looking and acting just like their insect parents—those apple-destroying pests!

Since I had not treated my apple tree with pest control products before Mama Moth and her Evil Sisters landed, there was really nothing I could do. Once the larvae started destroying, it was a done deal. I was doomed to have wormy apples. I had no one to blame but my own ignorance and negligence.

This season, however, I am prepared. That is why God brought into my life farmer-friends who know what creepy-crawler products are safe and effective. My backyard has turned into a battleground, with me as the Codling Moth Terminator.

What does all this have to do with anger? After over four decades of pastoral ministry I have observed that few things destroy the fruit of a Christian's testimony more than unrighteous anger. In fact, it is a major problem even among "peace-loving" Christians. Many of my friends in ministry agree with my observation that a great majority of our pastoral counseling situations are rooted in some form of ungodly anger. One cannot argue that anger truly is the worm eating away at the fruitfulness of many believers' lives.

Once the invasion force of unrighteous anger, in its many forms, lands on the outer skin of our unprepared and unprotected hearts, it burrows its way to our core, joins the corrupted seed already there, until it grows and emerges as an army of fruit-destroying pests in our lives and the lives of others. It's time to face these head-on, beginning with a close-up look at the enemy. We will then develop a strategy to seek and destroy them. I assure you; it is not going to be a pretty sight. Victory, however, will taste so sweet!

INSPECTING THE FRUIT

1. In what area is anger eating away at your faithfulness?

   At home? What do you hope to see change?

   At school? What do you hope to see change?

   At work? What do you hope to see change?

   Other? _____ What do you hope to see change?

2. Read Ephesians 2:1-10 below. Underline the key differences between what life is like for an unbeliever, and what life is like as a follower of Jesus Christ.

   My Life as an Unbeliever

   And you were dead in your trespasses and sins, in which you formerly walked according to the course of this world, according to the prince of the power of the air, of the spirit that is now working in the sons of disobedience. Among them we too all formerly lived in the lusts of our flesh, indulging the desires of the flesh and of the mind, and were by nature children of wrath, even as the rest (Ephesians 2:1-3).

   My Life as a Believer

   But God, being rich in mercy, because of His great love with which He loved us, even when we were dead in our transgressions, made us alive together with Christ (by grace you have been saved), and raised us up with Him, and seated us with Him in the heavenly places in Christ Jesus, so that in the ages to come He might show the surpassing riches of His grace in kindness toward us in Christ Jesus. For by grace you have been saved through faith; and that not of yourselves, it is the gift of God; not as a result of works, so that no one may boast. For we are His workmanship, created in Christ Jesus for good works, which God prepared beforehand so that we would walk in them (Ephesians 2:1-10).

FURTHER ADVICE FROM THE MASTER GARDENER

Read Galatians, Chapters 5-6. Write out three key verses:

_____

_____

_____

_____

_____

_____

_____

_____

_____

_____

_____

_____

_____

_____

_____

_____

_____

CHAPTER TWO

THE ABCs OF
HARVESTING ANGER

I grew up in Canada and moved to the United States when I was eleven. Although many think America and Canada speak the same language, I quickly learned to adjust my childhood alphabet so as to not be laughed at for pronouncing the American *zee* with the Canadian *zed.* Alphabets are nifty tools, not just for linguistics, but for making lists.

Let's begin with a list of some important presuppositions concerning the emotions, especially the emotion of anger. In deference to those of you green-thumbed, farmer-types who enjoy using impressive agricultural words, feel free to call them *The Fundamentals of Emotional Pomology and Spiritual Fruit-Growing.* I am going back to basics and choosing to call them *The ABCs of Harvesting Anger,* as we consider a practical theology of the emotions.

A. THE EMOTION OF ANGER WAS CREATED BY ALMIGHTY GOD.

Many treat the emotions as part of our human weakness. We've been taught to think the emotional side of being human is our worst feature. On the popular television and movie series, Star Trek, one of the characters was a half-human, half-Vulcan named Mr. Spock. He was constantly fighting off his human side because it was, in his thinking, too emotional and therefore, illogical.

We really do have many who feel this way about the emotions. Why else do we hear people sometimes say in an accusing way, "You're so emotional!" as if to say, "You're such a weakling!" But when Almighty God created humans with intellect, will and emotion,

7

He said "It is good" (Genesis 1:4). In fact, when speaking of everything He created, He said, "It is *very* good" (Genesis 1:31, emphasis added). Therefore, I am convinced we have no right to say otherwise.

I have been challenged for decades by the heart-searching words of one of my favorite writers, A.W. Tozer, who spoke of the essence of idolatry as the entertainment of thoughts about God that are unworthy of Him. My goal is to have us say, as a form of God-honoring worship, "Thank you, Heavenly Father, for my emotions." As fully human and emotional beings, I would want us to express with King David: "I will give thanks to You, for I am fearfully and wonderfully made" (Psalm 139:14). As we are about to see, we were made by an all-wise, all-knowing, all-loving God to get angry, the way He designed us to get angry! On to letter B.

B. THE EMOTION OF ANGER WAS CREATED BY ALMIGHTY GOD FOR A PURPOSE.

Our Creator doesn't do anything without a divine purpose. Why then did He give us emotions such as fear, love, loneliness, jealousy, anger and a host of others? Very simply stated, He gave them to us to generate energy within us to do something. Our English word *emotion* comes from the Latin word *emotio* which means to move out! That's what the emotions do. They move us out. They motivate us. They stimulate us!

In Albert Einstein's famous scientific formula, the symbol "E" in the formula $E=MC^2$ represents energy. I find this to be a helpful reminder when it comes to understanding God's design for our emotions. Energy plus motion equals emotion. The emotions truly are God's energizers! Let's consider a few of the many human emotions in this light:

- **The God-given emotion of fear** generates energy to respond to power—to run from danger and run to safety. It also motivates us to worship ["to run to," Greek: *phobeo*] Almighty God.

- **The God-given emotion of love** generates energy for self-sacrifice and service. It also stimulates us to obey God and to submit to biblically-ordained authorities in our lives.

- **The God-given emotion of loneliness** generates energy to find fulfillment in intimate relationships with God, a spouse, and others. It was also designed by our Creator to eradicate our sinful self-pity and self-fulfillment.

- **The God-given emotion of jealousy**—the same Hebrew and Greek words for *zeal*—generates energy to protect righteous standards and to imitate godly behavior. It also controls our sinful desire to have what others possess and moves us to imitate their positive qualities.

Without the emotions we would be lifeless blobs, having no desire or motivation. We would be nothing but a few reflexes to identify us as being alive. Does God want us to be emotional creatures? Absolutely. Imagine heaven's celebration without emotion. Imagine seeing Jesus without the ability to respond in adoration. Imagine life without the powerful energy the emotions produce.

Almighty God created us to be emotional, but He also created us to be emotionally sound, emotionally healthy and emotionally in control. On his deathbed, Jacob (also called Israel), assembled his sons to bestow on them a blessing appropriate to each one's unique personality (Genesis 49:28). He spoke of Reuben, his firstborn, as "uncontrolled as water" (Genesis 49:3). That is not quite the blessing we would expect from our dying father, but it was nonetheless true. I am reminded of the ancient wisdom of King Solomon: "Like a city that is broken into and without walls is a man who has no control over his spirit" (Proverbs 25:28). Like an unfortified city, susceptible to all kinds of attacks, is someone who is emotionally out of control.

What then is the God-intended purpose for the emotion of anger? Very simply, anger generates energy to make changes. We were made by God to get angry at our children's disobedience as the emotion of anger generates energy to make appropriate changes in their lives. We were made to be angry at injustice and have the emotion motivate us to promote just laws. Too often we have allowed evil to flourish in the world because we have not been angry enough about it. It was this God-given emotion of anger the apostle Paul talks about when he commands: "Be angry, and yet do not sin; do not let the sun go down on your anger, and do not give the devil an opportunity" (Ephesians 4:26-27).

Here we find four imperatives—four lifestyle commands. They are not suggestions!

Lifestyle Command #1: "Be angry . . ." (Greek: *orgizethe*)

Lifestyle Command #2: "do not sin . . ." (Greek: *hamartanete*)

Lifestyle Command #3: "do not let (Greek: *epidueto*) the sun set on your anger . . ."

Lifestyle Command #4: "do not give (Greek: *didote*) the devil an opportunity."

Let me paraphrase. The apostle Paul is commanding us to keep on getting angry at the right things and to make sure we continually express anger in a righteous way. He is urging us to never let the day end with unrighteous anger in our hearts and to not give the devil an open door into our lives (and the lives of those around us) by allowing unresolved anger to fester. Those are imperatives we all need to heed daily.

I am thankful for the God-given emotion of anger in my life. It has stimulated me to stay the course in correcting my children, guiding my foster-children and now maintaining biblical standards for over a dozen grandchildren (The number keeps growing). It has moved me to speak and write publicly against sin and antagonism towards God's holy standards. It is also the emotion that keeps me on the treadmill when I look, in anger, at the scale!

Unfortunately, as is often the case, we humans take that which God created for good and misuse, abuse and confuse it. So it is with the emotion of anger. The misuse of the emotion of anger, as well as jealousy, drove Cain to kill his brother—to *change* him from being alive to being dead (Genesis 4:3-15; 1 John 3:11-12).

Although we may never have killed, our sinful anger has most certainly driven us to act like raging fools. In fact, it is one of the clearest demonstrations of our foolishness: "Do not be eager ["terrified and fearful," Hebrew: *bahal*] in your heart to be angry, *for anger resides in the bosom of fools*" (Ecclesiastes 7:9, emphasis added). On to letter C.

C. THE EMOTION OF ANGER IS NEITHER RIGHT NOR WRONG, GOOD NOR BAD.

In general, the rightness or the wrongness of an emotion depends on two issues: the object of the emotion and how it is expressed. Whereas God created anger to generate energy to make appropriate changes, we have turned it into an excuse for lashing out and hurting others, ourselves, and even trying to hurt God. This is what is meant when James, the brother of our Lord, writes, "for the anger of man does not achieve the righteousness of God" (James 1:20).

Later, we will spend a great deal of time learning how to understand and deal with unrighteous anger, the kind of anger that is destroying our effectiveness as Christians. Being angry at the unrighteousness and sin in our own lives or in the lives of others is right. To use it, however, as an excuse to abuse or mistreat others violates its God-intended purpose. Also, the rightness or the wrongness of the emotion of anger depends not only on the object of the emotion, but the manner in which the anger is expressed. A student's anger at being bullied stimulates him to bring a kitchen knife to school. His anger—his God-given desire to *change* the situation—is understandable. But his ungodly plan for making that change is not.

So that's the simple ABCs of it all. The emotion of anger was created by Almighty God, created for a purpose and is neither right, nor wrong, good nor bad. It depends on the object of our anger and how it is expressed.

In the words of the children's song: "*Now I know my ABCs . . .*" Now begins the life-long lesson in spelling out how to avoid ungodly anger and the rotten fruit it produces, while enjoying the abundant fruit of righteous anger.

INSPECTING THE FRUIT

1. In general, how were you raised to respond to your emotions?

Anger?

Fear?

Love?

Loneliness?

Jealousy?

Other emotions?

2. What was the toughest season of your life when you most struggled with dealing with your emotions?

3. What is your view concerning the following statements:

"Anger is rooted in fear." Agree   Disagree   Comment:

"Fear is rooted in anger." Agree   Disagree   Comment:

FURTHER ADVICE FROM THE MASTER GARDENER

Look in a concordance and write down a few verse references related to each of the following emotions.

Anger:

Fear:

Love:

Loneliness:

Jealousy:

CHAPTER THREE

IS IT OKAY TO SPREAD MY ANGER?

Let's think of the many forms of our anger as a variety of fruit laid out at a farmer's market. Some of it is healthy-looking; some of it doesn't quite look right. It is obviously rotten and unnoticed, or even hidden, by the farmer. Anyone who has placed healthy fruit next to a rotting piece of fruit knows the old axiom is true. Eventually, one bad apple will spoil the whole bunch.

When it comes to our own anger, most of us are ill-equipped fruit inspectors. Many of us grew up in homes where any kind of anger was seen as rotten fruit, even healthy anger. We lived in a family system with its unspoken rule: "Good kids don't get mad." Or do they?

I grew up in what can be more succinctly summarized as an angry home. Before I was six years old my father left my mother to care for six children by herself. Prior to his leaving, I recall the verbal and physical abuse she experienced from him. Five years later I moved to California to live with my father. In between a few periods of calm, there were the verbal and sometimes physical altercations, often stimulated by my pre-teen and teenage propensity to disrespectfully speak my mind. In other words, I was a really mouthy kid! I had learned well from my father the deadly art of relational warfare. Although I expressed my rage differently, I became very much like him. I now understand even my healthy anger had issues!

In 1971, at the age of twenty-one, I came to a saving knowledge of the Lord Jesus Christ, trusting in Him alone for my salvation. That began a life-long process of Holy Spirit-empowered transformation (often called sanctification), as He endeavored to change me—quite literally, to make me more like Jesus Christ, one day at a time (2 Corinthians 3:18). After forty-five years of marriage and four decades of being a pastor, parent, foster-parent, and now a grand-parent, I am assured by my parishioners and my family that I am not guilty of displaying the abusive anger around which I grew up. By God's grace, I can declare I am "a new creature; the old things passed away; behold new things have come." (2 Corinthians 5:17).

Of course, I have had and still have my own anger issues. It has just taken me years to understand that although I was not a screamer, yeller, biter, or kicker, I was, nonetheless, an angry man. I had grown up learning to be more internal in my rage. I had become a master at masking my emotions in more inward, passive-aggressive responses. It took quite some time to understand it is really okay to get angry—the right way.

DOESN'T GOD GET ANGRY AT ANGRY PEOPLE?

If you had asked me prior to becoming a Bible student, I would have said, "Absolutely! Anger is always a sin." Now, after forty-five years of examining the Scriptures, I have a new answer. "Does God always get angry at angry people?" "Absolutely not!"   To suggest all anger is sinful would be to accuse God Himself of sin, for He is also an angry Person—albeit a Perfectly Angry Person. In other words, God has a righteous temper! Before you get angry with me, let me explain.

The Bible is filled with references about the fierce wrath of a Holy God (e.g. Revelation 19:15; etc.). In Romans 1:18 the apostle Paul speaks of God expressing His righteous anger toward ungodliness. In Mark 3:5, we find Jesus Christ angry and grieved at the hard-hearted crowd. In other gospel accounts we have the record of the sinless Son of God expressing His righteous indignation—His godly temper—at the people who were abusing the Holy Temple:

> And He [Jesus] found in the temple those who were selling oxen and sheep and doves, and the money changers seated at their tables. And He made a scourge of cords, and drove them all out of the temple, with the sheep and the oxen; and He poured out the coins of the money changers and overturned their tables; and to those who were selling the doves He said, 'Take these things away; stop making My Father's house a place of business.' His disciples remembered that it was written, 'ZEAL FOR YOUR HOUSE WILL CONSUME ME' (John 2:14-17).

Don't think for a minute Jesus did this in a gentle way. The Son of God, at times, was consumed with anger, divine zeal and godly jealousy. And it showed! This wood-cutting Nazarene carpenter (quite literally, a *tekton*, a rugged construction-worker) was certainly capable of getting their attention quickly.

Throughout biblical history the Bible also records God's people—patriarchs like Abraham and Moses, anointed kings like David, leaders like Nehemiah and prophets like Jeremiah—all expressing righteous anger God's way. It is this same kind of divine anger with which we are to make changes in our lives and in the lives of those around us. Once again, we heed the command of the apostle Paul: *"Be angry,* and yet do not sin; do not let the sun go down on your anger . . ."* (Ephesians 4:26, emphasis added).

We are commanded to get angry at the things that anger God, without it resulting in sin. Later, in the same passage the apostle Paul reminds us of one of the deeper spiritual results of choosing to express our God-given anger in an ungodly way: "Do not grieve ["offend, cause deep sorrow to," Greek: *lupeo*] the Holy Spirit . . . " (Ephesians 4:30).

RIGHTEOUS VS. UNRIGHTEOUS ANGER

We need not go far in Scripture to recognize there are many righteous expressions of anger illustrated and that serve as our example:

- God gets angry at those who disobey and reject Him (John 3:36; Hebrews 3:11; 4:3; 1 Thessalonians 2:16; Revelation 6:15-17; 16:19).

- Governments have been given the God-given authority to "bring wrath on those who practice evil" (Romans 13:14).

- Parents are commanded to discipline their children (Ephesians 6:1, 4; Colossians 3:20; Hebrews 12:9-11).

But how do we know the difference between righteous and unrighteous, godly and ungodly expressions of the emotion of anger? My friend, labeling something "righteous indignation" or "justifiable anger" doesn't necessarily make it righteous or justifiable. Nor does it make it godly. Again, I remind us of James' clear distinction: "for the anger of man does not achieve the righteousness of God" (James 1:20).

THE RIGHTEOUS ANGER OF JESUS

Twice in his three and a half years of public ministry, Jesus entered the Temple and demonstrated the holy wrath of God. We considered the earlier account in John 2:14-17. Now reflect on a similar encounter in the last week of His earthly life:

> Then they [Jesus and His disciples] came to Jerusalem. And He entered the temple and began to drive out those who were buying and selling in the temple, and overturned the tables of the money changers and the seats of those who were selling doves; and He would not permit anyone to carry merchandise through the temple. And He began to teach and say to them, "Is it not written, 'MY HOUSE SHALL BE CALLED A HOUSE OF PRAYER FOR ALL THE NATIONS'? But you have made it a ROBBERS DEN.' The chief priests and the scribes heard this, and began seeking how to destroy Him; for they were afraid of Him, for the whole crowd was astonished at His teaching (Mark 11:15-18).

When we look at how Jesus expressed His sinless anger and what most of our anger looks like, we see the obvious differences between His righteous wrath and our unrighteous anger.

1. Christ's righteous anger was controlled.

Jesus did not lash out with blind rage nor did He express emotional human energy without supernatural patience. We do not read about Him screaming at anyone with reckless abandon, mindless outbursts, or uncontrolled passion. We see clearly He only dealt with those with whom He was angry. His anger did not spill over into the crowd of innocent bystanders. Did He confront sin? Absolutely! But He did so with immeasurable self-control.

2. Christ's righteous anger was exercised in love.

His anger was an expression of His jealous love—His zeal for His Father's House (John 2:17). Such is the case with us. His anger toward our sin and His discipline of our lives is an amazing expression of His love for us (Hebrews 12:6-11).

16

3. Christ's righteous anger was restorative.

Notice the text pointing out that Jesus "began to teach . . ." (Mark 11:17). Jesus used His anger as the beginning of His teaching moment and as an opportunity to remind those distracted worshipers what they should have remembered. His intent was to start the process of helping them make appropriate changes in their thoughts and behaviors. In fact, with the exception of the religious leaders, the whole crowd responded positively and was "astonished at His teaching" (Mark 11:18).

THE UNRIGHTEOUS ANGER OF MAN

1. Unlike Christ's anger, our sinful anger is uncontrolled.

Look at the response of the leaders. Their fear, jealousy and anger drove them to seek to destroy Jesus (Mark 11:18). Unrighteous anger drives us to do what we will someday regret.

2. Unlike Christ's anger, our sinful anger is selfish.

In contrast to how Christ expressed His anger, we often seek to satisfy our own desires; not God's. It is more about us than about others. It is SELF-focused, SELF-defensive, SELF-promoting and, if the truth be told, SELF-defeating.

3. Unlike Christ's anger, our sinful anger is destructive.

The goal of our unrighteous anger is to lash out and hurt any way and any one we can. In fact, it can quickly move us blindly into random acts of aggression. Creating resentment and bitterness, these are hardly teaching moments. In those times, restoration is far from our thinking. His anger is always perfect. Our anger most often needs some work. I often remind folks of two of the great realities in life: There is a God. We are not Him!

That brings us to an even more basic question, one we church folk are often afraid to ask:

IS IT EVER OKAY TO GET MAD AT GOD?

Cain was outraged at God for not accepting his offering (Genesis 4:5-6). King David was angry at God for striking down Uzzah for his irreverence (2 Samuel 6:7-8). Jonah was mad at God for forgiving the Ninevites (Jonah 4:1, 4). Satan is still furious at God because he knows he has only a short time before he is judged for eternity (Revelation 12:12). King Solomon spoke of the foolish one whose life is ruined because "his heart rages against the Lord" (Proverbs 19:3). We would acknowledge these to be cases of unrighteous anger. But is it ever okay to be angry with God in a righteous way?

Perhaps we are grieving over a loss of a loved one. Maybe we have experienced a life of abuse or great disappointment. Some of us, if we are being honest, have felt abandoned, even by God Himself. How, then, should we feel?

Examine this compound word carefully: **GODISNOWHERE.** It poses two options. Hopefully, we know theologically <u>God</u> is <u>now here</u> (Psalm 139:1-18). Emotionally, however, it can sometimes feel like <u>God</u> is <u>nowhere</u>. It can feel like He is a deserting father, who took a break from our lives, and has never come back!

It is quite common for our lives to be filled with moments and even seasons of asking, "Why me, God?" And we are not alone. Jesus, hanging on the cross and bearing the full weight of all our sin, expressed in a moment of isolation: "My God, My God, Why have You forsaken Me?" (Matthew 27:46; Mark 15:34).

If the sinless Son of God can openly express His feelings, we should feel free to do the same with ourselves, others and even with our Heavenly Father. Like Jesus, we can even ask Him, "Why Lord?" But expect Him to have a good answer He may or may not choose to reveal, in His perfect timing and in His sovereign way.

Let me also assure all of us, while we wait for His answer, Almighty God will accept our disappointment and our anger, as long as it is controlled, exercised in love, and drives us to seek restoration in our fellowship with Him.

INSPECTING THE FRUIT

1. Reflect on your bouts with anger during the seasons of your life.

• Between age 2 to 10, was your anger:

Controlled?   Uncontrolled?
10 9 8 7 6 5 4 3 2 1

Exercised in love?   Selfish?
10 9 8 7 6 5 4 3 2 1

Restorative?   Destructive?
10 9 8 7 6 5 4 3 2 1

• Between age 11 to 17, was your anger:

Controlled?   Uncontrolled?
10 9 8 7 6 5 4 3 2 1

Exercised in love?   Selfish?
10 9 8 7 6 5 4 3 2 1

Restorative?   Destructive?
10 9 8 7 6 5 4 3 2 1

• Between age 19 to young adulthood, was your anger:

Controlled?   Uncontrolled?
10 9 8 7 6 5 4 3 2 1

Exercised in love?   Selfish?
10 9 8 7 6 5 4 3 2 1

Restorative?   Destructive?
10 9 8 7 6 5 4 3 2 1

(Continued on next page)

• During adulthood, has your anger been:

  Controlled?   Uncontrolled?
  10 9 8 7 6 5 4 3 2 1

  Exercised in love?   Selfish?
  10 9 8 7 6 5 4 3 2 1

  Restorative?   Destructive?
  10 9 8 7 6 5 4 3 2 1

2. Have you seen any substantial changes in the way you express anger? Why? Why not?

3. Has there been a time when you were angry or disappointed at God? Why? Is that still an issue?

FURTHER ADVICE FROM THE MASTER GARDENER

Read at least five of the following passages regarding those who expressed anger. Try to determine whether it was righteous or unrighteous anger.

- Cain (Genesis 4:5)
  Controlled? Uncontrolled? Exercised in love?
  Selfish? Restorative? Destructive?

- Esau (Genesis 27:41-45)
  Controlled? Uncontrolled? Exercised in love?
  Selfish? Restorative? Destructive?

- Jacob (Genesis 31:36)
  Controlled? Uncontrolled? Exercised in love?
  Selfish? Restorative? Destructive?

- Reuben, Simeon and Levi (Genesis 49:4-7)
  Controlled? Uncontrolled? Exercised in love?
  Selfish? Restorative? Destructive?

- Moses (Exodus 11:8; 32:19; Leviticus 10:16; Numbers 16:15)
  Controlled? Uncontrolled? Exercised in love?
  Selfish? Restorative? Destructive?

- King Ahab (1 Kings 21:4)
  Controlled? Uncontrolled? Exercised in love?
  Selfish? Restorative? Destructive?

- Naaman (2 Kings 5:11)
  Controlled? Uncontrolled? Exercised in love?
  Selfish? Restorative? Destructive?

- Asa (2 Chronicles 16:10)
  Controlled? Uncontrolled? Exercised in love?
  Selfish? Restorative? Destructive?

- Uzziah (2 Chronicles 26:19)
  Controlled? Uncontrolled? Exercised in love?
  Selfish? Restorative? Destructive?

- Nehemiah (Nehemiah 5:6; 13:17, 25)
  Controlled? Uncontrolled? Exercised in love?
  Selfish? Restorative? Destructive?

- Haman (Esther 3:5-6)
  Controlled? Uncontrolled? Exercised in love?
  Selfish? Restorative? Destructive?

- King Nebuchadnezzar (Daniel 3:13)
  Controlled? Uncontrolled? Exercised in love?
  Selfish? Restorative? Destructive?

- Jonah (Jonah 4:1-4)
  Controlled? Uncontrolled? Exercised in love?
  Selfish? Restorative? Destructive?

- Herod (Matthew 2:16)
  Controlled? Uncontrolled? Exercised in love?
  Selfish? Restorative? Destructive?

- James & John, the "sons of thunder" (Mark 3:17; Luke 9:51-56)
  Controlled? Uncontrolled? Exercised in love?
  Selfish? Restorative? Destructive?

- The People in Jesus' home town of Nazareth (Luke 4:16, 28-29)
  Controlled? Uncontrolled? Exercised in love?
  Selfish? Restorative? Destructive?

- The High Priests (Acts 5:17; 7:54)
  Controlled? Uncontrolled? Exercised in love?
  Selfish? Restorative? Destructive?

Comments: _____

_____

_____

CHAPTER FOUR

GETTING TO THE ROOT
OF MY ROTTEN ANGER

One particular day, early in my marriage, our cat decided to tear up our rented apartment carpet. I went ballistic. I grabbed a newspaper and began swinging at the running cat. I finally caught up with her and swatted her behind. She released her bowels and whatever else cats release. I immediately called my wife, weeping and shocked at my lack of self-control. I exclaimed to her, "How could I ever think of becoming a father, knowing I could treat this creature that way?"

Well, I am pleased to say, after three daughters, twenty-three foster-children and over a dozen grandchildren, the physical revenge exacted on the poor cat was never demonstrated to my family. That is not to say I was still not tempted to take on the cat and dog when they did what cats and dogs do. By God's grace and my wife's encouragement, they survived my expectation they act like civilized creatures. (I, for one, am grateful our pets will not be in heaven; that is, unless their glorified little bodies have sanctified bowels!)

Obviously, this is a small illustration of a much larger problem. But it begs a fundamental question: How is it we can so quickly move from being in a great mood to seething with anger? Perhaps I can help by sharing some of what I have observed over almost seventy years of life and four decades of pastoral ministry.

THE ROOTS BELOW THE SURFACE:
OUR BASIC NEEDS

I often ask why God called me to minister in Fresno, California, located in the agriculturally-blessed San Joaquin Valley. It is well known to my family and my congregation that I am not a farmer. One of the proofs of my agricultural ineptitude is the story of the time I tried to grow a peach tree in my backyard. The fact that I planted it in the shade and too far from the sprinklers was the least of my problems. I was intent on being a successful grower of a prolific peach tree, on my own terms. When, surprisingly, the tree produced its first tiny pink blossoms, I did what any agriculturally-ignorant city boy would do. I plucked them off—all of them. After all, I wanted peaches, not flowers!

I told this story to my congregation and suffered through the laughter and groans. One old fruit farmer, however, came to me after the service and told me I had actually done the right thing. He explained that plucking off the first season's flowers would help stimulate better growth the next season. He went on to explain the importance of timely watering, supplying soil nutrients, and observing the trunk and leaves for disease. He also explained the need for proper pruning to allow more sunlight. His lessons were specific and applicable to matters beyond fruit-growing. Things grow best when cared for properly.

What does this have to do with dealing with our anger? Quite often, when we disciple people, we are confronted with anger-fruit in many forms, expressed and repressed. It is tempting to just deal with the symptoms—the rotten fruit—and not get to the root of the problem. It is even more challenging to take time to examine the underlying disease or the lack of proper nutrients. In the words of one of my farmer-friends, those of us who have been counseling angry people for decades can testify that relationships do best when cared for properly "from the root to the fruit."

I want us to imagine a fruit tree. Let's call it "The Ungodly Anger Tree." It has three major roots, each of them below the surface of the ground. Those roots represent our basic, God-given needs. We were created with physical needs for air, food, water, clothing, shelter, sleep and exercise. We were born to need physical comfort and appropriate touch. We have also been created by God with a deeply emotional need for love and security, belonging and acceptance. We even have the emotional need for excitement. Call it hope and expectation.

Fundamentally, it is not a sin to be physically or emotionally needy. Even the sinless Lord Jesus Christ needed food and water (Matthew 4:2; Mark 11:12; John 19:28). He expressed the need for a donkey on which to ride into Jerusalem (Mark 11:3). He experienced the emotion of loneliness (Matthew 27:46; Mark 15:34). He certainly exuded hope (Matthew 12:21) and joy in the midst of unimaginable adversity (Hebrews 12:2). As we saw earlier, He even demonstrated godly jealousy and zeal (John 2:17).

The fully divine Son of God left Heaven's glory and took on the form of the fully human Son of Man (John 1:14; Philippians 2:6-8). In so doing, He chose to become, like all of us, physically and emotionally needy.

Along with our physical and emotional needs, we were created with spiritual needs. First and foremost, we have a need for a right relationship with God, our Creator and Heavenly Father. The French philosopher, Blaise Pascal, stated his often-quoted belief that every man is born with a God-shaped vacuum. The Lord Jesus Christ came to fill that void and give us abundant life (John 10:10). We who have trusted in Christ alone for our salvation also have a spiritual need for fellowship with God's people (Hebrews 10:24-25). We also have a Holy Spirit-led need to worship and serve the Lord (John 4:24; Ephesians 2:10). It is certainly not a sin to be spiritually needy. The impeccable Son of God craved private fellowship with His Heavenly Father (Matthew 14:23; Mark 1:35; Luke 5:16). He also had a passionate desire to serve others (Mark 10:45).

Below the surface of our lives, at root level, we are a bundle of needs. Although it is certainly not a sin to be needy, let me hasten to say that some of what we believe to be needs are not necessarily God-given needs. They are often only imagined or even wrongly declared as such. God certainly did not create us with the need to be self-sufficient, self-reliant and self-absorbed. Our sinful flesh may prompt us with the need to be Number One, but God's Spirit has a different plan. God did not place in us the need to be wealthy. In fact, He may have chosen us to be materially poor, so that we would have a richer faith and a greater focus on His eternal riches (James 2:5). We do not have a God-given need to have everyone agree with us. That's just not going to happen. In fact, as believers, we can expect the opposite and it may even result in suffering and persecution (2 Timothy 3:12). Let's not confuse real God-instilled needs for imagined needs of our own making. We need food. We need to be right with God. We also need a hug every once in a while!

Now back to the central issue. If it isn't a sin to have physical, emotional and spiritual needs, then what's the problem? Where does our unrighteous anger come from? We now move up, past the roots, and stop at the base of the trunk.

THE BASE OF THE TRUNK:
OUR HUMAN EXPECTATIONS

God asked Cain a question each of us should be asking ourselves: "Why are you angry?" (Genesis 4:6). Sometimes we do not really know the answer. We know we are enraged but we just don't know why. When it comes to understanding our anger, one of the primary questions we must ask is: "Who is it we expect to meet our physical, emotional and spiritual needs?" More often than not, we have come to expect a host of people and things to meet our needs, be it parents or spouses, friends and family, society or churches, employers or government agencies. I believe that is where the problem with unrighteous anger begins.

Yes, I agree that Almighty God, by His amazing grace and providential goodness, may use parents, spouses, families, and churches, and a number of others to mitigate our concerns and fulfill some of our needs. But, ultimately, it is God Himself who meets those needs directly or through others. Take a moment to reflect on some familiar passages:

The *Lord* is my shepherd, I shall not *want* . . . (Psalm 23:1, emphasis added).

. . . *your* [*Heavenly*] *Father* knows what you *need* before you ask *Him* . . . (Matthew 6:8, emphasis added; cf. Matthew 6:25-34).

And my *God* shall supply *all* your *needs* according to *His* riches in glory in Christ Jesus (Philippians 4:19, emphasis added).

Like a burrowing moth larva, unrighteous anger often begins its destructive journey to our core when we expect anything or anyone other than God to meet our needs. Even when He uses others, He still deserves the praise and glory. Being needy isn't a sin; not being grateful for God's direct or indirect provision is (Philippians 4:11-13; 1 Thessalonians 5:18).

Sometimes we have needs God chooses not to meet, in order to produce greater fruit in our lives. He may choose, for His glory, to keep us needy and dependent, leading to a fruitful life of suffering (Proverbs 30:7-9; Romans 8:18). He may even choose, because of our disobedience, to withhold what we need. I love one translation of God's word to the people in Haggai's day: "you expected much and it amounted to little" (Haggai 1:9; Holman Christian Standard Bible).

Sadly, we humans are filled with so many expectations that are not godly, nor are they very realistic.

- We expect everyone to meet our needs the way we demand they be met.

- We expect everyone to agree with us or suffer our wrath.

- We expect people to understand our behaviors and our motives.

- We expect others to adjust their lives to ours.

- We expect others to live up to our standards and be patient with us, even when we do not live up to those same standards.

For example, we expect others to be more attentive drivers than we are. We expect our boss to overlook our mistakes. We expect our children to be perfectly obedient. We expect dinner at six o'clock. We expect our spouse to hand over the remote control. It is fundamentally flawed to think Almighty God has the same list of expectations for others that we have.

INSPECTING THE FRUIT

Read the following list of typical human expectations, commenting on how these unreasonable expectations are a catalyst for your unrighteous anger.

- I expect others to meet my needs the way I demand they be met.

    Often   Sometimes   Rarely
    10 9 8 7 6 5 4 3 2 1

    The reality is: _____

- I expect others to agree with me.

    Often   Sometimes   Rarely
    10 9 8 7 6 5 4 3 2 1

    The reality is: _____

- I expect others to understand my behaviors and my motives.

    Often   Sometimes   Rarely
    10 9 8 7 6 5 4 3 2 1

    The reality is: _____

- I expect others to adjust their lives to mine.

    Often   Sometimes   Rarely
    10 9 8 7 6 5 4 3 2 1

    The reality is: _____

- I expect others to live up to my standards.

    Often   Sometimes   Rarely
    10 9 8 7 6 5 4 3 2 1

    The reality is: _____

• I expect others to be patient with me when I don't live up to my own standards.

Often   Sometimes   Rarely
10   9   8   7   6   5   4   3   2   1

The reality is: _____

• I expect others won't make the same mistakes I make.

Often   Sometimes   Rarely
10   9   8   7   6   5   4   3   2   1

The reality is: _____

• I expect God to fulfill all my desires according to my will.

Often   Sometimes   Rarely
10   9   8   7   6   5   4   3   2   1

The reality is: _____

• I expect my life to be without suffering and trials.

Often   Sometimes   Rarely
10   9   8   7   6   5   4   3   2   1

The reality is: _____

• I expect my sin to have no lasting consequences.

Often   Sometimes   Rarely
10   9   8   7   6   5   4   3   2   1

The reality is: _____

• I expect my realities to exceed my expectations.

Often   Sometimes   Rarely
10   9   8   7   6   5   4   3   2   1

The reality is: _____

Add your own:

• I expect: _____

       Often   Sometimes   Rarely

     10 9 8 7 6 5 4 3 2 1

       The reality is: _____

FURTHER ADVICE FROM THE MASTER GARDENER

Read the story of Nabal in 1 Samuel 25:2-42

1. What were his needs?

2. What were his expectations?

3. What was David's response?

4. What was Abigail's response?

5. What lessons do you gather from this account?

CHAPTER FIVE

UP THE TRUNK WHERE REAL HURT AWAITS

My wife loves tree trunks. Don't ask me why. Give her a charcoal pencil and a piece of gritty paper and eventually a tree will appear. While I do not draw tree trunks, I appreciate the knowledge I have received from my farmer-friends, especially those who make their living growing citrus fruit, almonds and pistachios. Like my wife, they also love tree trunks—for more lucrative reasons. (Then again, I could try to sell her drawings!)

It was not too long ago one of my friends noticed a fungus growing on one of my trees. She expressed great concern. Apparently, this kind of tree fungus threatened not only the life of the whole tree, but all the trees in my backyard. My wife would have to leave home to draw tree trunks.

Whereas, I used to ignore tree trunks, I now know the bark-covered trunk protects a tree from the elements and is the support system for the whole tree. It receives much-needed nutrients from the soil and transfers them to the branches and leaves. In other words, a healthy trunk supports the growth of healthy fruit. I get this.

Back to our Ungodly Anger Tree. At the root level, we have physical, emotional and spiritual needs. Above the surface and up the trunk we have expectations as to how those needs might be met. When our expectations get frustrated we get hurt. Fundamentally, a hurt is a frustrated expectation that comes out of a real or imagined need. It is our common human experience, expressed in words such as: "I'm not angry yet; I'm just hurt!" I recall the lyrics of an old song we sang in the college ministry of the church I attended in the 1970s: "We all get hurt. We all lay down with our face in the dirt." Who among us has not been wounded by someone or something?

The problem is, when the inevitable hurt happens, we deal with it in a variety of ways. Some people suppress and bury it deep in their souls: "I'm okay. Honest!" But we're not okay, whether we know it or not. Others express it openly: "I'm hurt and I am not okay." Many of us do little about it, hoping in some moment of self-control, it will go away. And it doesn't. Ever. Later, in some season or moment of emotional memory, the hurt creeps back in, often with more intensity and emotional pain. Unresolved hurt incubates with time, like the spores of fungus on a tree trunk. If left unchecked and unresolved, it can affect the whole forest of our lives.

As Bible-believing people, we are clearly instructed concerning what to do with our inevitable hurts, which are a consequence of being born human and living among sinful, hurtful people. We do well to recall the comforting words of Jesus Himself:

> Come to Me, all who are weary and heavy-laden, and I will give you rest. Take My yoke upon you and learn from Me, for I am gentle and humble in heart; and you shall find rest for your souls. For My yoke is easy, and My burden is light (Matthew 11:28-30).

We also remember the words of the apostle Peter who spoke of "casting all your anxiety upon Him [Jesus], because He cares for you" (1 Peter 5:7).

Yes, we might know these things, but we just don't believe them—really. Or if we do believe them, we just don't do them—completely. Or if we do choose to do them, we often give God a time-limit in which to do His work:

> *"Okay, God, here's what I expected and here's what didn't happen. So, here's my hurt. I cast it on Your shoulders. Now, You take care of it, just like You promised in Scripture. Ready. Set. Go. I'll give You ten seconds to handle this."*

Then we pause. After all, we do want to give Him a chance. But our patience wears out quickly: *"Okay, God, Your time is up. Now, it's my turn to take care of this!"*

Casting our cares on Him makes for wonderful church-talk and pontificating on spiritual platitudes, but it is rarely a life-long practice. As painful as it is to admit, some of us need to confess we are addicted to the hurt and wouldn't know how to live without it. It truly has become our new normal. No wonder the hurt so quickly turns into the many forms of anger.

Let's review:

We have needs we forget only God can choose directly or indirectly to meet or not to meet, in order to produce healthier fruit in our lives. We have biblical or, more often, unbiblical expectations as to how those needs should be met. When those expectations get frustrated, we get hurt. What happens when we don't deal with the hurt the way God designed us to do—by casting our cares on Him? We get angry!

In summary, let me say in a single sentence what may, at first, seem like a mouthful. I'll explain this in much more detail along the way:

Unrighteous anger is an outward or inward expression of an unresolved hurt, based on a frustrated expectation that comes out of a real or imagined need.

INSPECTING THE FRUIT

Reflect on some of the resolved and unresolved hurts in your life. How do you feel these influence your responses to others today?

FURTHER ADVICE FROM THE MASTER GARDENER

1. Read all of 1 Peter. Underline those passages that relate to how Jesus dealt with hurts and concerns. Pick one to write out below:

2. Underline in a different color those passages that teach us how to deal with our hurts and concerns. Pick one to write out below:

CHAPTER SIX

THE MANY BRANCHES OF UNRIGHTEOUS ANGER

My only memorable knowledge of branches comes from an experience as a child, when my brothers and I decided to build a treehouse. I suppose there was nothing wrong with the idea, except for a few key matters. First, we were apartment-dwelling kids with no way to pay for or gather wood. So, we did what too many kids in our condition would do. We stole it. Secondly, our choice of location for our treehouse was in a park next to our apartment—the very same park and the very same tree under which the newly crowned Queen Elizabeth II was celebrated as the Queen of Canada!

I still remember that moment, looking down from those big old branches and seeing the black boots of a motorcycle cop. Oh, I also forgot to mention that this particular tree in Coronation Park was just yards from the police station. Poor planning indeed!

The policeman took us to the station where he opened a giant book and pretended to read, "Ah, yes, boys. We know all about you. Come with me." He actually placed us in an unlocked jail cell for a few minutes, which seemed like an eternity. The sight of large branches can still stir up that unforgettable experience.

Continuing with our analogy, let's move up the ungodly fruit tree to the weak branches that bear the rotten fruit of unrighteous anger. Once again, I am told by my agriculturally-blessed friends that a tree needs to have good branches in order to have structural integrity, and to provide a canopy for the life-giving leaves. Unhealthy branches divert nutrients from healthy branches and are often weakened by disease, making them incapable of producing the smaller branches that can bear the weight of an abundance of healthy fruit.

THE WEAK BRANCHES:
REPRESSED AND EXPRESSED ANGER

I want us to imagine our ungodly anger tree with six major branches, all of them unhealthy and diseased. Each of these branches represents a way we express unrighteous anger. Some are more outwardly expressive than others, but all of them are dangerous to us—physically, emotionally and spiritually. Specifically, they are incapable of providing what is needed for the tree to bear the fruit of the indwelling Holy Spirit's ministry in our lives: love, joy, peace, patience, kindness, goodness, faithfulness, gentleness and self-control (Galatians 5:22-23). Instead, they make it possible for the tree to bear the foul-smelling fruit of the flesh: enmity, strife, jealousy, outbursts of anger, disputes, dissensions, factions, envyings, anger, malice, slander, abusive speech, bitterness and clamor (Galatians 5:20; Colossians 3:8; Ephesians 4:31).

Anger Branch #1: Scapegoating

"Picking on the Innocent Victim"

Perhaps you recall the Old Testament accounts of how the High Priest would, on the Day of Atonement (called *Yom Kippur*), symbolically lay on an innocent goat the full weight of the combined sin of Israel. He would then cast the poor goat out of the camp (Leviticus 16:7-10, 20-22). It was called the scapegoat or, quite literally, "the goat of removal." In Hebrew it is called the *Azazel*.

To some degree this is how many of us express our anger. We pick on the innocent victim, especially those closest to us or who do not have the power to punish us or defend themselves. They are the scapegoats—the *Azazel* in our lives. There are plenty of examples in Scripture. Cain's sinful anger at God's rejection of his sacrifice and jealousy of his innocent brother, Abel, turned to hatred and ultimately murder (Genesis 4:3-8). Joseph's older brothers were enraged by and envious of their father's favoritism toward their younger brother. They initially planned to kill Joseph, but settled for selling him into slavery (Genesis 37:4, 8, 26-27).

Certainly, these are extreme reactions. Most of our scapegoating isn't so murderous and cruel. It certainly can, however, be devastating to those on the other end of our scapegoating wrath—

those who feel, in the way they have been treated, like they have been branded "goats of removal." Their theme song might just be, *"Why Is Everybody Always Pickin' on Me?"*

As foster-parents for many years, we saw this kind of displaced anger in a number of the abused children who came to live with us. Understandably angry at the way their lives were unfolding, they lashed out to hurt even those who were now trying to help them.

Here's how scapegoating anger looks in our everyday lives. We head off to work. Our boss yells at us for some undeserved or deserved infraction. We restrain ourselves from kicking back for fear of losing our job. Instead, we hold it in until we get home, where the scapegoating begins. We snap at our spouse for some silly reason. She doesn't respond back for fear the whole evening will be one big argument. So, she picks on her oldest daughter. The oldest daughter can't scream back at Mom, so she hits her little brother. Little brother is too small to retaliate against his big sister, so he kicks the dog. The dog then bites the unsuspecting father. And the cycle of scapegoating continues, sometimes for years, even for generations. Simply stated, if you are prone to express your anger by picking on innocent or weaker victims, you are a scapegoater. Anyone want to admit that today? I will.

I am rarely explosive in my anger. As I shared earlier, I am most drawn to anger when the cat and dog engage in their "potty" mistakes, usually discovered by my bare feet in the middle of the night. In those cases, I would rather be physically expressive but have settled for more repressed ways to engage in my childish fits of rage. Scapegoating seems to fit the need of the moment.

I get irritated at my sleeping wife, simply because she is the only one in range. The dog is hiding under the chair and the cat couldn't care less, remaining in bed. My wife sides with the cat, having observed my bark is bigger than my bite. The dog returns to sleeping on the chair. All will be well in the morning. So they think! As you will see later, I am not just a scapegoater.

Anger Branch #2: Stamp Saving

"Building Up and Blowing Up"

I am old enough to remember S&H Green Stamps. The popular marketing idea prompted us to make a purchase at a participating store or gas station. The clerk would hand us a few stamps that could be stored up to exchange for items at an S&H Redemption Store. It took hundreds of single stamps to buy a clock radio or a lava lamp (Anybody remember those?). Normally, you would put the stamps one-by-one in a kitchen drawer. Then came the day when the drawer was full enough. It was now time to open the drawer, place the stamps in a redemption book and head off to spend the stockpile.

Some of us have spent a lifetime collecting emotional trading stamps. Others have just begun. We go through the day, refusing to outwardly express our anger and hurt. We just bury all those frustrated expectations in the kitchen drawer of our life, all the while insisting, "I'm not angry. Really, I'm not." Then subconsciously we whisper, *"Now, let me just stuff some stamps in this drawer."* Then one day we come home and someone does something that would normally seem insignificant. Our drawer full of emotional trading stamps cries out, *"It's now time to buy that lava lamp!"* And, boy, is it expensive! We redeem every stamp in the drawer. We let loose, "And remember when you did this . . . and that . . . and you said this . . . and that . . . and now . . ."

My dear wife regularly laments the fact that she cannot find her glasses nor her car keys. It amazes me when we are having a heated discussion (aka: an argument) and she remembers everything I said or did the last time we argued about this same issue, even if it was three months or three years ago. Who can win against someone with a stamp saving, supersonic memory for relational details?

It is time to be honest when we realize our anger is out of proportion to the action that precipitated it. In the words of an English proverb I once read: "Anger is often more hurtful than the injury that caused it." If we are prone to build up and then blow up, we are stamp savers. If we often find the issue over which our argument started is not the issue we end up arguing about, we, too, are emotional stamp collectors.

I am sure at this point many of us are saying, "Lord, my drawer is really full. Please, help me to keep it closed. Better yet, help me to learn not to even save those stamps!"

Anger Branch #3: Stress Illness

"Getting Sick"

The emotion of anger has intense physical repercussions. It affects the flow of blood. It causes our glands to secrete adrenalin and other hormones. It truly can be quite "gut-wrenching" and "heart-breaking." As we will see later, unresolved anger can literally destroy our bodies. Medically speaking, it is sometimes described as a slow death. As a pastoral counselor, I agree with many of my colleagues who suggest anger can even be a slow form of suicide.

Sadly, too many of my fellow Christians express their unresolved anger in a physical way. It shows up in stress illnesses whose root cause is hidden and unresolved anger. As such, it is correct to call them *psychosomatic* (psychologically and emotionally induced) and *pneumasomatic* (spiritually induced). No matter the source, they are nonetheless real illnesses. I once heard, "Your ulcers are not due to what you are eating but what's eating you." Although certainly not all illnesses are anger-based, some of us have become quite fooled by anger, disguising itself in physical symptoms.

I have been attending prayer meetings for over forty-five years. I have observed many who go to church meetings, rightly asking for prayer for high blood pressure, insomnia, ulcers, headaches, heart disease, colitis and a host of other illnesses. In most cases they receive at least some empathy and, hopefully, a substantial amount of prayer. Rarely have I heard people ask for prayer for what might be the real reason for some of these illnesses: "I am here to confess I am really angry—at my family, at my work situation, at the way my life is, at my church, and even at God. And the anger is destroying my body. Please pray for my anger!" But that is not what happens in most public church gatherings or even behind the closed doors of a pastor's office. Many have come to realize when they get overtly angry, people reject them. When they get sick, however, people treat them nicely. Which one are they more likely to choose? To get sick, of course. Stress illness is often one of those games that gets played whenever we don't win playing other forms of anger.

If we are internalizing our anger and our body seems to be responding physically, with immediate headaches, stomach pains or, in the long term, other physical ailments, it is worth considering we might be suffering from stress illness. Even if we are trying to keep this hidden, our body may be shouting, *"I'm angry and I feel it."* Or maybe our gut is whispering, *"I'm sick and tired of being sick and tired."*

Anger Branch #4: Withdrawal

"Running Outwardly. Retreating Inwardly"

Who among us has not wanted to run from conflict? Some of us do. We leave the room or the house. Sometimes we leave town. Some of us leave it all behind and never come back! Others of us retreat inwardly, deep within our souls. For us, it is our "hiding place," where we can shut out the world of conflict. Our response to the angry person or situation is silence. It's safer that way! It's what I call the "emotional cold," because it feels like we have an impenetrable emotional bubble surrounding us. I sometimes describe it as that deep feeling where we are tempted to take our little spiritual blanket, stand in the corner and suck our thumbs, while we wait for the Lord's return.

For some of us, our unresolved anger is expressed in inactivity. Like Elijah, we try to sleep away the pain (1 Kings 19:4-5). For many it is the kind of anger that gets buried in a book, television, the Internet, or listening to music. Others retreat to their Bibles. There is nothing fundamentally wrong with these activities, unless they are ways to escape from dealing with unresolved hurts and frustrated expectations.

Then there are those sad souls who, instead of expressing the hurt to God and working through the conflict, turn inwardly to what is often called "a dark night of the soul." It feels like an inner blackness, a seemingly impossible-to-resolve hopelessness—deep depression.

If we are prone to withdraw—to run outwardly or retreat inwardly, or both, it is time for us to learn how to come out with it and deal with it openly. Real help is available for the asking.

INSPECTING THE FRUIT

1. How are you most prone to run <u>outwardly</u> from conflict?

    __ I move to a corner of a room.
    __ I move to another room.
    __ I go outside.
    __ I leave the premises and go to: _____.
    __ Other: _____.

2. How are you most prone to retreat <u>inwardly</u> from conflict?

    __ I get quiet.
    __ I take a nap.
    __ I read a book.
    __ I read my Bible or a devotional book.
    __ I watch television or a video.
    __ I run to social media.
    __ I listen to music.
    __ I retreat to the "hiding place" of my soul.
    __ I experience a temporary "dark night of the soul."
    __ I admit I have contemplated suicide.
    __ I have attempted suicide.
    __ Other: _____.

CHAPTER SEVEN

MORE OF THOSE WEAK LIMBS

The San Joaquin Valley, in which I live, is presently being invaded by an incurable wood rot fungus, called *ganoderma*. This mysterious disease devours trees from the inside out and is threatening the 1.2 billion dollar almond industry in our valley. It is merciless, as it eats slowly away at the tree's heartwood, root structure, trunk and branches. Although it is normally seen in older trees, it is now causing even young trees to snap and fall over.

The desperate farmers have yet to find a fungicide to kill it. The mushroom-like growths (called *conks*) at the base of the tree are the only evidence the fungus has invaded. The disease is spreading as trillions of spores are released into the air. Many farmers are simply knocking the infected trees down in hopes of saving their other trees. It is an epidemic of destruction and there is no end in sight.

So far we have considered four of the diseased branches that help produce the rotten fruit of unrighteous anger.

Anger Branch #1: Scapegoating: "Picking on the Innocent Victim"

Anger Branch #2: Stamp Saving: "Building Up and Blowing Up"

Anger Branch #3: Stress Illness: "Getting Sick"

Anger Branch #4: Withdrawal: "Running Outwardly. Retreating Inwardly"

Unlike real branches that have been invaded by a mysterious, hard-to-diagnose, incurable fungus, our infected anger branches are hardly mysterious, easily diagnosed and, thankfully, very curable. Before we get to that, let's talk about more of those weak limbs.

Anger Branch #5: Passive-Aggression

"Getting Even"

The passive-aggressive is the person who rarely expresses anger on the outside. But, oh, how he or she gets even! Clarence Darrow said it this way, "I've never killed anyone, but I have read some obituary notices with great satisfaction."

The passive-aggressive is often the person who is not allowed to express anger publicly:

- It is the medical professional who cannot tell a patient what he or she is really thinking, *"Will you stop whining! What do you expect when you abuse your body and now you are sick?"* Then he or she makes the patient wait an extra thirty minutes, just because it feels good to get even.

- It is the public servant who, because of the ever-present, watchful eyes of the community, cannot let his guard down. He suffers public scorn when he openly expresses anger and frustration. Instead, he puts certain people on his "unusable list."

- It is the teacher who is afraid to express genuine frustration with a student for fear of the principal or the parents' wrath. The report card becomes her tool of quiet revenge.

- It is the waitress who spits in your soup: *"Don't mess with me, people!"*

- It is the police officer who smiles at a rude driver as he writes the traffic ticket and says, "Have a nice day!"

- It is the minister who cannot share his feelings: *"Will you people stop being so critical and start acting more like Jesus!"* Instead, he gets even any way he can and still look fairly holy on the outside.

Even the children of such public people can often fall prey to this same form of anger. They had to learn to control their emotions in public, for fear of embarrassing their family. They may even have secretly expressed their hurt and frustration by open defiance of all their parents stood for.

Many forms of quiet revenge are also forms of passive-aggressive behavior. Fault-finding, spreading rumors, rejoicing in hearing something bad about a person and even tardiness can be forms of passive-aggressive anger. Indifference—the "I don't care" attitude that shows up in too many ways to mention—is also a common form of anger. In fact, it is often rage under some measure of temporary control.

The expressions of the passive-aggressive vary; the results are often the same. They look perfectly okay on the outside. On the inside, however, they are seething with anger, that is, until they get even. Then they quietly smile. Any passive-aggressives in our midst? Yes, I know there are. I am one of them!

One day, after a challenging sermon, one of my church attendees greeted me at the door. I asked, "So what did God teach you through today's message?" His response took me back, "Not much. There was really nothing I hadn't heard before. Actually, I heard a much better message on that passage by . . ." (He then mentioned a pastor-friend of mine.)

My seasoned pastor's mouth whispered, "Well, thank you for your honesty. I'll try to do better next time." But my well-honed passive-aggressive heart shouted in my brain, *What a mean thing to say, even if it is true. Why don't you just go to my friend's church? Let him deal with you."*

The next week, as he came to the back of the church, I turned away from him to give a hand to an older lady. It felt really good, not to help the lady, but to spurn him! On the outside, I looked so kind and caring. On the inside, I was seething. On the outside, I just smiled. Later, on the inside, God dealt with my heart. On the outside, I stopped smiling at my passive-aggressive, sinful anger.

On the home front, my wife of almost five decades can attest to my ongoing issues with being passive in my anger. I am an expert in withholding blessings from those who disappoint me. Sometimes, I withdraw my plans about which they had no knowledge. It just feels good to say to myself, *"Well, I am not going to do what I had in mind to do for them."* My wife is keenly aware of my subtle punishments to which she is known to respond, "I know you are angry. Don't passive-aggressive us." Ouch! Passive-aggressive people are not used to getting caught!

Anger Branch #6: Expressed Anger

"Letting It Show"

As we have seen, unrighteous anger expresses itself in insidious ways: picking on the innocent victim (scapegoating), building up and blowing up (stamp saving), getting sick (stress illness), running outwardly and retreating inwardly (withdrawing) and getting even (passive-aggression). Our sinful rage is not always so subtle. We are all aware of people who scream, yell, bite and kick. They throw things, slam doors and sometimes strike out even more dramatically at their fellow humans or even their animals. When they are angry everyone around them knows it.

By the way, people who are repressive in their anger in public (e.g. scapegoaters, stamp savers, passive-aggressives, etc.) can often be explosive in their anger at home. Most who express their anger outwardly do so with some measure of self-control. This is not always the case, however, as evidenced by the many incidences of domestic violence and family assaults. Sadly, most are not reported but certainly are felt deeply in the hearts of the silent victims.

If you mostly express your anger outwardly, raise your hand. Imagine crowds of people raising their hands in solidarity with the imaginary I.E.A.S.—the International Expressed Anger Society. As compared to those who tend to demonstrate their anger in more hidden, inwardly repressive ways, you might applaud yourselves as being more emotionally healthy. "After all, at least we let it out." Well, not so fast in letting yourselves off the hook. Some three thousand years ago King Solomon wrote: "An angry man stirs up strife, and a hot-tempered man abounds in transgression" (Proverbs 29:22).

ALCOHOL AND DRUGS:
THE ANGRY MAN'S NEMESIS

Permit me a few comments about the effects of alcohol and drugs on our anger. In Proverbs 20 King Solomon warned: "Wine is a mocker, strong drink a brawler, and whoever is intoxicated by it is not wise" (Proverbs 20:1). He is quite graphic in the words he used to warn his son, and us, about the foolishness of being drunk, especially as it relates to our expressions of anger. The Hebrew word for mocker is *luts*, which means to scorn, mock or deride people. Oh, the alcohol and drug-induced, poisonous things folks have said to those closest to them. Alcohol is said to loosen the tongue—often too much!

King Solomon then uses another word to describe a brawler. The Hebrew word *hamah* speaks of shouting, creating an uproar and making a commotion. It is more graphically used to speak of those who howl like a mad dog (Psalm 59:6, 14), and growl like bears (Isaiah 59:11). In other words, Solomon wants us to know being intoxicated makes us act like animals. Remember that the next time you think you can handle your "drug of choice." Those around you cannot. Better to pay close attention to the mandate of the apostle Paul: "Do not get drunk with wine, for that is dissipation ["excessive, riotous actions," Greek: *asotia*], but be filled with the Spirit" (Ephesians 5:18).

Hopefully, most of us have chosen the road of temperance, sobriety, or, at least, moderation. In so doing, we will only have ourselves to blame for our outbursts of anger and not some ungodly percentage of blood-alcohol.

A WORD TO ALL OF US ANGRY PEOPLE— NO MATTER HOW WE EXPRESS IT.

If we are ever going to deal properly with our anger we must acknowledge the hot-tempered person is not just the expressive—the screamer, yeller, verbal, or physical abuser. An angry person who stirs up strife and abounds in sin is anyone who is controlled by any of the forms we have spoken about.

It is time to admit with the rest of fallen mankind, "I am an angry, hot-tempered person. I also live around, at last count, over seven billion of us." Perhaps, we should reduce the number to allow for those young children who have yet to discover the world of conflict. But, just wait!

WHEN BRANCHES COLLIDE

Imagine a scapegoater having to live or work with a stamp saver. One picks on the other; the stamp saver waits for the right time in his or her mind and then explodes. The scapegoater doesn't know what hit him. Consider a person whose repressed anger shows up in stress illness who is married to one who withdraws. One is always sick while the other simply hides. Nothing gets dealt with. How about a passive-aggressive having to work with an expressive? One ultimately finds ways to exact a quiet revenge on the other who is constantly screaming or lashing out. Mathematically, there are scores of possible combinations of angry people, each with their own unique interactions, depending on the levels of intensity.

INSPECTING THE FRUIT

Identifying the Anger Branches in My Life

Pick the anger branch (or branches) you engage in and indicate the place where it most often occurs.

Anger Branch #1: Scapegoating (Picking on the Innocent Victim)

    At home____ At work/school____ In public____ Other: ____

In what situation are you most likely to express anger in this manner? How has this most affected you/them?

Anger Branch #2: Stamp Saving (Building Up and Blowing up)

    At home____ At work/school____ In public____ Other: ____

In what situation are you most likely to express anger in this manner? How has this most affected you/them?

Anger Branch #3: Stress Illness (Getting Sick)

    At home____ At work/school____ In public____ Other: ____

In what situation are you most likely to express anger in this manner? How has this most affected you/them?

Anger Branch #4: Withdrawal (Retreating Inwardly)

At home___ At work/school___ In public___ Other: ___

In what situation are you most likely to express anger in this manner? How has this most affected you/them?

Anger Branch #5: Passive-Aggression (Getting Even)

At home___ At work/school___ In public___ Other: ___

In what situation are you most likely to express anger in this manner? How has this most affected you/them?

Anger Branch #6: Expression (Letting It Show)

At home___ At work/school___ In public___ Other: ___

In what situation are you most likely to express anger in this manner? How has this most affected you/them?

So, now it's time to 'fess up—all of us—no matter what anger branch we perch on the most:

"I _____ am a hot-tempered person!"
        (Your Name)

Identifying the Anger Branches in Others

Pick the anger branch (or branches) your closest relative, companion or fellow worker engages in the most and share how their anger branch interacts with yours.

Anger Branch #1: Scapegoating (Picking on the Innocent Victim)

Relationship of that person to you:

Relative__	Spouse__	Companion__	Co-worker__
Supervisor__	Teacher__	Friend__	Other:_____

How has their expression of this form of anger most affected you?

Anger Branch #2: Stamp Saving (Building Up and Blowing up)

Relationship of that person to you:

Relative__	Spouse__	Companion__	Co-worker__
Supervisor__	Teacher__	Friend__	Other:_____

How has their expression of this form of anger most affected you?

Anger Branch #3: Stress Illness (Getting Sick)

Relationship of that person to you:

Relative__	Spouse__	Companion__	Co-worker__
Supervisor__	Teacher__	Friend__	Other:_____

How has their expression of this form of anger most affected you?

Anger Branch #4: Withdrawal (Retreating Inwardly)

Relationship of that person to you:

Relative__	Spouse__	Companion__	Co-worker__
Supervisor__	Teacher__	Friend__	Other:_____

How has their expression of this form of anger most affected you?

Anger Branch #5: Passive-Aggression (Getting Even)

Relationship of that person to you:

Relative___   Spouse___   Companion___   Co-worker___
Supervisor___   Teacher___   Friend___   Other:_____

How has their expression of this form of anger most affected you?

Anger Branch #6: Expression (Letting It Show)

Relationship of that person to you:

Relative___   Spouse___   Companion___   Co-worker___
Supervisor___   Teacher___   Friend___   Other:_____

How has their expression of this form of anger most affected you?

FURTHER ADVICE FROM THE MASTER GARDENER

Read the following biblical accounts of people who expressed (or repressed) their anger. Try to identify their anger branch.

• Cain and Abel (Genesis 4:1-8)

• King Saul (1 Samuel 20:30-33)

• Pontius Pilate (Matthew 27:24-26; Mark 15:14-15; John 19:12-16)

• The Jewish Leaders (John 8:58-59)

• Paul and Barnabas (Acts 15:36-39)

CHAPTER EIGHT

THE FRUIT OF THE FLESH

Entomologists tell us there are millions of insects that invade trees, plants and flowers. In our area we have resilient trees that have been struck by lightning, suffered through earthquakes and fire, but are succumbing rapidly to bark beetles, wreaking havoc on the drought-stricken forests in California.

Have you ever had the chance to take a close look at some of these destructive bugs? I made the mistake of looking online at the larva, pupa of the adult Codling Moth that attacked my apple tree. I then researched further and examined some magnified pictures of the rotten, worm-infested fruit piled in a decaying mess on the ground. It provided me with substantial motivation to continue my battle against these insect-invaders. It also provided a graphic image of the fruit of my sinful heart.

In the fifth chapter of Paul's epistle to the Galatians, he addresses the fleshly infestation every born-again believer experiences throughout their earthly lives. Prior to coming to a saving knowledge of Jesus Christ, we were completely receptive to sin's decaying impulses. Now, by the power of the indwelling Holy Spirit, we can have daily victory over these fleshly invaders:

> But I say, walk by the Spirit, and you will not carry out the desire of the flesh. For the flesh sets its desire against the Spirit, and the Spirit against the flesh; for these are in opposition to one another, so that you may not do the things that you please. But if you are led by the Spirit, you are not under the Law (Galatians 5:16-18).

The apostle Paul moves on to speak about the nature of the daily struggle between our flesh, the inward desire to do what we want and the Spirit, whose desire it is for us to do what He wants, as He endeavors to make us more like Jesus:

> Now the deeds of the flesh are evident, which are: immorality, impurity, sensuality, idolatry, sorcery, enmities, strife, jealousy, outbursts of anger, disputes, dissensions, factions, envying, drunkenness, carousing, and things like these, of which I forewarn you, just as I have forewarned you, that those who practice such things will not inherit the kingdom of God (Galatians 5:19-21).

In his close-up catalog of the ugliness of sin, the apostle Paul presents five basic categories of the deeds of the flesh: sexual sins (immorality, impurity, sensuality), religious sins (idolatry, sorcery), social sins, (enmities, strife, jealousy, outbursts of anger, disputes, dissensions, factions, envying), sins of personal excess (drunkenness, carousing), and other miscellaneous sins ("things like these").

Since this is a book about dealing with anger, I want us to more closely examine the words he uses related to social sins. Here we have eight very powerful words that form what could rightly be called *The Ugly Faces of Interpersonal Conflict*. Staying with our agricultural theme, let's call them *The Fruit of the Flesh*. Without the restraining power of the Holy Spirit of God in our lives (Galatians 5:16-18), this sinful fruit will come out in abundance.

All of us know what it's like to have anger and wrath well up from deep inside our hearts. It comes flying out of our lives in a number of repressed and expressed forms, reminding us of the flies and gnats escaping decaying fruit when we hit them with a stick.

Whether we are talking about conflicts in marriage, fights between parents and children, sibling rivalries, squabbles among church members, conflicts at work, or skirmishes between groups of people, we must readily admit— we are a warring people. Many of us are one continuous temper tantrum after another, just waiting to fly off the handle! And we don't get to blame anybody but ourselves. James, the brother of our Lord, was spot on when he penned these words: "What is the source of quarrels and conflicts among you? Is not the source your pleasures that wage war in your members?" (James 4:1).

Humanists try to tell us, "War is obsolete . . ." They are quick to add, ". . . if men would just get along." As William Shakespeare reminded us, "Therein lies the rub." I remember an old cigarette commercial that expressed what could well be the battle cry of our flesh: "I'd rather fight than switch." It's the nature of our sinful flesh to fight. Oh, how our sinful hearts love a scuffle or two. The first chapter in Paul's epistle to the Romans speaks of the human heart as "full of envy, murder, strife . . ." (cf. Romans 1:29-31). It doesn't matter who we are. Every one of us was born "full of flesh" and therefore full of fight.

With this in mind, look with me at each of these social sins found in our fleshly hearts. I will refer us to some key New Testament passages. In keeping with our agricultural theme, I am calling this:

THE FRUIT OF THE FLESH CATALOG

Fruit of the Flesh #1: Enmities

Now the deeds of the flesh are evident, which are . . . **enmities**,
strife, jealousy, outbursts of anger, disputes, dissensions,
factions, envying . . . (Galatians 5:19-21, emphasis added).

The Greek word the apostle Paul uses is *echthra*. Notice the word translated is plural—enmities. In its basic form it speaks of inward hostilities, even to the point of murderous intentions and "hatreds" (as the King James Version rightly calls them). We try, but often fail, to keep these enmities well hidden. I recently read about a classified advertisement that obviously had a whole story behind it: "Wedding dress for sale. Never worn. Will trade for .38 caliber pistol."

Fleshly enmities are stored deeply in the flesh factory of our hearts and tend to show up in all those phony words we use: "I'm not mad. Really, there's nothing wrong. No problem." The truth is, sometimes our flesh doesn't get angry on the outside; it just gets even. Like the old Quaker who was steaming mad at his cow for kicking him, "Thou dost know that I am a Quaker and I cannot strike thee . . . but if thou dost not stop kicking me I will sell thee to a Presbyterian who will beat thee to death."

These kinds of inward hostilities we so try to hide are not just directed toward our fellow humans; they are often directed toward God Himself. We don't often say it, but it nonetheless shows up in acts of disobedience and, especially, in our attraction to the godless things of the world—so said Paul and James:

. . . the mind set on the flesh is *hostile* toward God; for it does not subject itself to the law of God, for it is not even able to do so . . . (Romans 8:7, emphasis added).

You adulteresses, do you not know that friendship with the world is *hostility* toward God? Therefore whoever wishes to be a friend of the world makes himself an enemy of God (James 4:4, emphasis added).

Fruit Flesh #2: Strife

Soon those inward, passive-aggressive enmities and hostilities toward man and God spill out in more blatant outward forms. The apostle Paul calls one of them "strife":

Now the deeds of the flesh are evident, which are . . . enmities, **strife**, jealousy, outbursts of anger, disputes, dissensions, factions, envying . . . (Galatians 5:19-21, emphasis added).

The Greek word Paul uses is *eris*. The King James Version translates it "variance"; the New International Version calls it "discord" and other translations refer to it as "contentions." They are all rather mild words to describe the quarreling, fighting and lashing out to hurt those with whom we are at odds.

Our flesh is so very cruel. And this is certainly not just a problem among unbelievers. To his fellow Christians in the Corinthian Church the apostle Paul wrote:

For I have been informed concerning you, my brethren, by Chloe's people, that there are quarrels [strifes] among you (1 Corinthians 11:1).

. . . for you are still fleshly. For since there is jealousy and *strife* among you, are you not fleshly, and are you not walking like mere men? (1 Corinthians 3:3, emphasis added).

In his second letter to these same brothers and sisters in Christ, he was concerned that the problem continued to exist:

For I am afraid that perhaps when I come I may find you to be not what I wish and may be found by you to be not what you wish; that perhaps there may be *strife*, jealousy, angry tempers, disputes, slanders, gossip, arrogance, disturbances . . . " (2 Corinthians 12:20, emphasis added).

Closely linked to strife is the next in the apostle Paul's list of deeds of the flesh directed toward each other. It is one quite guilty of creating inter-personal conflict.

Fruit of the Flesh #3: Jealousy

Now the deeds of the flesh are evident, which are . . . enmities, strife, **jealousy**, outbursts of anger, disputes, dissensions, factions, envying . . . (Galatians 5:19-21, emphasis added).

The Greek word the apostle Paul uses is *zelos*, which can be both positive and negative. Jealousy, in and of itself, is neither right nor wrong, good nor bad. In a positive way it speaks of being zealous, of having a godly jealousy that drives us to possess good qualities, to protect God's holy standards and even to become like Jesus Christ (2 Corinthians 11:2). But here in Galatians 5:20, apostle Paul is referring to the sinful kind of jealousy, the kind that is hateful and destructive. It is the envy the classical poets referred to as "the fiery, green-eyed monster." Paul simply called it "fleshly," one of the worst parts of being human (1 Corinthians 3:3). James, the brother of our Lord, would agree with how very ugly and harmful this deed of the flesh really is:

But if you have bitter jealousy and selfish ambition in your heart, do not be arrogant and so lie against the truth . . . For where jealousy and selfish ambition exist, there is disorder and every evil thing" (James 3:14, 16).

The King James Version translates the word as "emulations." Today, we speak of an emulation as synonymous with imitation. But, in the 1700s, it was an English word that more often spoke of ambitious rivalries. The apostle Paul's use of the word refers to the deep-seated need we have in our jealous hearts to try to be better than others, at any cost.

Fruit of the Flesh #4: Outbursts of Anger

Just as inward enmities and hostilities result in underline{outward} strife and quarrels, so this underline{inward} jealousy manifests its rotten fruit in more outward ways:

> Now the deeds of the flesh are evident, which are . . . enmities, strife, jealousy, **outbursts of anger**, disputes, dissensions, factions, envying . . . (Galatians 5:19-21, emphasis added).

In Genesis 4:3-5, it was this inward jealousy that pushed Cain to his outburst of anger, resulting in the murder of his brother, Abel. In Acts 13:4-5, it was this ungodly envy that led the Jews to try to kill the apostle Paul.

Here in Galatians, the word Paul uses is the plural form of the Greek word *thumos*. In its verb form, *thumoo*, it refers to being provoked to wrath. It is often connected to the Greek word *machomai* which can quite literally be translated as "an anger-fight" (cf. Acts 7:26), "a war of words" (cf. 2 Timothy 2:24), and "a hand-to-hand struggle" (cf. James 4:2). The Greek word *thumos* is also synonymous with the word *aganaktesis,* which spoke of the compounded irritation the other ten disciples felt when the mother of their fellow apostles, James and John, requested her sons be placed in the highest position when Christ ushered in His Kingdom (Matthew 20:24). Here in his list of the fruit of the flesh—the ugly faces of interpersonal conflict—the apostle Paul is picturing piles of uncontrolled passion, loads of angry and uncontrolled temper-tantrums, a long line of inflammatory indignations, countless fits of rage, and a mountain of ungodly emotion.

Modern philosophers are wrong when they suggest mankind is basically good. We are a quick-tempered bunch, each with a load of ungodly anger waiting to dump on others. Our sinful flesh has no ability to reason. It has no ability to forgive. It has no ability to show mercy. It has no ability to express remorse. It only knows how to pile it on and bury others, one outburst of anger at a time.

INSPECTING THE FRUIT

Mark as many as apply.

1. Where do you most get angry?

At home___ At work___ At school___ At sporting events___
At church___ On the road___ In public___ In private___ Other:___

2. In what circumstances do you most get frustrated?

Dealing with spouse___   Dealing with family___
Raising children___   Driving/Parking___
Waiting in lines___   Repairing things___
Dealing with friends___   Handling finances___
Shopping___   Losing a competition___
Poor performance___   Other: _____

3. Are you more prone to handle your anger inwardly (repression) or outwardly (expression)?

4. Specifically, how do you most often express your anger?

5. What would you most like to change about the way you deal with anger?

FURTHER ADVICE FROM THE MASTER GARDENER

Read 2 Corinthians 7:8-12 and consider the story of the apostle Paul's rebuke to the church.

Comment about the positive results of his righteous anger in the lives of his brothers and sisters in Christ.

How does his godly anger differ from our fleshly anger?

CHAPTER NINE

MORE FRUIT OF THE FLESH. REALLY?

As I mentioned earlier, our valley is known for its abundant and award-winning fruit. From table grapes and raisins to a variety of citrus fruit, our growers pride themselves on being a part of a multi-billion dollar industry that brings the area international recognition. There is, however, a fruit factory that dwells within every human heart. It is the secret place where the deeds of the flesh produce their rotten fruit. So far we have examined a short list:

Fruit of the Flesh #1: Enmities (Greek: *echthra*)
Fruit of the Flesh #2: Strife (Greek: *eris*)
Fruit of the Flesh #3: Jealousy (Greek: *zelos*)
Fruit of the Flesh #4: Outbursts of anger (Greek: *thumos*)

Enmities prompt us to lash out at those we love. Strife generates the energy to unleash the wrath we have stored up in our sinful hearts. Jealousy is the "fiery, green-eyed monster" in each of us, urging us to better ourselves, even at the expense of others. Outbursts of anger are . . . well . . . outbursts of anger!

I was recently sent a quote: "When you get angry take a breath and count to 10. Throw a punch at 8. Nobody expects that!" Maybe our flesh isn't prone to punch someone out unexpectedly, but it is more than willing to drive us to actively engage in the fifth ugly face of conflict the apostle Paul mentions.

Fruit of the Flesh #5: Disputes

Now the deeds of the flesh are evident, which are . . . enmities, strife, jealousy, outbursts of anger, **disputes**, dissensions, factions, envying . . . (Galatians 5:19-21, emphasis added).

The Greek word is the plural form of *eritheia*. It originally referred to candidates for public office, campaigning for political support with only their own personal benefit in mind. The best evidence indicates this word should be translated not so much as disputes but as selfish ambitions. We all know people who have loads of selfish ambition they throw at others in the form of rivalries and disputes. Maybe you are one of them.

Let's be honest. It is the nature of our flesh to promote ourselves—to look out for Number One. My sinful flesh enters a daily, "I've-got-to-win every battle." The war cry is familiar to all of us: "It's my way or the highway." In his letter to the Philippians, the apostle Paul precisely described our disputing, selfishly ambitious hearts: "For they all seek after their own interests, not those of Christ Jesus" (Philippians 2:21).

In any given conflict, our flesh does everything in its power to win, even if it means beating another person down. Our flesh loves disputes. In fact, some of us have developed it into an art-form. In 1 Timothy 6 the apostle Paul spoke of those who have "a morbid interest in controversial questions and *disputes* about words, out of which arise envy, strife, abusive language, evil suspicions . . . (1 Timothy 6:4, emphasis added). He then tells us what we are to do about this: "But avoid foolish controversies and genealogies and strife and *disputes* about the Law; for they are unprofitable and worthless" (Titus 3:9, emphasis added). Instead, we are to follow the pattern set by Jesus: "Do nothing from selfishness or empty conceit, but with humility of mind let each of you regard one another as more important than himself . . ." (Philippians 2:3). Being the selfish brutes we are, that's not something we can do in our own power.

Fruit of the Flesh #6: Dissensions

Now the deeds of the flesh are evident, which are . . . enmities, strife, jealousy, outbursts of anger, disputes, **dissensions**, factions, envying . . . (Galatians 5:19-21, emphasis added).

The Greek word, *dichostasia*, speaks literally of standing apart or splitting something in two. My two-faced, fleshly heart loves to divide over issues. It loves gossip, slander, lying and making absurd exaggerations regarding people and events, all in hopes of separating people and tearing them apart from each other. No wonder the King James Version calls this deed of the flesh "seditions." We are warned to stay away from such people: "Now I urge you, brethren, keep your eye on those who cause *dissensions* and hindrances contrary to the teaching which you learned, and turn away from them" (Romans 16:17, emphasis added). The problem is that we can run from others, but how do we run from our own fleshly hearts that love dissensions just as much?

Fruit of the Flesh #7: Factions

Now the deeds of the flesh are evident, which are . . . enmities, strife, jealousy, outbursts of anger, disputes, dissensions, **factions**, envying . . . (Galatians 5:19-21, emphasis added).

Here the Greek word the apostle Paul uses is *hairesis*, from which we get our word heresies. Sometimes the word is translated in the New Testament as sects. Let me explain why. This is the deed of the flesh that loves to rally troops and start a war. Whereas fleshly dissension in our heart pushes us to take sides, fleshly factions prompt us to gather whole groups of people to our way of thinking. Thus, it is also translated as causing divisions or "having a party-spirit." You know what I mean. Who among us has not started a "Take my side" party, a "We don't agree with them" convention, and a "They're wrong; we're right" rally?

A number of churches in Paul's day had been invaded by this fruit of the flesh. They were engorged with fleshly factions (1 Corinthians 11:19). No surprise. It can happen anywhere—in the family, in the workplace, or in any group, including (or some say, especially) in a church.

Fruit of the Flesh #8: Envying

Another deed of the flesh in the apostle Paul's *Catalog of Relational Sins* is the one Euripides called "the greatest of all diseases among men." Another called it "the twin brother of jealousy."

Now the deeds of the flesh are evident, which are . . . enmities, strife, jealousy, outbursts of anger, disputes, dissensions, factions, **envying** . . . (Galatians 5:19-21, emphasis added).

The Greek word he uses is the plural form of *phthonos*. He is not just talking about envy, but envy heaped upon envy. Whereas jealousy is the desire to have what others have, envy is the desire to not want anyone else to have it, either. Unlike jealousy that has some positive aspects to it, envy is its completely evil twin. The envy in our fleshly hearts wants others to be unhappy and miserable.

The worldly philosophers of our day insist there will come a day when the world will share its resources generously. Not as long as the flesh is active. It's just not in our depraved nature. Our envy-filled hearts cry out from deep within: *"If I can't have it, you can't have it either!"* No wonder many call envy "the most corroding of the vices." Philip Bailey, the English poet, described it as "a coal [that] comes hissing hot from hell." But, my friends, it's not just from the pit of hell. It also comes straight from the depths of our fleshly hearts.

And things like these . . .

Later in Paul's *Fruit of the Flesh Catalog*, he adds a disclaimer, of sorts. Accepting the fact he cannot list out every category of sin, he leaves room for miscellaneous sins he simply calls "things like these."

> . . . and *things like these*, of which I forewarn you, just as I have forewarned you, that those who practice such things will not inherit the kingdom of God (Galatians 5:21, emphasis added).

Frankly, we could go through a number of other lists of sins in the Bible. But, even at that, we would have to include *"and things like these. Et cetera. Et cetera. Et cetera. Ad infinitum. Ad nauseum."* There is a plethora of sin attacking us from the inside out and from the outside in.

I would like to quickly list some other fruit of the flesh the apostle Paul presents in his epistles to his fellow believers, especially those that relate to anger and our interpersonal conflicts. Take, for example, his words to the Colossians that are so very timely for us: "But now you also, put them all aside: **anger**, wrath, **malice**, **slander**, and **abusive speech** from your mouth" (Colossians 3:8, emphasis added).

Without repeating the words the apostle Paul used in Galatians 5:19-21, (e.g. "wrath" is the same word as "outbursts of anger"), we add to our list of the fruit of the flesh from Colossians 3:8:

Fruit of the Flesh #9: Anger

Here the apostle Paul uses the common Greek word *orge*, meaning temper, agitation, angry impulse, and violent indignation. It has its root in the word to tremble and quiver (Psalm 4:4), and is related to the word *parorgimos* used in Ephesians 4:26 that speaks of being enraged. This is the kind of anger that provokes us to hold a grudge and take revenge. It is the lasting kind of anger, not necessarily the immediate outburst. In Romans 12:19, the related verb and noun for taking revenge [*ekdikeo* and *ekdikesis*] are used. Frankly, this is the long term kind of anger we have all come to hate—just not enough.

Fruit of the Flesh #10: Malice

The Greek word *kakia* refers to our ill-will, evil thoughts, and malicious behavior. This is the hurtful kind of anger that sometimes remains in our thoughts for long periods. Eventually, it manifests itself in our actions that lash out to hurt, even the most innocent.

Fruit of the Flesh #11: Slander

Here the apostle Paul presents us with the Greek word *blasphemia*, which speaks of using injurious speech, seeking evil, casting judgment on people, and stating things as fact that are not true. In this sense, it is related to gossip and innuendo. The definitions speak for themselves. The long term consequences are familiar to us all.

Fruit of the Flesh #12: Abusive Speech

The apostle Paul chooses this Greek word *aischrologia* to describe our filthy language, our foul and obscene speech, and our anger-induced profanity. Earlier in his letter to the Galatians he also described some of our speech as cannibalistic, as we consume each other, one abusive word at a time: "But if you bite and devour one another, take care that you are not consumed by one another" (Galatians 5:15).

Let's move on to consider the apostle Paul's additional words from Ephesians 4:31, as we add a few more deeds of the flesh to our list: "Let all **bitterness** and wrath and anger and **clamor** and slander be put away from you, along with all malice" (Ephesians 4:31, emphasis added).

Fruit of the Flesh #13: Clamor

The Greek word *krauge* graphically pictures us crying out loud, creating an uproar and starting a brawl. It's the New Testament equivalent of the Hebrew word *hamah* which speak of shouting, making a commotion, and howling like a wild animal. Not a pretty sight, for sure.

Fruit of the Flesh #14: Bitterness

We would also be remiss if we did not take some time to address one of the biggest and ugliest of all the fruit of the flesh—bitterness. The Greek word most commonly used is *pikria*. It's a graphic word, describing a bitter root that produces bitter fruit. Consider some of the dramatic ways it is used to describe the bitterness of the heart produced by anger:

> Let all *bitterness* and wrath and anger and clamor and slander be put away from you, along with all malice (Ephesians 4:31, emphasis added).

> See to it that no one comes short of the grace of God; that no *root of bitterness* springing up causes trouble, and by it many be defiled . . . (Hebrews 12:15, emphasis added).

> . . . are you angry ["filled with bitter anger," Greek: *cholao*], (John 7:23).

> For I see that you are in the *gall of bitterness* and in the bondage of iniquity (Acts 8:23, emphasis added).

The gall of bitterness is the apostle Paul's dramatic way of explaining the deep rooted, long lasting poison of bitterness that expresses itself alongside the many forms of anger:

> Enmities. Strife. Jealousy. Outbursts of anger. Disputes. Dissensions, Factions. Envyings. Anger. Malice. Slander. Abusive speech. Clamor. Bitterness.

What a list! It should make our skin crawl. Worse yet, it should make us worry that, if left unchecked, this rotten fruit of the flesh will keep growing, increasing our harvest of putrid, rotten fruit. It's time for a fruit inspection of the heart. It's time to do an honest evaluation of the condition of our souls. Going back to the worm analogy, it's also time to stop biting into worms and get to the bitter root of the problem.

INSPECTING THE FRUIT

Taking each word (and not adding repeats) identify the frequency of any of these in your life.

We begin with those words found in Galatians 5:19-21:

Fruit of the Flesh #1: Enmities (Greek: *echthra*, meaning many forms of hatred and inward hostilities).

Often		Sometimes				Rarely			
10	9	8	7	6	5	4	3	2	1

Fruit of the Flesh #2: Strife (Greek: *eris*, meaning discord, contention, quarrel, wrangling, at odds and variance with others).

Often		Sometimes				Rarely			
10	9	8	7	6	5	4	3	2	1

Fruit of the Flesh #3: Jealousy (Greek: *zelos*, meaning envy, ambitious rivalry, fierce indignation, and emulations).

Often		Sometimes				Rarely			
10	9	8	7	6	5	4	3	2	1

Fruit of the Flesh #4: Outbursts of Anger (Greek: *thumos*, meaning wrath, fierce fits of rage, boiling outbursts, inflammatory indignation, piles of uncontrolled temper, and ungodly passion).

Often		Sometimes				Rarely			
10	9	8	7	6	5	4	3	2	1

Fruit of the Flesh #5: Disputes (Greek: *eritheia*, meaning self-seeking, self-promotion, selfish ambition, using unfair methods to win, putting oneself forward, and insisting on one's own way).

Often   Sometimes   Rarely
10 9   8   7   6   5   4   3   2   1

Fruit of the Flesh #6: Dissensions (Greek: *dichostasia*, meaning creating division, encouraging sedition, standing apart, taking sides, causing splits, and "rallying troops").

Often   Sometimes   Rarely
10 9   8   7   6   5   4   3   2   1

Fruit of the Flesh #7: Factions (Greek: *hairesis*, meaning engaging in storm-like activities, expressing divergent opinions, and creating sectarian division).

Often   Sometimes   Rarely
10 9   8   7   6   5   4   3   2   1

Fruit of the Flesh #8: Envyings (Greek: *phthonos*, meaning envy heaped on envy and a sinful desire to not want others to have what you do not have).

Often   Sometimes   Rarely
10 9   8   7   6   5   4   3   2   1

Now consider additional words from Colossians 3:8:

Fruit of the Flesh #9: Anger (Greek: *orge*, meaning temper, agitation, angry impulse, and violent indignation).

Often   Sometimes   Rarely
10 9   8   7   6   5   4   3   2   1

Fruit of the Flesh #10: Malice (Greek: *kakia*, meaning ill-will, evil thoughts, and malicious behavior)

Often   Sometimes   Rarely
10 9   8   7   6   5   4   3   2   1

Fruit of the Flesh #11: Slander (Greek: *blasphemia*, meaning using injurious speech, seeking evil, casting judgment, and stating things as fact that are not true. It is related to gossip and innuendo).

Often		Sometimes				Rarely			
10	9	8	7	6	5	4	3	2	1

Fruit of the Flesh #12: Abusive Speech (Greek: *aischrologia*, meaning filthy language, foul, obscene speech, and profanity).

Often		Sometimes				Rarely			
10	9	8	7	6	5	4	3	2	1

And now consider additional words from Ephesians 4:31 (cf. Acts 8:23; Hebrews 12:15):

Fruit of the Flesh #13: Clamor (Greek: *krauge*, meaning a loud outcry, an uproar, and brawling).

Often		Sometimes				Rarely			
10	9	8	7	6	5	4	3	2	1

Fruit of the Flesh #14: Bitterness (Greek: *pikria*, meaning a deeply-rooted, long-lasting poison that expresses itself in many forms of anger).

Often		Sometimes				Rarely			
10	9	8	7	6	5	4	3	2	1

Which of these are infesting your heart the most?

FURTHER ADVICE FROM THE MASTER GARDENER

Understanding there is an interaction with all the deeds of the flesh (Galatians 5:19-21), evaluate how you are presently doing.

	Under Holy Spirit Control						Out of Control			
Sexual Sins										
Immorality	10	9	8	7	6	5	4	3	2	1
Impurity	10	9	8	7	6	5	4	3	2	1
Sensuality	10	9	8	7	6	5	4	3	2	1
Religious Sins										
Idolatry	10	9	8	7	6	5	4	3	2	1
Sorcery (drugs)*	10	9	8	7	6	5	4	3	2	1
Enmities	10	9	8	7	6	5	4	3	2	1
Social Sins										
Strife	10	9	8	7	6	5	4	3	2	1
Jealousy	10	9	8	7	6	5	4	3	2	1
Outbursts of anger	10	9	8	7	6	5	4	3	2	1
Disputes	10	9	8	7	6	5	4	3	2	1
Dissentions	10	9	8	7	6	5	4	3	2	1
Factions	10	9	8	7	6	5	4	3	2	1
Envying	10	9	8	7	6	5	4	3	2	1
Sins of Excess										
Drunkenness	10	9	8	7	6	5	4	3	2	1
Carousing	10	9	8	7	6	5	4	3	2	1
Things like these:										
(Add to the list)										
_____ :	10	9	8	7	6	5	4	3	2	1
_____ :	10	9	8	7	6	5	4	3	2	1
_____ :	10	9	8	7	6	5	4	3	2	1
_____ :	10	9	8	7	6	5	4	3	2	1
_____ :	10	9	8	7	6	5	4	3	2	1

* (Greek: *pharmakeia,* which refers to the use of drugs, sometimes in connection with sorcery and idolatry)

CHAPTER TEN

THE ROTTEN HARVEST
OF SINFUL ANGER

Using the ungodly anger tree as an analogy, we have learned how to identify some of the many forms of unrighteous and unresolved anger in our lives. Below the surface are the roots, representing our real or imagined physical, emotional and spiritual needs. Above the surface are our biblical or unbiblical expectations as to how we desire those needs to be met. Further up the trunk, where the branches begin to spread, are the inevitable hurts we experience when those expectations are not met. The unresolved hurts can easily result in many branches of repressed or expressed forms of ungodly anger—picking on the innocent victim (scapegoating), building up and blowing up (stamp saving), getting sick (stress illness), running outwardly and retreating inwardly (withdrawing), and getting even (passive-aggression). Of course, we are also quite familiar with the many forms of expressed anger—the ones that show the world, "I'm really mad!"

In the last two chapters we listed some fourteen different fruit of the flesh, found in Galatians 5 and other passages. No need to repeat those. I do, however, want to remind us of our summary:

Unrighteous anger is an outward or inward expression of an unresolved hurt, based on a frustrated expectation that comes out of a real or imagined need.

THE STENCH OF UNGODLY ANGER

In my international travels I have had the opportunity to savor a number of kinds of fruit, many unfamiliar to us in the West. I have had my taste buds delighted, especially in Southeast Asia, with the likes of atis, kalamansi, mangoes, mangosteen, papaya, and my favorite, seniorita bananas. How sweet they are!

I was also invited to partake of a fruit that was, quite frankly, disgusting. It is called durian (Latin name: *Durio zibethinus*), apparently a cousin to the giant jackfruit. The old priests were known for speaking of durian as the fruit that "smells like hell and tastes like heaven." I am still waiting to taste the heavenly part. Many airlines, subways and trains will not allow the smelly fruit to be brought on board. No one is expected to travel well with the all-pervasive stench of this "onion-flavored custard," apparently a favorite food among elephants and orangutans!

Imagine assigning a smell to the fruit of our sinful flesh. Like durian, I think it would clear a room! The Bible is specific that our self-righteous deeds are like filthy garments (Isaiah 64:6)—dirty diapers in the nostrils of our Holy God. Before we get to the much-needed solution, I want us to briefly examine the stinky, rotten harvest of sinful anger in our lives, the kind that neither smells nor tastes like heaven. Quite the opposite.

THE STENCH OF UNGODLY ANGER—
EMOTIONALLY

Most people love the taste of freshly squeezed orange juice. Some of us swear by the health benefits of juicing, whereby fruit and vegetables are ground into a pulpy liquid. The Book of Proverbs, however, speaks graphically of the inward grinding of sinful anger as it slowly squeezes the life out of us. In fact, three times in the same verse the same Hebrew word is used:

> For the *churning* ["pressing, squeezing, wringing," Hebrew: *mits*] of milk produces butter. And the *pressing* [*mits*] the nose brings forth blood; so the *churning* [*mits*] of anger produces strife (Proverbs 30:33, emphasis added).

I am certain all of us can testify to the dramatic and emotional impact of conflict. Think of the last heart-wrenching argument we had with a loved one. Perhaps it was as recently as today. Our stomach churned like one of those old buckets with the wooden rod in the center that produced butter from cream—up and down, up and down, up and down! Our heart bled like we got pinched or

72

punched in the nose. We felt squeezed and wrung out. The only thing it produced was more quarrelling and anger. In fact, Round Two may shortly follow! In the meantime, we keep churning day and night.

Mark Twain remarked in similar fashion, "Anger is an acid that can do more harm to the vessel in which it is stored than to anything on which it is poured." I also agree, in general, with Ralph Waldo Emerson, "For every minute you remain angry, you give up sixty seconds of peace of mind." Actually, I think his estimates are off. For every minute of unresolved anger, I believe we give up a lifetime of peace, until the conflict is resolved.

Unresolved conflict, prompted by the deeds of the flesh, can turn our once-comfortable mattress into a bed of nails and our favorite dinner into a stale piece of bread and lukewarm water. In other words, it can ruin the best things in life.

It has been well said that he who angers us conquers us. We become a slave to every person upon whom we pour the vials of our wrath. The person with whom we are angry lives in our hearts all day and night. I have heard from fellow counselors that unresolved anger is, in their thinking, a temporary form of insanity, defined as repeating the same behaviors and hoping for a different outcome. In the words of Horace, the Roman poet during the time of Augustus Caesar, "Anger is a momentary madness, so control your passion or it will control you." That's worth considering.

THE STENCH OF UNGODLY ANGER— SOCIALLY

We also must consider the high cost of anger on our social lives. We don't need reminders of the far-too-painful reality that angry people are horrible to be around. Their anger can be highly contagious and easily fuel our wrath. King Solomon agreed: "Like charcoal to hot embers and wood to fire, so is a contentious man to kindle strife" (Proverbs 26:21).

Many of us could give testimony of being in a public place and hearing someone spout off their vitriolic language at some undeserving clerk, waitress or airline attendant. I confess my Italian blood boils and I want to mount my white horse and rush to the rescue. Instead, I just hold my nose at the stench of this ungodly treatment of the innocent.

If the truth be told, others of us don't have to leave the house to experience the rotten smell of unrighteous anger. It reeks daily:

Better is a dry morsel and quietness with it than a house full of feasting with strife (Proverbs 17:1).

It is better to live in a corner of a roof than in a house shared with a contentious woman . . . . It is better to live in a desert land than with a contentious and vexing woman (Proverbs 21:9; 25:24; 21:19).

Of course, King Solomon was writing instructions for his son, Rehoboam. He could have just as easily addressed this as a man-problem, as well as a kid-problem, or an everybody-problem. Angry people don't necessarily live longer. It just feels like they do to those who have to live around them.

My botanist friends have told me trees actually talk to each other when invaded by insects. They secrete a hormonal chemical, called pheromones, that trigger a response in members of their own species. In other words, wounded trees spread the word. I could not help but think of how true that is among humans. Although there is far too much abuse that goes unnoticed, sometimes those who have suffered get the last word. I recently read a brutally honest obituary of a vitriolic man, written by the victims of his lifelong abuse. I have edited it here but it would be well worth taking the time to read it in total:

Leslie Ray "Popeye" Charping was born in Galveston, Texas on November 20, 1942 and passed away January 30, 2017, which was 29 years longer than expected and much longer than he deserved. He leaves behind 2 relieved children . . . along with six grandchildren and countless other victims including an ex-wife, relatives, friends, neighbors, doctors, nurses and random strangers . . . . Leslie's hobbies included being abusive to his family, expediting trips to heaven for the beloved family pets . . . . Leslie's life served no other obvious purpose . . . he did not contribute to society or serve his community and he possessed no redeeming qualities . . . With Leslie's passing he will be missed only for what he never did; being a loving husband, father and good friend. No services will be held, there will be no prayers for eternal peace and no apologizes to the family he tortured. Leslie's remains will be cremated and kept in the barn until "Ray", the family donkey's wood shavings run out. Leslie's passing proves that evil does in fact die and hopefully marks a time of healing and safety for all. (Adapted from the actual obituary posted on the website of Carnes Funeral Home. <http://obit.carnesfuneralhome.com/leslie-ray-charping>).

Reading this sad obituary, one cannot avoid the unmistakable smell of ungodly anger still lingering on this abused family. It begs the question: What will our family write about us, if they were to tell the truth?

THE STENCH OF UNGODLY ANGER— PHYSICALLY

Observing his own life and the lives of those around him, King Solomon could well give this sage advice: "So, remove grief and anger from your heart and put away pain from your body, because childhood and the prime of life are fleeting" (Ecclesiastes 11:10).Scores of books have been written, detailing how anger and unresolved conflict literally destroys the body. Of course, some people know this and don't care. In fact, they have become quite addicted to both its effects and its cause. And there is a huge physical price to pay.

Almighty God has given us an emergency alarm system called the adrenal glands that produce the hormone epinephrine, also called adrenalin. When we are faced with a threat, an emergency or even an anticipated challenge, our adrenal glands shoot adrenalin into our blood stream. Our heart begins to beat faster and faster, increasing our blood circulation. Our blood pressure rises. Our minds go on high alert. Our vision is laser-focused. Every muscle is prepared for extreme exertion. Our whole body is now functioning at its optimum efficiency. We've all heard stories of athletes doing extraordinary feats and mothers lifting cars off of children. We have adrenalin to thank for that. Adrenalin is also the fuel behind the "fight or flight" response many of us have experienced in a crisis.

Doctors tell us adrenalin will not harm the body because after the emergency is over the glands settle to their normal function and the body relaxes. But consider the impact on one who treats everything like an emergency, one who is continually angry over work, relationships, money, or a host of things. His glands continue pumping adrenalin. His blood pressure stays up. His heart continues to beat faster. In fact, his body may even be addicted to "the rush." In reality, it has become an obsession. He literally wears his body out before its time.

It is a medical fact that, in many cases, high blood pressure, heart trouble, kidney disease, arthritis, headaches and strokes have a direct link to unresolved anger. It is also well known that a healthy approach to the challenges of life improves our resistance, even to such dreaded diseases as cancer. Sadly, in some cases, unresolved anger is properly diagnosed as a prolonged form of suicide.

THE STENCH OF UNGODLY ANGER—
SPIRITUALLY

Unrighteous and unresolved anger is not just physically, emotionally and socially debilitating; it also stinks spiritually. Consider the timeless words of the apostle Paul to the Ephesians. I think you will agree his words strike straight and true: "Be angry, and yet do not sin; do not let the sun go down on your anger, and *do not give the devil an opportunity*" (Ephesians 4:26-27, emphasis added). He went on to say in the same letter:

> Let no unwholesome word proceed from your mouth, but only such a word as is good for edification according to the need of the moment, *that it may give grace to those who hear. And do not grieve the Holy Spirit of God*, by whom you were sealed for the day of redemption. Let all bitterness and wrath and anger and clamor and slander be put away from you, along with all malice. *And be kind to one another, tender-hearted, forgiving each other, just as God in Christ also has forgiven you* (Ephesians 4:29-32, emphasis added).

Both of these passages are clear. Ungodly, unrighteous, unresolved, and unconfessed anger is a highly spiritual issue. The fruit of the flesh reaps lasting spiritual consequences. Drawing our principles from what the apostle Paul wrote in Ephesians 4, let's be more specific regarding:

THE FOUR SPIRITUAL CONSEQUENCES OF UNRIGHTEOUS AND UNRESOLVED ANGER

Consequence #1: It gives the devil an open door into our lives.

As shocking as this may be, ungodly and unresolved anger can open the door to demonic influence. In essence, it says, "Satan, you are welcome into my life and my family for generations. Have your evil way with all of us! "

Consequence #2: It does not extend grace to others.

The Gospel of Grace involves receiving the unmerited gift of eternal life which we don't deserve and could never earn. Our treatment of others also needs to be an underserved gift, a reflection of the grace of God we have received (Ephesians 2:8-9; Titus 3:5). Sadly, our sinful anger is, in reality, the anti-gospel— the opposite of the good news proclaimed by the apostle Paul: "But God demonstrates His own love toward us, in that while we were yet sinners, Christ died for us" (Romans 5:8).

Consequence #3: It grieves the Holy Spirit.

Our fleshly anger saddens the One who dwells in us, the One who gave us the emotion of anger as His energizer to make positive change, and the One who desires to fill us with His life-giving Spirit. In fact, He feels about our sin the way we feel when attending a funeral of a precious loved one. Our sinful anger grieves Him deeply.

Consequence #4: It mocks the very kindness and forgiveness we have received from God in Christ.

What disrespect to declare ourselves forgiven by God as objects of His mercy and kindness while, at the same time, allowing the fruit of anger to prevail in our lives. Few Scriptures say this better than the apostle Paul's words here in his letter to the Ephesians. It's worth repeating:

Let all bitterness and wrath and anger and clamor and slander be put away from you, along with all malice. Be kind to one another, tender-hearted, forgiving each other, just as God in Christ also has forgiven you (Ephesians 4:31-32).

Unrighteous and unresolved anger neither smells good on the outside, nor tastes great on the inside. Like a rotting piece of fruit, it stinks on many levels—emotionally, socially, physically and spiritually. Rather than settle for the stench and rotten taste of the fruit of the flesh as being our new normal, we need to spend our days walking by the Spirit and pursuing the sweet-smelling and sweet-tasting fruit of the Holy Spirit of God: love, joy, peace, patience, kindness, goodness, faithfulness, gentleness and self-control (cf. Galatians 5:19-23).

INSPECTING THE FRUIT

1. In what one area has your anger been the most costly? Briefly explain.

- Emotionally___
     Specifically, _____

- Socially: ____
     Specifically, _____

- Physically: ____
     Specifically, _____

- Spiritually: ____
     Specifically, _____

2. Reflect on the following counsel from King Solomon as it relates to your foolish anger: "Do not be eager in your heart to be angry, for anger resides in the bosom of fools" (Ecclesiastes 7:9).

FURTHER ADVICE FROM THE MASTER GARDENER

Complete the assignment in the Appendix, titled *Ancient Wisdom Related to Anger.*

CHAPTER ELEVEN

PRUNING THE
DISEASED ANGER TREE

Permit me to share a few quotes I find true to my experience:

"A garden is a thing of beauty and a job forever."

"People who think they can run the earth should begin with a small garden."

"A gardener is a woman who loves flowers and marries a man who hates weeds."

My wife, who grew up around horses and barns, gardens and fruit trees, decided to marry an ill-equipped city boy. As such, even after forty-five years of marriage and over twenty-five years living in the same house, she refuses to let me loose in the backyard with anything resembling a garden tool. She has learned well from painful experience.

In my enthusiastic but inexperienced hands, garden clippers and pruning shears are grim reapers. It is no surprise she will not let me prune our Nanny Tree, the apple tree we planted in memory of my fruit-loving mother. But pruning is needed nonetheless, which is why God brought into my life my wife's sister, as well as our skilled gardener and patient botanist friends. With their guidance and step-by-step instructions, pruning has become both simple and effective.

The process for dealing with our unresolved and unrighteous anger involves five simple, but very effective pruning steps. In each of these you will find the key word: TODAY. There is a sense, biblically-speaking, the noun today can be seen as an action verb, calling us to pray often, "Lord, help me to *DO TODAY* well." I am encouraged by a number of key passages:

> See, I have set before you *today* life and prosperity, and death and adversity . . . . I call heaven and earth to witness against you *today*, that I have set before you life and death, the blessing and the curse. So choose life in order that you may live, you and your descendants (Deuteronomy 30:15, 19, emphasis added).

> If it is disagreeable in your sight to serve the Lord, choose for yourselves *today* whom you will serve . . . but as for me and my house, we will serve the Lord (Joshua 24:15, emphasis added).

> So do not worry about *tomorrow*; for *tomorrow* will care for itself. *Each day* has enough trouble of its own (Matthew 6:34, emphasis added).

Oh, how life would be so much smoother if we admitted and dealt with today's anger—today! If we want healthy fruit, timely pruning is essential.

Pruning Step #1: Trace it TODAY

Using the anger tree we talked about earlier, we can trace our anger by the associated behaviors—scapegoating, stamp saving, stress illness, withdrawal, passive-aggression or the many forms of expressed anger. First, we trace it back through the hurt. Then we try to identify the expectation. Ultimately, we must get to the root—the physical, emotional or spiritual need, remembering that if it is a real need our Heavenly Father knows about it (Matthew 6:8) and promises to meet that need (Philippians 4:19) in His way and in His time.

I recently communicated my frustration to my wife when she did not answer her phone or respond to my many texts. I was especially angry when she returned home late, even though I discovered she had a very good reason. Even so, why such an unusual over-reaction on my part? Tracing my anger helped me understand.

As I wrote in the preface, at the age of nineteen, my forty-nine year old father died of a heart attack. It was sudden and shocking. It was also disturbing because the night before we had a pretty typical teenager-parent argument. We both went to bed angry and never finished the argument with the usual hugs. I never saw him again.

In my role as a minister, my life has been full of unexpected hospital visits and funerals. By tracing my anger at my wife's lack of immediate response, I was soon able to figure out why I was so upset. I imagined her in a hospital emergency room or, worse, in a morgue. I shared with her the anguish I felt at the deaths I've experienced. I expressed my very unrealistic expectation that she respond immediately when I call. I was able to admit that the anger comes out of an emotional need, one I, of course, know should be left in the loving hands of our sovereign God. My wife's days are numbered by Him. My worry and anger is, therefore, misplaced. She also came to more fully understand my desire that she be more careful to respond to my calls as soon as possible. Tracing my anger helped her as much as it did me.

Pruning Step #2: Admit it TODAY

A newspaper reporter once asked the popular English writer, G.K. Chesterton, "What's wrong with the world?" He replied, "I am." The essential problem in dealing with anger is to begin with ourselves; not others. James, the brother of our Lord, called it like it really is:

> What is the source of quarrels and conflicts among *you*? Is not the source *your* pleasures that wage war in *your* members? (James 4:1, emphasis added).

> But *each one* is tempted when he is carried away and enticed by his *own* lust. Then when lust has conceived, it gives birth to sin; and when sin is accomplished, it brings forth death. Do not be deceived, my beloved brethren (James 1:14-16, emphasis added).

True repentance from our sinful anger involves admitting it. It means taking responsibility and not blaming others. It means not even blaming the flesh, the devil or the world. Oh, they certainly tempt us, but they don't force us. Even if you hurt me, my explosive reaction is still under my control. No one steals the fruit of the Spirit from my life unless I let it happen.

I draw this conclusion from the many biblical uses of the Greek word *noutheteo* which refers to admonishing and warning someone by causing them to bring the matter to the front of the mind (Acts 3:19). King David demonstrated the practice clearly, when after a long season of keeping his sin secret, he cried out to the Lord, "Acquit me of hidden faults" (Psalm 19:12).

As stated in an earlier chapter, when we sin we grieve the Holy Spirit of God (Ephesians 4:30). The Greek word *lupeo* the apostle Paul uses means to cause the Holy Spirit deep sorrow, like the anguish we feel at the loss of a loved one. When we sin and fall short of God's glory and holy standards, we cause God to grieve. The first step to true repentance is to admit our sin and how much it brings sorrow to our Creator.

I remind us of the story in 2 Samuel 11-12 where King David's sin of adultery with Bathsheba and murder of Uriah, her husband, should be familiar to all of us. David could not truly experience the fullness of renewed fellowship with God until he repented. The process of repentance began when David finally made a full and complete admission of his sin. After living about a year of lies and self-deception, he finally came to grip with the truth and admitted, "I have sinned against the Lord" (2 Samuel 12:13). Later in the Psalms he described the folly and pain of trying to hide his sin for so long: "For I know my transgressions, and my sin is ever before me" (Psalm 51:3).

Let's consider also Psalm 32, another Psalm written by David. By the way, the title presents this psalm as a *maskil*, the Hebrew word for a teaching psalm. You also will see him use the word *Selah,* which means pause. I like to translate it as "Stop and think about that." Let the words of David's testimony be our teaching psalm and our pondering moment, as we deal with our ungodly anger:

> How blessed is he whose transgression is forgiven, whose sin is covered! How blessed is the man to whom the LORD does not impute iniquity, and in whose spirit there is no deceit! When I kept silent about my sin, my body wasted away through my groaning all day long. For day and night Your hand was heavy upon me; My vitality was drained away as with the fever heat of summer. Selah. I acknowledged my sin to You and my iniquity I did not hide. I said, "I will confess my transgressions to the LORD" and You forgave the guilt of my sin. *Selah* (Psalm 32:1-5, emphasis added).

Selah. Stop and think about that. And while we are still pondering Psalm 32 let me remind us of the first part of Psalm 51. Remember this psalm was written after the prophet Nathan confronted King David. He finally stopped running and admitted his sin:

> Be gracious to me, O God, according to Your lovingkindness, according to the greatness of Your compassion blot out my transgressions. Wash me thoroughly from my iniquity and cleanse me from my sin. For I know my transgressions and my sin is ever before me. Against You, You only, I have sinned and done what is evil in Your sight, so that You are justified when You speak and blameless when You judge (Psalm 51:1-4).

King David went on to say:

> Behold, You desire *truth in the innermost being,* and in the *hidden part* You will make me know wisdom (Psalm 51:6, emphasis added).

The God who searches and knows our hearts is calling us to tell the truth in our innermost being and in our hidden part about our unrighteous and unconfessed anger. It's time to stop the pretending, the blaming, the hiding and the cover-up. It's time to stop the rationalizing and the minimizing. It's time to listen to the promptings of the Holy Spirit and admit our sin of anger. That is a major step in the process of repentance and the subsequent restoration to fellowship with our God and others. In fact, there really can be no true repentance without it.

A number of years ago I was teaching a seminar to a group of about four hundred men. After a few hours of teaching, I was giving an invitation for the men to repent of their unconfessed sin. Before I could finish, one of the men stood with arms outstretched, as if hanging on a cross. He made his way to the aisle and literally fell at my feet. In full admission of his sin, and recognizing the true consequences to himself and his family, he began to wail, "Oh God, what have I done?" A few of the men came forward and piled on top of him, trying to console him. Without any prompting, the entire crowd of men stood quietly. They knew they could just as well be where that man was.

The acknowledgement of the depth of his sin before God was his first step to legitimate confession and spiritual renewal. When we recognize the depths of our sin of anger and its full effects, repentance begins to happen. Speaking from his own experience, King David would say to any of us who are living in the mire of unacknowledged sin, "I acknowledged my sin to You, and my iniquity I did not hide . . ." (Psalm 32:5).

By the way, years later I was able to meet with that dear brother. His life and his family have been restored. With confidence, I believe I can share what I truly believe he would say to all of us: "Stop hiding. Stop making excuses. Stop lying to yourself and others. Stop blaming your dysfunctional family, your tough breaks in life or your high blood pressure. You sinned. Now admit it today."

Pruning Step #3: Confess it TODAY

After bringing the reality of our sin to the front of our mind and admitting it, it now needs to move from our mind to our mouth. Again, we learn from King David's own words:

> I acknowledged my sin to You, and my iniquity I did not hide; I said, '*I will confess my transgressions to the Lord*'; and You forgave the guilt of my sin. Selah (Psalm 32:5, emphasis added).

> For I *confess* my iniquity; I am full of anxiety because of my sin (Psalm 38:18, emphasis added).

I also remind us of the familiar New Testament passage:

> If we *confess* our sins, He is faithful and righteous to forgive us our sins and to cleanse us from all unrighteousness (1 John 1:9, emphasis added).

Here in the apostle John's first epistle we find the Greek word *homologeo*. It comes from two words: *homo*, meaning the same and *logeo*, meaning to speak. To confess is to express the same words about a matter God would say. The apostle Paul declared in his epistle to the Romans, "If you *confess* [Greek: *homologeo*] with your lips that *Jesus is Lord* . . ." (Romans 10:9, emphasis added). Jesus is Lord! That is exactly what the Father would confess about His Son.

(Perhaps we would do well to confess this once more in our heart of hearts: Jesus is truly Lord!)

Here is the point. Sincere confession of our sinful anger, in all its forms, is not saying: "I am sorry I got caught" or "If I offended you" or the ever popular, "Maybe I was wrong." True confession says what God would say about an ungodly thought or sinful action; not what others or our excuse-making heart would say. The word *homologeo* demands we confess what we believe our Holy and Righteous God would declare:

"That sin of anger you are finally admitting falls short of My character, My attributes, and My glory!"

"That sin of anger is inconsistent with who you are as My child."

"That sin of anger deeply grieves My Holy Spirit."

When I was a little boy of nine I memorized a prayer I still believe to be quite precious. In some churches it is called *The Act of Contrition* Prayer. I often recite it deeply within my soul:

O, my God, I am heartily sorry for having offended Thee; and I detest all my sins because of Thy just punishments, but most of all, because they offend Thee, my God, Who art all good and deserving of all my love . . .

Trace it today. Admit it today. Confess it today. I can think of no better way to begin to prune our angry hearts. But it is just the beginning. There are more pruning steps ahead.

INSPECTING THE FRUIT

1. Why is dealing with anger today so important?

2. Reflect on a time when you let your anger fester. What happened?

3. Read the following passage and underline the key words for getting along with others.

> To sum up, all of you be harmonious, sympathetic, brotherly, kindhearted, and humble in spirit; not returning evil for evil or insult for insult, but giving a blessing instead; for you were called for the very purpose that you might inherit a blessing. For, "The one who desires life, to love and see good days, must keep his tongue from evil and his lips from speaking deceit. He must turn away from evil and do good; he must seek peace and pursue it. For the eyes of the Lord are toward the righteous, and His ears attend to their prayer, but the face of the Lord is against those who do evil" (1 Peter 3:8-12).

FURTHER ADVICE FROM THE MASTER GARDENER

Read in the Appendix the detailed study online of 1 Peter 3:8-12 titled *A Life Skills Outline for Getting Along With Others: A Biblical Guide to Living in Peace with Others.*

CHAPTER TWELVE

PRUNING EVEN MORE OF THE DISEASED ANGER TREE

I love my weed-wacker, my hedge-clipper and my container of herbicide. As you have already figured out, that does not mean I am skilled in their use. To my unskilled eye, every stray shoot without a flower is a weed, deserving of being wacked or poisoned. Every tree or shrub deserves a military haircut.

I do know pruning is a multi-step process. Unlike my propensity to slash and cut anything that appears out of place, pruning is a precise process that, if done correctly, does more good than harm. So it is with pruning our ungodly anger tree.

So far we have seen the first three steps in God's process for pruning the diseased anger tree.

• Pruning Step #1: Trace it TODAY

• Pruning Step #2: Admit it TODAY

• Pruning Step #3: Confess it TODAY

Let's continue with our final two pruning steps.

Pruning Step #4: Turn from it TODAY

The process of repentance for the believer involves tracing, admitting and confessing our sinful anger and ungodly wrath. It also involves true repentance—turning immediately from that sin. Many of us are quick to confess and slow to repent. No wonder we keep repeating the same sins over and over again. Yes, King David was completely broken and contrite. He also had every intention of never returning to his sin again. Consider his heartfelt prayer:

For You do not delight in sacrifice, otherwise I would give it;
You are not pleased with burnt offering. The sacrifices of God
are a broken spirit; a broken and a contrite heart, O God, You
will not despise (Psalm 51:16-17).

God doesn't want our phony words of confession, nor our
insincere religious commitments. He wants the sacrificial
commitment to a true repentance that only comes from a broken
spirit and a contrite heart. Anything less is not true repentance. The
apostle Paul made a clear distinction between regret and repentance:
"For the sorrow that is according to the will of God produces a
repentance without regret, leading to salvation, but the sorrow of the
world produces death" (2 Corinthians 7:10).

One of my favorite passages of Scripture is found in Luke's
Gospel where he records the words of Jesus both confronting and
encouraging proud, but soon-to-be broken, apostle Peter: "Simon,
Simon, behold, Satan has demanded permission to sift you like
wheat; but I have prayed for you, that your faith may not fail; and
you, when once you have *turned again* strengthen your brothers"
(Luke 22:31-32, emphasis added).

Here we find the Greek word *epistrepho* that refers to turning
back, turning around, and turning away. In simple terms, it means to
repent and return to where you were. In modern Greece, if you were
to examine the back of a glass soda bottle, you will find this same
word *epistrepho*. It makes sense because the word most completely
means: "Return for Filling." It is also related to the word *metanoeo*,
meaning to change our minds as we change our behaviors.

Isn't that what we need to do? The sin of unrepentant anger
empties us out of the fruit of the Spirit and our intimacy with God.
Like a dirty soda bottle we lay in the gutter. Once we admit and
confess our sin and return to God, He cleanses us and fills us with
His Holy Spirit, the One who produces the fruit of love, joy, peace,
patience, etc. (Galatians 5:22-23). We have both a change of mind
and a change of behavior.

True repentance involves more than being sorry we got caught. It
involves a deep resolve to do our best to never do it again. It means
putting ourselves in a place where we can be held accountable to not
repeat the same offense. This is exactly what happened to King
David. May his familiar prayer also be ours:

Behold, I was brought forth in iniquity, and in sin my mother conceived me. Behold, You desire truth in the innermost being and in the hidden part You will make me know wisdom. Purify me with hyssop, and I shall be clean; wash me, and I shall be whiter than snow. Make me to hear joy and gladness; let the bones which You have broken rejoice. Hide Your face from my sins and blot out all my iniquities. Create in me a clean heart, O God, and renew a steadfast spirit within me. Do not cast me away from Your presence and do not take Your Holy Spirit from me. Restore to me the joy of Your salvation and sustain me with a willing spirit. Then I will teach transgressors Your ways and sinners will be converted to You. Deliver me from blood guiltiness, O God, the God of my salvation. Then my tongue will joyfully sing of Your righteousness. O Lord, open my lips, that my mouth may declare Your praise. For You do not delight in sacrifice, otherwise I would give it. You are not pleased with burnt offering. The sacrifices of God are a broken spirit. A broken and a contrite heart, O God, You will not despise (Psalm 51:5-17).

Let's also consider the redemptive side of this process of pruning our anger, as Jesus declares to Simon one of the fruitful results of true repentance—ministering to others. Jesus consoled Peter with the words: "when once you have turned again, *strengthen* your brothers" (Luke 22:32, emphasis added).

Here we find the Greek word *sterizo*. It speaks of fixing things that are broken, making firm things that are shaky, and strengthening things that are weak. That's the goal. As we truly turn from unrighteous anger, we pray we will be used of God to strengthen others and point them to the One who can fix them, as He fixed us.

Experience teaches the love of fruit is not enough to make us good gardeners. We must also learn to deal with the things that threaten the health of the fruit. Pruning our sinful anger involves a process that can be easily remembered as:

The A.C.T.S. of Repentance

A. ADMITTING the sin of anger in our <u>mind</u>.
C. CONFESSING the sin of anger with our <u>mouth</u>.
T. TURNING from the sin of anger in our <u>manner</u>.
S. STRENGTHENING others in our <u>ministry</u>.

I love the redemptive result. The fruit of that pruning process is clearly presented in Scripture: "Therefore repent [Greek: *metanoeo*] and return [Greek: *epistrepho*], so that your sins may be wiped away, in order that *times of refreshing* may come from the presence of the Lord" (Acts 3:19, emphasis added). May our sin of anger be wiped away and those times of refreshing be ours in abundance.

Let's review:

Pruning Step #1: Trace it TODAY.

Pruning Step #2: Admit it TODAY.

Pruning Step #3: Confess it TODAY.

Pruning Step #4: Turn from it TODAY.

Now comes one final pruning step.

Pruning Step #5: Handle it TODAY

Most every day we will face situations that produce anger. It is the consequence of living on a planet filled with fellow sinners. We must know ourselves enough to observe what anger branches we are perching on. We must then deal with the inevitable hurts that come from frustrated expectations. Ultimately, we must daily acknowledge Who it is that meets our physical, emotional and spiritual needs. Again I remind us of the timeless counsel of the apostle Paul: "Be angry, and yet do not sin; do not let the sun go down on your anger, and do not give the devil an opportunity" (Ephesians 4:26-27). It coincides with the relationship-building words in 1 Corinthians 13 many rightly call the Love Chapter: "love . . . does not take into account a wrong suffered" (1 Corinthians 13:4-5). In the words of Billy Graham, "Learn to balance the books at the end of each day."

There is an old Latin proverb: "He who goes to bed angry has the devil as a bedfellow." My wife and I made a commitment when we got married we would never go to bed when there is strife between us. We have never regretted that decision, even though, in the early years, it meant some painful nights of long and sometimes heated discussions. We have followed our early agreement to end those intense conversations in prayer, followed by a season of forgiveness. We have committed ourselves to the practice of taking care of today's anger today, knowing that in so doing, we won't ever have to worry about yesterday's unresolved anger. Truthfully, after almost forty-five years of marriage, either of us could die and there would be no unresolved issues.

INSPECTING THE FRUIT

A vital step to dealing with conflict involves tracing our anger. Reflect on a recent situation where you expressed what you know to be ungodly anger. Now trace it from the root of the problem to its consequences.

1. What were my basic needs?
   (Review *Our Basic Needs* in Chapter Four, titled *Getting to the Root of My Anger*).

   Physically: _____

   Emotionally: _____

   Spiritually: _____

2. What were my expectations?
   (Review *Frustrated Expectations* in Chapter Four, titled *Getting to the Root of My Anger*)

3. What were my unresolved hurts?
   (Review *Up the Trunk Where the Real Hurt Awaits* in Chapter Five)

4. In what ways did I repress or express my anger?
   (Review *The Many Branches of Unrighteous Anger* and *More of Those Weak Limbs* in Chapters Six and Seven)

(Continued on next page)

Scapegoating (Picking on the Innocent Victim): ___

Stamp Saving (Building Up and Blowing Up): ___

Stress Illness (Getting Sick): ___

Withdrawal (Running Outwardly. Retreating Inwardly):___

Passive-Aggression(Getting Even): ___

Expression (Letting It Show): ___

5. What kind of ungodly fruit came out?
(Review *The Fruit of the Flesh* in Chapters Eight and Nine)

Enmities: ___

Strife: ___

Jealousy: ___

Outbursts of anger: ___

Disputes: ___

Dissensions: ___

Factions: ___

Envyings: ___

Anger: ___

Malice: ___

Slander: ___

Abusive Speech: ___

Clamor: ___

Bitterness: ___

6. What were the consequences of the conflict?
    (Review *The Rotten Harvest of Sinful Anger* in Chapter Ten)

    The stench of my anger emotionally: _____

    The stench of my anger socially: _____

    The stench of my anger physically: _____

    The stench of my anger spiritually: _____

Once I have traced it, it is now time to:

    Admit my anger TODAY.

    Confess my anger TODAY.

    Turn from my anger TODAY.

    Handle it TODAY.

(Review *Pruning the Diseased Anger Tree* in Chapters Eleven and Twelve)

FURTHER ADVICE FROM THE MASTER GARDENER

Read the Story of David's process of repentance in 2 Samuel, Chapters 11 and 12, as well as what he said about it in Psalm 32, 38 and 51.

Specifically identify the passages related to:

• The progression of his spiritual rebellion.

• The pattern of his spiritual renewal.

• The results of his spiritual restoration.

(For further study, I refer you to Chapter 41 and 42 of *The Purity War: A Biblical Guide to Living in an Immoral World* by James Cecy, available through www.puritywar.com or www.jaron.org)

CHAPTER THIRTEEN

GARDENING TIPS FOR DEALING WITH ANGER DAILY

Who am I to give gardening tips? There was a time when I spent a great deal of money buying lady bugs, the natural enemies of many insects. I was told they would control the aphids that were destroying our roses. I released hundreds. It would have been prudent to tell my wife. The next day I jumped out of my chair as the pest exterminator was finishing his routine spraying of our yard. A costly oversight, for sure.

I recall another time when I was feeling impressed with myself because my front lawn was greener than all of our neighbors. I decided to cut it even shorter than recommended by my wife and her "know-it-all" gardener friends. On the first day it looked like a manicured masterpiece. On day three it was scorched earth. (Oh yes, I forgot to mention it was well over 108 degrees outside—over 42 degrees Celsius.) Apparently, those "know-it-alls" really do know it all!

My frustration also became a lesson for dealing with the heat of anger and helping keep our lives from becoming parched and dry. I remind us of our anger tree pruning steps from the last two chapters:

Pruning Step #1: Trace it TODAY.

Pruning Step #2: Admit it TODAY.

Pruning Step #3: Confess it TODAY.

Pruning Step #4: Turn from it TODAY.

Pruning Step #5: Handle it TODAY.

How do we take care of today's anger TODAY, before it becomes tomorrow's unresolved conflict? Early in my Christian life I designed some reminders I have used for many years to help keep my anger in check on a daily basis. I'd like to share those with you.

In times past, I referred to them as *My Ten Commandments for Dealing With Anger.*" In keeping with the fruit tree analogy, I was tempted to call these *My Ten Principles of Spiritual Pomology* or even *The Ten Steps of Effective Fruticulture* (Yes, that's a word). I even tried out *The Ten Gardening Tips for Dealing with Stinky, Rotten, Worm-Infested Anger-Fruit.*" I think it is best to stick with the condensed version: *Gardening Tips for Dealing with Anger Daily.*

Gardening Tip #1: Be more tolerant of other's shortcomings.
"Lighten up!"

Settle it, folks. People are going to make mistakes. After all, only God can use a pencil without the need for an eraser. We are going to get hurt today. Some of our expectations are not going to be fulfilled today. We need to learn to relax our expectations, to be more tolerant of other's shortcomings and overlook some of the slips people around us will make today. Some of us have become consumed with high expectations and it is no surprise we have become disgruntled by the low realities. Listen to some ancient but wise counsel:

> A man's discretion makes him slow to anger, and it is his glory to overlook a transgression (Proverbs 19:11).

> Above all, keep fervent in your love for one another, because love covers a multitude of sins (1 Peter 4:8).

In the more modern words of four-star General Colin Powell, "Get mad, then get over it!" In other words, don't take every offense as personal. Daily we need to pray for a softer heart and thicker skin. Daily we need to ask the Lord for more laughter before we die as miserable old souls. Perhaps some help with this prayer is in order:

> "Lord, help me to be more tolerant of other's shortcomings. Dear God, help me to lighten up a bit!"

Gardening Tip #2: Don't provoke others to anger.

"Don't push each other's button!"

This you know, my beloved brethren. But everyone must be quick to hear, slow to speak and slow to anger (James 1:19).

If we are going to be honest today, we have to admit that each of us has an anger button—that thing people do to push us over the edge. Maybe it's someone tailgating us. Perhaps it's someone misjudging our motives or embarrassing us. Think about this for a moment. If someone wanted to, how could they get us really angry?

In the early years of my marriage, if I was losing an argument, I would often push my wife's anger button. My goal was sinfully planned. I would try to get her to over-react, so I could win. I'd look at her with a smirk and say, "You know you are just like your mother." She'd get furious and scream. Then I would say, "You see. I was right. You are just like her!" It did not go well from there. I quickly learned to stay clear of those anger-inflaming words.

Recently, I was discussing this portion of the book with my wife and our married children. Our normally quiet daughter spoke up and said to her husband, who is known for his strong opinions: "I know I have anger buttons; you installed them!" We all laughed, including him. I then read a text I had received a few weeks earlier: "I'm sorry. I didn't mean to push all your buttons. I was just looking for mute." We had a lively discussion and quickly acknowledged that provoking others to anger is not always so humorous. We all wish we had pushed the mute button, instead.

We do not have to be around people very long before we learn how to push the anger button of a loved one. In his letter to the Ephesians and the companion epistle to the Colossians, Paul warns fathers: "Do not provoke your children to anger . . ." (Ephesians 6:4) and "Do not exasperate your children, so that they will not lose heart" (Colossians 3:21).

The Greek words he uses are quite explicit. In Ephesians 6 he is calling fathers to not provoke [Greek: *parogizo*] their children in such a way that rouses them to wrath. In Colossians 3, he is commanding fathers not to exasperate [Greek: *erethizo*] their children and embitter them to a point of losing heart and becoming dispirited [Greek: *athumeo*]. Paul's point is clear. A father's role is to exercise godly anger that breaks his child's <u>will</u> and produces godly change. It is not to express ungodly anger that breaks his child's spirit. In other words, don't push your children's buttons!

Provoking those close to us, or anyone else, for that matter, is not only sinful; it can also be dangerous. Consider the ancient words from Proverbs: "The terror of a king is like the growling of a lion; he who provokes him to anger forfeits his own life" (Proverbs 20:2).

Gardening Tip #3: Don't knowingly put yourself in a situation where you know you'll get angry.

"Don't grab the dog by the ear!"

Sometimes our anger feels justified and it is; other times it feels right and it isn't. Our anger can start out as righteous indignation (controlled, exercised in love and restorative), just as God intended our anger to be. But it can so easily become unrighteous anger (uncontrolled, selfish and destructive), especially when we are confronted by an angry situation and angry people. Knowing when it is time to leave the scene of a conflict takes divine wisdom and supernatural courage. Once again, we rely on the ancient wisdom literature to provide instruction: "Keeping away from strife is an honor for a man, but any fool will quarrel" (Proverbs 20:3).

Some people are addicted to chaos. They cannot live without it and create it quite intentionally. Most even admit their chaos is contagious. In dealing with such people our best bet is to heed these words: "Do not associate with ["befriend," Hebrew: *ra'ah*] a man given to anger; or go with a hot-tempered man, or you will learn his ways, and find a snare for yourself" (Proverbs 22:24-25).

If we hang out with an angry person, we will learn his angry ways and become as trapped as he is. Run, baby, run! Get out of that situation as quickly as possible. This can be especially hard when we live in the same house or work in the same place. In that case, we do the best we can to not become like them. We need to take to heart the apostle Paul's counsel: "If possible, so far as it depends on you, be at peace with all men" (Romans 12:18).

This Gardening Tip also means staying out of other people's business. Some of us rescuing-type people need to heed the wisdom of Solomon: "Like one who takes a dog by the ears is he who passes by and meddles with strife not belonging to him" (Proverbs 26:17).

Who among us doesn't understand the simple truth? Grab the ear of a dog fighting with another dog and those angry critters are most certainly going to forget their own quarrel and turn their raging fury on you. Ask any seasoned law enforcement officers you know. They will share that the greatest threats to their safety are domestic quarrels. Many officers, trying to break up fights between family members, have found themselves in the hospital or even dead from wounds inflicted by the very people they were trying to protect.

So it is when we meddle with matters best left to the quarreling parties to work out themselves or with the help of a counselor better suited for the task. Do not knowingly put yourself in a situation where you know you'll get angry. "Don't grab fighting dogs by the ear!" A valuable lesson in the dog park and in life!

Gardening Tip #4: Stop a quarrel before it gets out of control.

"Don't let the water out of the dam!"

Perhaps you have heard the story of the little Dutch boy with his finger in the dike, holding it there for fear if he let go the dam would break and all the water would destroy everything in its path. Whether it is a myth or based on a true story still remains a matter of debate. What is not debatable is the lesson it teaches. We need to take responsibility for not letting things get out of control, including an argument. This principle is not new. Three thousand years ago King Solomon used a similar illustration: "The beginning of strife is like letting out water, so abandon the quarrel before it breaks out" (Proverbs 17:14).

Most of us know when disagreements are getting out of control. Instead of doing what we should do to stop the onslaught, we often roll up our sleeves and get ready for battle. We need to learn to stop an argument before it goes too far. The old saying is also true when it comes to fighting: "If one will not; two cannot!" When we feel ourselves ready to over-react, we need to take a breath. It's not rocket science. Or maybe it is. They always count down before blast-off! Perhaps we might even say:

"I know I'm getting angry and defensive. Let me re-phrase what I just said."

"I don't want to argue. Let me calm down for a moment."

And during that time we need to put our finger in the dike and pray:

"Lord, help me to back off."

"God, help me to not let the water out of the dam!"

Gardening Tip #5: Don't talk behind another's back.

"Don't rally troops!"

Today, we often talk about "fueling the fire." The expression comes from the three-thousand year old proverb: "For lack of wood the fire goes out, and where there is no whisperer, contention quiets down" (Proverbs 26:20). King Solomon is saying angry situations are troubling enough, but when people talk about the situation to others, it fuels the conflict. How true this is.

After decades of pastoral ministry, I have come to the conclusion most churches do not split over doctrinal issues, as much as they would like to use that as their spiritual rationale. Most churches split over a violation of this proverb. In modern terms, it is a common problem I call "rallying troops." I am very certain we all recognize some form of this.

For example, two people have a substantial disagreement and instead of dealing quietly and directly with each other, they begin a virtual campaign. One side rallies their troops, those who support their side (or, in many cases, just don't like the person on the other side). Sadly, the other side does the same, gathering their own army of supporters.

As is often the case, the two original parties decide the conflict isn't worth it and they decide to make up. They reconcile with each other. Praise the Lord! But, even though time has passed, we are naïve to think the matter is over. By now, troop members from one side have started battling with the well-outfitted army from the other side. There are even traitors who have, by now, switched armies. They are sometimes called *frenemies*. These are people who pretend to be friends and actually have joined the other side. These group wars are never simple! The more backbiting and gossip that occurs the more the conflict is fueled, often beyond easy solution and sometimes for generations. Remember the Hatfields and McCoys and the War of the Roses.

This is also one of the major reasons business partnerships break up. The partners are quick to share their work frustrations at home but they forget to inform their spouses they have resolved their differences at work. The spouses build up resentment and begin to chip away at the partnership, until it dissolves.

Much of this angry division could have been avoided if folks refused to talk behind each other's backs and dealt with their conflict directly. Realize, my friends, conflict between you and another is just that—between you and another. And that's all. Do not share with those people who are not directly involved. If they are not a positive part of the solution, they will easily become a substantial part of the problem—potentially, a whole regiment of them!

INSPECTING THE FRUIT

1. Look at the first five of the ten principles for dealing with anger daily and choose the one or two you most need to work on today.

    __Gardening Tip #1: Be more tolerant of other's shortcomings. "Lighten up!"
    __Gardening Tip #2: Don't provoke others to anger. "Don't push each other's button!"
    __Gardening Tip #3: Don't knowingly put yourself in a situation where you know you'll get angry. "Don't grab the dog by the ear!"
    __Gardening Tip #4: Stop a quarrel before it gets out of control. "Don't let the water out of the dam!"
    __Gardening Tip #5: Don't talk behind another's back. "Don't rally troops!"

2. What are some of the mistakes others make that you need to learn to overlook?

3. What do you do that makes those closest to you react negatively and hope they would learn to overlook?

4. What is your greatest anger button? Why?

5. Do you know "the anger button" for the people closest to you? In other words, what gets them angry?

6. Reflect on the last time you interfered with a conflict between two other people. What did you learn from the experience?

7. In this conflict, what could you have done to be a part of the solution, rather than a part of the problem?

8. What phrases can you practice using to help diffuse an argument?

9. Reflect on your last experience with "rallying troops" and calling people to your side of a disagreement. Have you resolved your differences with the individual with whom you had conflict?

10. What do you need to do with those who have taken sides?

FURTHER ADVICE FROM THE MASTER GARDENER

Read the story of the Prodigal Son (Luke 15:11-32). Which of these first five of the Gardening Tips were properly or improperly used by anyone in the story?

Gardening Tip #1: Be more tolerant of other's shortcomings.
Properly Used? ____ Improperly Used? ____

Gardening Tip #2: Don't provoke others to anger.
Properly Used? ____ Improperly Used? ____

Gardening Tip #3: Don't knowingly put yourself in a situation where you know you'll get angry.
Properly Used? ____ Improperly Used? ____

Gardening Tip #4: Stop a quarrel before it gets out of control.
Properly Used? ____ Improperly Used? ____

Gardening Tip #5: Don't talk behind another's back.
Properly Used? ____ Improperly Used? ____

CHAPTER FOURTEEN

MORE GARDENING TIPS FOR DEALING WITH ANGER DAILY

I have a dear friend who is a pastor and a key leader in eastern Europe. He and I were both invited to speak at a leadership conference, held in Kiev, Ukraine. After many hours of travel, I was confronted by a rather grumpy flight attendant who refused to allow me to board with my carry-on luggage, containing all my notes and materials for the conference. At the check-in counter the airline clerk had declared my luggage was within their required size and weight limits but at the gate this lady declared, without measuring or weighing, it was too large and over-weight.

As an experienced traveler, I am used to such inconsistencies. This time, however, as she insisted I be separated from my carry-on, I exploded. Standing in line, getting ready to board, I gave her a piece of my mind. Even as I was speaking I was well aware I was now acting like those very people I frown upon when they do such rude things. To make matters worse, my pastor-friend even commented about my lack of self-control. The sadder part? I was headed to teach a seminar to hundreds of pastors on the subject of anger! The story isn't over.

We arrived in Kiev (with my luggage) and the hotel had no record of my friend's reservation. Although he showed them the paperwork, the hotel was now full. He blew his stack! I felt somewhat vindicated. And then again, here we were—two clergymen—desperately in need of practicing what we preach, and applying these *Gardening Tips for Dealing with Anger Daily.*

Let's review the first half of our tips for dealing with anger, even at airports and hotels, or wherever our anger buttons are pushed.

Gardening Tip #1: Be more tolerant of other's shortcomings.

Gardening Tip #2: Don't provoke others to anger.

Gardening Tip #3: Don't knowingly put yourself in a situation where you know you'll get angry.

Gardening Tip #4: Stop a quarrel before it gets out of control.

Gardening Tip #5: Don't talk behind another's back.

Now, we move on to five more principles for dealing with anger daily.

Gardening Tip #6: Think before you talk.

"Engage your brain before opening your mouth!"

Don't we wish we had a little computer apparatus in front of our face that screens our thoughts before the words are spoken. Fancy ones would have a Morality Check, a Kindness Check and a "Do You Really Want to Say That?" Button. Expensive ones would even print out what we were going to say so we can get a really good look at it. No such apparatus exists—except the human heart!

I read recently a quote from Ambrose Bierce that is worth pondering: "Speak when you are angry and you will make the best speech you will ever regret." Most of us have said things in anger we wish we had never said. We now live with the painful reality that "a word once spoken is forever history." If only we had heeded the apostle Paul's clearly-stated instructions: "Let no unwholesome word proceed from your mouth, but only such a word as is good for edification according to the need of the moment, that it may give grace to those who hear" (Ephesians 4:29).

The word unwholesome [Greek: *sapros*] means corrupt or completely rotten. It brings to my mind the image of the maggot-infested piece of fruit I once witnessed being eaten by a poor girl in the streets of Bombay. The apostle Paul is saying that any words that are not good for edification, that do not build people up, that are not according to the need of the moment and do not give grace are corrupt, rotten, maggot-infested words that are offensive to the nostrils of our Holy God. Let's think about that before we speak!

Here's the simple taste test for godly speech. Before we speak we need to ask ourselves:

- Is what I am about to say good for edification? Is it meant to build up or destroy?

- Is what I am about to say according to the need of the moment? Is this really the best time to say this, or can it wait for a more receptive moment?

- Is what I am about to say a "grace gift" to any who hear?

(For more specific questions, review *The Taste Test for Godly Speech* in the Appendix.)

Gardening Tip #7: Lower your voice.

"Talk to others as if you are talking to God!"

The world says, "If you can't be right then be wrong at the top of your voice." God says: "Lower your voice!" We do well to consider the timeless words from Proverbs: "A gentle answer turns away wrath, but a harsh word stirs up anger" (Proverbs 15:1). There is really something about a soft voice. It soothes. It gets people's attention. It makes them listen more carefully. It quiets the whole room!

Many years ago, when I graduated from seminary, a man entered my new church office. He was obviously upset and asked to speak to a pastor. Well, I was one of those—just barely. No seminary training could have prepared me for what was next.

I closed my office door and immediately he began screaming, "Pastor, you are not going to like what I am about to say. I hate my wife! I hate her! I hate her! I really hate her! In fact . . . Pastor . . . .I want her gone . . . I mean it . . . I want her . . . dead!" I responded, "Calm down and let's talk about this."

There was nothing I could do to quiet him down as he paced around my office. Finally, I said to him, "I don't know what to do for you since you won't quiet down enough to listen. So, why don't we pray."

Surprisingly, he began to pray . . . well . . . scream, "God, I hate her so much. I want her out of my life." He went on babbling about all the things she had done to hurt him. But as he was praying, his voice softened. It is hard to pray and scream at the same time.

As his voice softened, so did he. Pretty soon he was on his knees (I know because I had wisely chosen not to close my eyes!). His voice softened even further, and I watched as he fell on his face with outstretched arms and softly cried out, "No, God. Don't hurt my wife. Heal me. Help me to forgive her. Lord, help me . . . (By now he is sobbing) . . . to love her again."

I learned a lifelong principle. In the midst of intensity we need to learn to talk as if I we are praying. Whisper it softly to yourself a few times: "Thou shall lower your voice." Like this angry man, it will soften your countenance and your heart. It might even turn away the other person's anger before the matter gets out of control.

Why not give it a try? For the next few days, practice lowering your voice when talking to the clerks or waiters who serve you, especially those whose faces announce they are having a bad day. Be sure to look them in the eyes as you give a greeting and thank them for their service. Who knows? Maybe your soft voice and affirming words, along with a generous tip, will make their day better. Then again, even if it doesn't, it can make your day what God intended it to be. Besides, it is good practice for the home-front and the workplace!

Gardening Tip #8: Forgive and seek forgiveness.

"Be the first to ask forgiveness!"

I'm sure none of us remember the supposedly globally unifying event in 1984: International Forgiveness Week. For those of us who were around then, we were not surprised it died for lack of interest. I agree with Dr. Charles Swindoll's observation that we would rather "sit on a judgment seat than on a mercy seat."

We have little interest in forgiving people, especially those who have hurt us. And no program is going to change our minds or behavior. The battle rages within as much of our unresolved anger, and its devastating consequences, stems from our inability to ask forgiveness of others. We keep waiting for others to come to us: "After all, they hurt me more than I hurt them." But God isn't interested in percentages of who is more wrong or more right. Even if it could be determined we are to blame for a very small portion of the conflict, we have the responsibility to go that person and ask,

"Will you forgive me?" Consider the kingdom principles Jesus taught in the Sermon on the Mount:

> You have heard that the ancients were told, 'You shall not commit murder' and 'Whoever commits murder shall be liable to the court.' But I say to you that everyone who is angry with his brother shall be guilty before the court; and whoever shall say to his brother, '*Raca*,' [Aramaic for "empty-head" or "good-for-nothing"] shall be guilty before the supreme court; and whoever shall say, 'You fool,' shall be guilty enough to go into the fiery hell. "If therefore you are presenting your offering at the altar, and there remember that your brother has something against you, leave your offering there before the altar, and go your way; first be reconciled to your brother, and then come and present your offering (Matthew 5:21-24, NASB 1975).

And let's not forget the apostle Paul's exhortation:

> Let all bitterness and wrath and anger and clamor and slander be put away from you, along with all malice. And be kind to one another, tender-hearted, forgiving each other, just as God in Christ also has forgiven you (Ephesians 4:31-32).

I think the apostle Paul might summarize this with a simple phrase: The forgiven make good forgivers. Let us be the first to ask, "Will you forgive me?" Then wait for the honest answer: "Yes." "No." or, "Not yet. I need some time."

Gardening Tip #9: Consider other's needs as more important than your own.

"Let others have it their way!"

I don't wait well—at doctors' offices, in checkout lines, or on freeways. I admit, I am guilty of an inner road rage that sometimes comes out in a disgruntled mumble and behind-the-closed-window ranting, "Really . . . YOU cut right in front of ME . . . you Dufus!" (That's pastor-profanity and certainly not the Hebrew word for saint!). No wonder I need these tips for dealing with anger daily, especially this one calling me to consider other people's needs as more important than my own.

Bear in mind the theological and practical implications of the apostle Paul's words in the second chapter of Philippians. Having written about the humility of Christ leaving Heaven's glory, the apostle challenges us with some life-changing words. Oh, the anger that would subside if we kept this perspective:

> Do nothing from selfishness or empty conceit, but with humility of mind let each of you regard one another as more important than himself; do not merely look out for your own personal interests, but also for the interests of others (Philippians 2:3-4).

Five hundred years ago the great reformer, Martin Luther, was making this point. He told the story of the mountain goats in the Alps. The paths are too narrow for two goats to pass, so one of them will lie down and actually let the other walk over him. Luther went on to say to his audience, "We don't have the sense of mountain goats."

He is so right. We continue today to play "King of the Mountain," fighting for our rights, having to win every argument, and scuffling to be the first in line, often at the expense of anyone near or far. It's time to act like a mountain goat, not in being bull-headed and stubborn, but by letting other people have their way, as a form of worship and imitation of Christ. So said the apostle Paul when he called us to "be subject to one another in the fear [the worship] of Christ" (Ephesians 5:21).

If the apostle Paul were sitting in the car with us whenever someone tries to crowd us out, he might just quote his simple words to the Ephesians. Then again, he might also say, "Don't miss your opportunity to act like a mountain goat." Or he might pose it in a form of a life-skills question: "So, what's so wrong with letting the other person win?"

My counsel to us is more personal. From one stubborn goat to another, it is time to give way on the freeway of life and let others have the right of way!

Gardening Tip #10: Love in word and deed.

"Soothe the other person with a gift in secret!"

Perhaps you recall the book or the movie, *The Cross and the Switchblade*, the story of David Wilkerson's ministry to gang members in the streets of New York City. In one account, gang leader Nicky Cruz holds a knife up to David's throat. He cries out, "I'm going to cut you, man!" David responds, "You could cut me up into a thousand pieces and lay them in the street, and every piece will still love you." That is the perspective we are to have with those who hurt us. And it's not a new perspective. Solomon reminded his son: "Hatred stirs up strife, but love covers all transgressions" (Proverbs 10:12). How many transgressions does love cover? All of them!

Listen also to his advice as to what to do after a conflict: "A gift in secret subdues ["soothes, pacifies," Hebrew: *kaphah*] anger, and a bribe in the bosom, strong wrath" (Proverbs 21:14). It's a curious passage, but it is quite important. When we are in an angry situation with another, King Solomon's counsel is to resolve the issue with them in words and then follow it up by giving a soothing secret gift to them. It is what he calls "a bribe in the bosom." In this context, it's a good bribe, a symbol and a constant reminder of the restoration of a relationship.

Consider the conflict between Jacob and his twin brother, Esau: "So Esau bore a grudge against Jacob because of the blessing with which his father had blessed him (Genesis 27:40); and Esau said to himself, 'The days of mourning for my father are near; then I will kill my brother Jacob'" (Genesis 27:41).

The conflict went on for decades, until Jacob decided to reconcile with his brother: "Then he [Jacob] selected from what he had with him a present for his brother Esau" (Genesis 32:13). Finally in Genesis 33 they meet. Jacob offered his gift in secret—his bribe in the bosom—but Esau refused, not fully understanding what this symbol really meant. Jacob begged his brother to accept:

> Jacob said, "No, please, if now I have found favor in your
> sight, then take my present from my hand, for I see your face
> as one sees the face of God, and you have received me
> favorably. Please take my gift which has been brought to you,

because God has dealt graciously with me and because I have plenty." Thus he urged him and he took it (Genesis 33:10-11).

When I was a youth pastor, I embarrassed one of the girls in my class. She confronted me with her hurt and I promptly asked her forgiveness. I then picked up a rock (No, not to throw at her!). I gave the rock to her and said, "Please accept this rock as a symbol of my love for you. Let it be a simple reminder that I am truly sorry for what I did to you." Many years later, I saw her and spoke of this incident. She shared, "I still have that rock!" That's the gift in secret. (Although now that I told you, it's no longer a secret!). You get the point!

You might be familiar with the love languages as outlined by Gary Chapman in his 1995 book, *"The Five Love Languages: How to Express Heartfelt Commitment to Your Mate."* There he presents some actions that uniquely convey love to others:

- Gifts
- Quality Time
- Words of Affirmation
- Acts of Service
- Physical Touch

These can also be the gifts in secret and the bribes in the bosom that pacify present anger and help prevent future conflict. It helps, of course, if you have taken the time to know the person in order to help with determining what kind of love gift would be most effective in communicating with them. These gifts in secret do not have to be big or grandiose. They are the small tokens that say, "I am grateful we are on the mend."

So, get on with it. Send that small gift, arrange to do something simple but special, take a few minutes to make a call, wash their car or give them a hug. Just be sure it stays between the two of you. It's a gift "in secret." Bragging about the gift to make yourself look better can fuel a future fire.

ONE FINAL GARDENING TIP

Recently my agronomist friend sat in my office at church and told me about "fruit mummies." Yes, it was as creepy as it sounds. Fruit mummies are dried up fruit that stay on the branch, even though they are dead. They are not the valuable "Dried on the Vine" fruit, purposely left on the tree and picked at just the right sweetness. These fruit are dead. Real dead. Unless knocked off the branches they continue to harden and become shelters for insects who live in this mummified fruit until the spring. Then they launch their invasion. She called them "time bombs." I could not help reflecting on the fruit mummies in our lives, those hardened caves, harboring a future invasion of sinful anger. It's time to knock them off!

INSPECTING THE FRUIT

1. Look at the second five of the ten principles for dealing with anger daily and choose one or two you most need to work on today.

   __Gardening Tip #6: Think before you talk. "Engage your brain before opening your mouth!"

   __Gardening Tip #7: Lower your voice. "Talk to others as if you are talking to God!"

   __Gardening Tip #8: Forgive and seek forgiveness. "Be the first to ask forgiveness!"

   __Gardening Tip #9: Consider other's needs as more   important than your own. "Let others have it their way!"

   __Gardening Tip #10: Love in word and deed. "Soothe the other person with a gift in secret!"

2. How would your conversations improve if you considered the following questions before speaking?

   • Is what I am about to say good for edification? Is it meant to build up or destroy?

   • Is what I am about to say according to the need of the moment? Is this really the best time to say this or can it wait for a more receptive moment?

   • Is what I am about to say a "grace gift" to any who hear?

111

3. Do you recall a time when your soft voice turned away someone's anger, argument or bad mood?

4. In what situation has it been most difficult for you to forgive others as God has forgiven you?

5. What is the difference between saying, "I'm sorry!" and "Will you forgive me?"

6. In what areas of life do you feel the need to always win?

7. In what areas of potential conflict would it be best to let others have their way?

8. Give some suggestions for some small "gifts in secret" as a means of follow-up to encourage the continued restoration of a relationship.

   • Gifts:

   • Quality Time:

   • Words of Affirmation:

   • Acts of Service:

   • Physical Touch:

FURTHER ADVICE FROM THE MASTER GARDENER

1. Read the story of the conflict between Jacob and Esau in Genesis, Chapters 27, 32 and 33).

   a. What caused the conflict?

   b. What were the long-term results?

   c. How did the brothers reconcile?

2. Read through the assignment in the Appendix titled *A Worksheet for Resolving Conflict*.

PART TWO

HARVESTING THE
TASTY FRUIT OF THE SPIRIT

CHAPTER FIFTEEN

SPIRITUAL POMOLOGY: GROWING HEALTHY FRUIT

While attending seminary in southern California, I was the constant brunt of jokes about my ignorance of growing "anything green." My friends challenged me to grow something—anything. I called a few nurseries and asked what would be the easiest fruit or vegetable to grow in a planter box on my apartment patio. Overwhelmingly, they encouraged me to grow carrots, insisting, "Anybody can grow them." Well, they had never met me!

I planted quality carrot seeds into store-bought, nutrient-rich soil. I placed the planter box in the sun and carefully watered, following the nursery worker's instructions meticulously. In just a few days, an amazing thing happened. Little green sprouts came up from the soil. I pranced down the hall of the seminary, saying to my buddies, "Yes, I am a farmer!" They laughed, as if to say, "Just wait!" And wait I did.

Soon I was asking a botanist friend, "Why aren't my carrots growing?" He asked me all the questions about seeds and sun and soil, to which I answered, "I did all that." He said, "Then, how do you know they are not growing?" I was surprised at the question and responded innocently, "Because every morning I pull them out of the soil and check them. Then I wipe off the little white hairs— or whatever they are. After all, I don't want hairy carrots. Then I shove them back into the soil." He just rolled his eyes and said, "What did you expect? Leave them alone and they'll grow."

I have never forgotten how silly I felt. Although I am still rather ill-equipped to plant a healthy garden or grow abundant fruit trees, I did learn a principle that has produced some amazing spiritual fruit: Things grow best when left alone in good soil. So it is with harvesting the tasty fruit of the indwelling Holy Spirit. So it is with dealing with generation-destroying anger and producing a generational legacy of love, joy and peace.

I am definitely not a seasoned farmer, nor a botanist, nor an agronomist. I am also not a pomologist, one who is an expert in producing fruit. I have lived in this San Joaquin Valley for over twenty-five years, and thankfully my gardening and landscaping skills have improved—slightly. Some things take a lifetime to master.

I have come to learn that fruit, by its very definition, is a seed-bearing structure that grows from a flower. I have also learned that, botanically-speaking, a strawberry is not a fruit. Technically-speaking, it is the swollen base of the flower and doesn't grow from that flower. Tomatoes are not a vegetable; almonds are in the fruit family and peanuts are in the vegetable family. Frankly, it's still a little confusing to me. It is, however, my divine calling to help people understand how a different kind of fruit grows—the fruit of the Spirit:

> But the fruit of the Spirit is love, joy, peace, patience,
> kindness, goodness, faithfulness, gentleness, self-control;
> against such things there is no law (Galatians 5:22-23).

I read this passage and immediately picture a beautiful tree with abundant fruit filling its lush branches. Perhaps the apostle Paul had the same image in mind as he considered the human heart overflowing with fruit that comes in the shape of love, joy, peace, patience, kindness, goodness, faithfulness, gentleness and self-control. (By the way, if you haven't already, I encourage you to memorize these).

In the following chapters we are going to perform a thorough inspection of all nine fruit of the Spirit-filled life. We will also show how daily harvesting the tasty fruit of the Holy Spirit is so very effective in dealing with the rotten fruit of the flesh—especially anger in its many forms. Before we do, I want to make sure we understand some of the basic principles of spiritual pomology—growing healthy spiritual fruit in our lives.

THE EIGHT PRINCIPLES OF SPIRITUAL POMOLOGY

Spiritual Pomology Principle #1: The fruit of the Spirit is not automatic.

As a very young boy I had experienced corn on the cob. For years, however, I thought corn primarily came in cans—niblet or creamed. Frankly, it was my favorite vegetable. What short Italian kid wouldn't be attracted to a can with a giant on it. (*"Ho! Ho! Ho! Green Giant!"*)

What human being wouldn't also benefit from an abundant harvest of fruit the apostle Paul is writing about? This passage, however, is not talking about <u>human</u> characteristics, nor is it talking about <u>super-human</u> qualities. They are not called the fruit of <u>man</u> nor the fruit of <u>human</u> potential. They are not even called the fruit of <u>religion</u>. Don't fail to notice the apostle Paul is quick to call them "the fruit of the *SPIRIT*" (Galatians 5:22, emphasis added). I love the simple words of Hosea 14:8 when God declares to His people, "From Me comes your fruit." This is not a light matter. This list of nine life-changing, anger-eliminating characteristics is the harvest that comes only from one source—the Holy Spirit of the One True God. He is the real Giant in our lives.

I am told by experts that most modern fruit are the result of selective breeding. Unfortunately, over time, plants that have been selectively bred tend to lose their vigor, hardiness, resistance to disease, and ability to reproduce.

Every human being has some level of fruit as a result of being created in the image of God (Genesis 1:26-27; 9:6). We can all produce some form of human love, human joy, human peace, etc., but because of our sinful human nature, it is, at best, a flawed love, joy, and peace. Like inbred fruit, these qualities of human effort can taste good for a while, but over time they lose their vigor, hardiness, resistance to sin and ability to reproduce anything worthwhile. On the other hand, the Holy Spirit of God produces an abundant harvest of divine fruit that is hardy and lasting.

How then does one become a candidate for reaping this amazing harvest? Every spiritual pomologist should strive to understand and apply the two step process of producing the supernatural fruit of the Spirit.

Fruit Production Step #1: The right seed must be planted in our hearts.

Suppose we are holding a handful of seeds in the palm of our hand. We don't have to be farmers to know that no growth will occur if we just set these little seeds on the table and wait for them to grow. First, they need to be planted in good soil.

In the same way, to reap a harvest of tasty and lasting spiritual fruit (love, joy, peace, etc.), the right seed must be planted in the soil of our hearts. For that to happen, we must have the Holy Spirit of God living inside of us. And for that to happen, we must respond to God's amazing grace and become born-again followers of Jesus Christ, by trusting in Him alone for our salvation. There is no other way! (John 1:12; 3:16; 14:6; Acts 4:12; Ephesians 2:8-9; Titus 3:5). The apostle Paul said it this way:

> However, you are not in the flesh but in the Spirit, if indeed the Spirit of God dwells in you. But if anyone does not have the Spirit of Christ, he does not belong to Him (Romans 8:9).

Even then, planting the seed is the start, but it is certainly not enough. Having a cornucopia of spiritual fruit is not automatic in the life of every born-again Christian. We must take special care of the soil of our now regenerated hearts. This brings us to our next step.

Fruit Production Step #2: The soil of our hearts must be properly cared for.

To put it in farming terms, if we are going to see the fruit of the Holy Spirit flowing from our regenerated hearts and the rotten fruit of the flesh, especially ungodly anger, destroyed, we need to take special care of the soil of our hearts. Let me make it as simple as possible:

- Daily, we must water our hearts by meditating on the Word of God (Psalm 1:1-2; Joshua 1:8).

- Daily, we must weed our lives by admitting, confessing and turning from sin (1 John 1:9).

• Daily, we must nourish our souls by seeking to obey God's will in every area of our lives (Colossians 4:12; 1Thessalonians 4:13; Hebrews 10:36).

Let's put this in biblical terms. In order to experience the fruit of the Spirit we must walk by, be led by, live by, and be filled with the Spirit. Those are the exact words Paul uses:

But I say, *walk by the Spirit*, and you will not carry out the desire of the flesh. For the flesh sets its desire against the Spirit, and the Spirit against the flesh; for these are in opposition to one another, so that you may not do the things that you please. But if you are *led by the Spirit*, you are not under the Law (Galatians 5:16-18, emphasis added).

Now those who belong to Christ Jesus have crucified the flesh with its passions and desires. If we *live by the Spirit*, let us also *walk by the Spirit* (Galatians 5:24-25; Romans 6:6; Galatians 2:20; 6:14; emphasis added).

. . . be filled *with the Spirit* (Ephesians 5:18, emphasis added).

Again, the fruit of the Spirit is not automatic. These qualities are the marks of a transformed life that is well-watered, well-weeded and well-nourished. They are the fruit of a regenerated life that is walking in obedience to the indwelling Holy Spirit of God. They are the results of the "crucified life" that has been freed from the *power* of sin (salvation), is daily being freed from the *practice* of sin (sanctification) and will someday be freed from the *presence* of sin (glorification) (Galatians 5:24-25; Romans 6:6, 14; Galatians 2:20; 6:14).

Spiritual Pomology Principle #2: The fruit of the Spirit is not limited.

Many of us are fruit lovers. We certainly have numerous kinds from which to choose:

• apples and oranges   • lemons and limes
• bananas and pineapples   • grapes and raisins

- plums and prunes
- pomegranates and apricots
- raspberries and blackberries
- cantaloupes and watermelons
- figs and dates

- tangerines and nectarines
- grapefruit and peaches
- mangoes and papayas
- cherries and blueberries
- guava and kiwi fruit

Perhaps some of us have even had the experience of eating jackfruit, a single fruit weighing in at over a hundred pounds (over forty-five kilos). Talk about a fruit-fest in one sitting!

Notice the apostle Paul adds to his list of nine fruit of the Spirit—"such things" (Galatians 5:23)—implying the fruit of the Spirit are not limited to this list in Galatians. Almighty God has given the world a large variety of fruit. In the same way, the Spirit of God has filled the harvest of our hearts with a large variety of spiritual fruit, even beyond this list of nine. What other fruit of the Holy Spirit's ministry in our lives can there be? It can also be said:

- The fruit of the Spirit-filled life is the conviction of sin we feel when we offend God (John 16:8).

- The fruit of the Spirit-filled life is enjoying empowered and abundant life (John 10:10; Acts 1:8; Romans 8:11).

- The fruit of the Spirit-filled life is everything that is the opposite of the deeds of the flesh (Galatians 5:19-21).

- The fruit of the Spirit-filled life is also . . .

- enduring hope
- lasting endurance
- impacting evangelism
- intimate fellowship

- ceaseless mercy
- effective service
- persevering prayer
- life-changing discipleship

. . . and a host of other "such things" (Galatians 5:23).

Simply stated, the fruit of the Spirit is the full work of the Holy Spirit of God in our lives as He corrects, equips, empowers and grows us. As such, it truly is a horn of plenty, a full harvest of the heart and a cornucopia of spiritual abundance. (A more detailed list of additional fruit will follow in Chapter Twenty-Four, under the section called *Other Windfall Fruit of the Holy Spirit*).

Spiritual Pomology Principle #3: The fruit of the Spirit is not fully produced in us immediately.

I was pretty disappointed when my new apple tree had so few apples in its first harvest season. In the second season I was pleased my young tree yielded tasty fruit but nowhere near the abundant fruit of the mature trees my friends had in their yards. My impatience was obvious. I wanted fruit and I wanted it now!

As young Christians, when we are filled with the Spirit and walking under His control, we likewise see fruit but not as fully as when we are older in the Lord. Just as the mature fruit tree produces fuller and more abundant fruit, so the mature Christian produces fuller and more abundant spiritual fruit. The fruit of love a mature Christian demonstrates will be even fuller than the fruit of love produced in the new Christian.

One of our local farmers was telling me about his family grapevines that are over a hundred years old and produce a copious amount of fruit. I was reminded of Psalm 92, I like to refer to it as *The Faithful and Fruitful Old Man's Psalm*:

> The righteous man will flourish like the palm tree. He will grow like a cedar in Lebanon. Planted in the house of the Lord. They will flourish in the courts of our God. They will still yield fruit in old age. They shall be full of sap and very green . . . (Psalm 92:12-14).

I want to be a constantly growing fruit tree—well planted, ever-flourishing, and bearing fruit. I even want to be sappy and green until I die. Don't you? Assuming our hearts are properly cared for, our capacity to produce fruit will increase as we grow. We will still yield fruit in old age. Manifesting the mature fruit of the Spirit is a life-long process. It is well worth the effort and the wait.

By the way, as we mature in the Lord, we will also be able to see a timeline of spiritual fruit-bearing throughout our lives. We older believers should be able to identify those seasons in our lives when God's Holy Spirit gave us an extra measure of:

• sacrificial love
• abiding joy
• incomprehensible peace

121

- enduring patience
- overwhelming kindness
- deep-seated goodness
- lasting faithfulness
- amazing gentleness
- unexpected self-control

Spiritual Pomology Principle #4: The fruit of the Spirit is all one harvest of the heart.

Attending the yearly Canadian National Exhibition in Toronto, Canada was one of the highlights of my youth. Surprisingly, I do not remember much about the rides and attractions, mostly because we couldn't afford the tickets. I do, however, remember the Agricultural Center where I had my first glimpse of an entire building with rows and rows of multi-colored fruit and vegetables. Although I did not take the time to walk down the aisles, I still recall that view of the full harvest of Canadian abundance. So it is with the fruit of the Spirit.

Some have tried to make much out of the fact there are nine in Paul's list, breaking them down into three groups of three. Some suggest the first three (love, joy and peace) are general habits of the mind, having to do with our relationship to God, the second three (patience, kindness, goodness) are social virtues, speaking of our relationship to others, and the third group (faithfulness, gentleness, self-control) are dealing with our relationship to ourselves. I believe it is better to consider all nine as addressing our relationship to God, to others and to ourselves. In other words, all nine form one crop.

In the Greek text the word fruit is the singular word *karpos*. (Remember, in English, the word fruit can refer to one fruit or lots of fruit). To avoid confusion, this text could well be translated, "the ONE fruit of the Spirit is love, joy, peace . . ." That's very curious, since the word the apostle Paul uses to describe the deeds of the flesh in the same chapter is plural (Galatians 5:19-21).

Over the years, much has been discussed about this singular use of the word fruit. Some argue the singular means all nine fruit flow into each other. In other words, "If you have love then you will have joy . . ." and, "When you have love and joy then you will have peace . . . " and, "When you have love, joy and peace then you will have patience, etc." If this were true, it would take longer to experience faithfulness, gentleness and self-control (the last three on the list) than it would be to experience love, joy, and peace (the first three on the list).

Notice also the list of nine begins with love. Some have tried to make a major point of this, explaining there really is only one fruit (love), and that love manifests itself in the other eight fruit (joy, peace, patience, etc.). Those that teach this often try to use 1 Corinthians 13 to support their view and show some similarities. Yes, the Love Chapter does say, "Love is patient. Love is kind . . ." The problem is that not all of 1 Corinthians, Chapter 13:4-8 fits with all of Galatians, Chapter 5:22-23.

I believe the apostle Paul is using the singular to speak of the fruit the Holy Spirit can produce as a single harvest of the regenerated and spirit-filled heart. Unlike the gifts of the Spirit, which are given to different people (1 Corinthians 12:1-11; Romans 12:6-8), all of the individual fruit of the Spirit listed in Galatians 5 are to be found in all Christians. We don't get to say "I am okay with love, joy and peace but, for now, I choose to stay clear of faithfulness and self-control." Simply stated: ALL of the fruit is to be found in ALL of the faithful! The apostle Peter clearly states the result: "For if these qualities are yours and are increasing, they render you neither useless nor *unfruitful* in the true knowledge of our Lord Jesus Christ" (2 Peter 1:8, emphasis added).

Spiritual Pomology Principle #5: The fruit of the Spirit represents the life of Christ in us.

I remember seeing a television interview where a woman was showing off her collection of fruit and vegetables that looked like famous people. She even had a potato chip that looked like President Richard Nixon!

As we will see, each of the nine fruit of the Spirit-filled life do look like a person—Jesus Christ! Each of them can be found perfectly exemplified in our Lord. As the Holy Spirit produces the fruit in our lives, we, too, look more like Jesus. The more we look like Jesus the more others, who imitate us, look like Him, too. So said the apostle Paul: "Be imitators of me, just as I also am of Christ" (1 Corinthians 11:1)

To talk about the fruit of the Spirit is to talk about imitating Christ-like love, Christ-like joy, Christ-like peace, etc. Although we often refer to this examination of Galatians as *The Fruit of the Spirit-Filled Life,* it could just as well be called *Becoming Like Jesus Christ.* It's the very reason He lives inside of us:

> But we all, with unveiled face beholding as in a mirror the glory of the Lord, are being transformed ["changed in stages," Greek: *metamorphoo*] into the same image from glory to glory ["godly attributes and qualities," Greek: *doxa*] just as from the Lord, the Spirit (2 Corinthians 3:18).

Instead of saying we are being transformed "from glory to glory," the apostle Paul could just as easily have said that we are being transformed from one Christ-like quality to the other, or from one fruit of the Spirit to the other—moment by moment, over a lifetime of obedience.

Spiritual Pomology Principle #6: The fruit of the Spirit is a sweet harvest.

The apostle Paul concludes this passage with what initially seems like a strange phrase:

> . . . against such things there is no law . . . (Galatians 5:23).

The apostle Paul is, in essence, saying the fruit of the Spirit-filled life is always a sweet harvest, a sweet work of grace. We don't need more religion or man-made regulations to sweeten our lives. We need the succulent ministry of the indwelling Holy Spirit, leading us moment by moment, using His Word to guide us.

I am told farmers recognize the sugar content in fruit is not always the same. It depends on the season, the amount of water and the intensity of the sun. In order to measure the sweetness, they use a piece of equipment called a refractometer. They drip some fruit juice onto the refractometer plate, hold it up to the light and see the light's angle of refraction on the scale, as it passes through the sugared fruit juice. Sometimes they hold it up to the sun. (I suppose this would be a good place to draw the analogy regarding our lives being held up and measured by the light of the Son of God).

We have all experienced biting into a peach that looked delicious on the outside, only to find it bitter on the inside. Well, that will never be the case with the fruit of the Spirit. What you see is what you get. Like some fruit manufacturers do, the Holy Spirit puts a sticker on our hearts that reads, "The Fruit of the Spirit is always the sweetest." In fact, they become sweeter as the days go by. Our spiritual taste-buds are always enjoying better fruit.

Spiritual Pomology Principle #7: The fruit of the Spirit attracts others to Christ.

There was a short season of my boyhood when I lived around Barrie, Ontario, Canada. Though I had spent my early life in inner-city Toronto, I was fascinated by the apple orchards in northern Ontario, especially in the fall. I can still remember the taste of those apples warmed by the after-school sun. (I also remember sneaking into the orchard and helping myself to pockets full of apples).

There is something about a tree full of luscious fruit that attracts me even today. (Although, now I grow them or pay for them). This is also true of a person whose life is filled with the fruit of the Spirit. There is a magnetism and an attractive sweet aroma. I remind us of the words of Solomon to his son, Rehoboam, as he prepared him to reach his world: "The fruit of the righteous is a tree of life, and he who is wise wins souls" (Proverbs 11:30). I am also blessed by the words of the apostle Paul: "But thanks be to God, who always leads us in triumph in Christ, and manifests through us the sweet aroma of the knowledge of Him in every place" (2 Corinthians 2:14).

I believe one of the greatest evangelistic tools for winning souls is "Living the Spirit-filled Life" evangelism. That's what I desire to see in all of us. I am praying our lives will be so filled with His abundant love, joy, peace, patience, kindness, goodness, faithfulness, gentleness and self-control that many of our unbelieving family and friends will be attracted to the fruit of the Spirit in our lives. Then, I trust, they will come running to the Savior who made such an abundant and fruitful life possible. May our lives be a horn of plenty, a cornucopia to the world, and overflowing with the sweet aroma of all of these Christ-like qualities.

I am biblically confident when I say that fruit of the Spirit is also God's definition of sexy. Show me a man or woman filled with Christ-like and Spirit-led love, joy, peace, patience, kindness, goodness, faithful, gentleness and self-control and I will show you an amazingly attractive person." Ponder that the next time you dress to impress:

> . . . all of you who were baptized into Christ have *clothed yourselves* with Christ (Galatians 3:27, emphasis added).

> . . . *put on the new self*, which in the likeness of God has been created in righteousness and holiness of the truth (Ephesians 4:24, emphasis added).

> So, as those who have been chosen of God, holy and beloved, *put on* a heart of compassion, kindness, humility, gentleness and patience; bearing with one another, and forgiving each other, whoever has a complaint against anyone; just as the Lord forgave you, so also should you. Beyond all these things *put on* love, which is the perfect bond of unity (Colossians 3:12-14, emphasis added).

> But since we are of the day, let us be sober, having *put on* the breastplate of faith and love, and as a helmet, the hope of salvation (1 Thessalonians 5:8, emphasis added).

Spiritual Pomology Principle #8: The fruit of the Spirit is evidence of victory over sin.

We are blessed in our area to have numerous farmers' markets where local growers line up their amazing produce. My problem? It all looks so good. How do I know which is the best fruit to buy? I have to admit I am guilty of faking it in order to impress my farmer-friends. I smell the fruit, give it a knowing squeeze and tap it with my finger. Truthfully, the only way I would know is if I bit into it. Understandably, not many vendors appreciate that.

Let's recap our eight principles of spiritual pomology:

> 1. The fruit of the Spirit is not automatic.

> 2. The fruit of the Spirit is not limited.

3. The fruit of the Spirit is not fully produced in us immediately.

4. The fruit of the Spirit is all one harvest of the heart.

5. The fruit of the Spirit represents the life of Christ in us.

6. The fruit of the Spirit is a sweet harvest.

7. The fruit of the Spirit attracts others to Christ.

8. The fruit of the Spirit is evidence of victory over sin.

What does all this pomology-talk have to do with dealing with my sin, especially anger? Everything. In fact, it is the key. Every manifestation of one of these nine fruit is the clear evidence we are living in the power of the indwelling Holy Spirit. The more we walk in the Spirit, the more we are not being overtaken by the power of the flesh. The rotten fruit of our flesh, such as all of our many expressions of sinful anger, are eliminated to the degree we harvest the fruit of the Spirit—all nine of them. Like a spiritual farmer's market, they will be on open display to the world (cf. Galatians 5:16-25).

With all eight principles in mind, we come to an operational definition of the fruit of the Spirit we can live by:

The fruit of the Spirit is the abundant harvest of Christ-like qualities the indwelling Holy Spirit produces in the regenerated and obedient heart.

INSPECTING THE FRUIT

Comment on each of these eight principles about growing spiritual fruit in our lives as they relate to dealing with your anger:

1. The fruit of the Spirit is not automatic.

What prevents this from happening in your life?

2. The fruit of the Spirit is not limited.

> Besides love, joy, peace, patience, kindness, goodness, faithful, gentleness and self-control, what else do you need to deal with anger?

3. The fruit of the Spirit is not fully produced in us immediately.

> What fruit have you most seen developing in your life? How has this affected your anger responses?

4. The fruit of the Spirit is all one harvest of the heart.

> As it relates to your anger, identify the inter-relationships with all nine fruit of the Spirit as one "basket of fruit." How would love affect your joy, how would joy affect   your peace, etc.?

5. The fruit of the Spirit represents the life of Christ in us.

> How have you seen any of these Christ-like characteristics grow in your life?

6. The fruit of the Spirit is a sweet harvest.

> Besides the nine fruit of the Spirit mentioned in Galatians 5:22-23, what other fruit have you seen in your life?

7. The fruit of the Spirit attracts others to Christ.

> Who has been most affected by the positive changes in your life?

8. The fruit of the Spirit is evidence of victory over sin.

> What proof are you seeing, as it relates to anger? Explain.

FURTHER ADVICE FROM THE MASTER GARDENER

Read the companion epistles, Ephesians and Colossians, underlining each passage relating to dealing with your anger.

CHAPTER SIXTEEN

THE TASTY FRUIT OF SPIRIT-FILLED LOVE

When it comes to growing healthy trees or harvesting fruit, my ineptitude has already been established. Actually, things have changed. Not without help. One of my favorite books to read is the *Old Farmer's Almanac*. It is truly an American icon, published every year since 1792, when George Washington was president. No other newspaper or magazine has been around longer. Up until recently the little book came with a hole in the upper left hand corner, presumably to hang on a nail in the old outhouses. It was the book with a double use. You read it and then . . . well . . . you used it.

Although, I especially enjoy the sections on astronomy, history, and gardening, not everything in the magazine appeals to me. For example, one year's version had an article on "How to Grow a Square Watermelon." Supposedly, this made them easier to store, slice and serve. Frankly, I am not really interested in growing square watermelons or, for that matter, round bananas. I am, of course, very interested in growing spiritual fruit.

In the fifth chapter of Galatians we come to the portion of this ancient epistle dealing with the empowering ministry of the indwelling Holy Spirit as He produces His harvest of luscious spiritual fruit. Again, we review, hopefully from memory:

> But the fruit of the Spirit is love, joy, peace, patience,
> kindness, goodness, faithfulness, gentleness, self-control;
> against such things there is no law (Galatians 5:22-23).

In order to benefit from each of these nine fruit of the Spirit in dealing with our anger, we will need to look at each in terms of its

Scriptural definition, supreme example, specific commands, spiritual source, substantial impact, and solutions to our anger. We begin with Galatians 5:22, at what can rightly be called "The First-fruit of the Fruit of the Spirit":

But the fruit of the Spirit is **love** . . . (Galatians 5:22, emphasis added).

THE SCRIPTURAL DEFINITION

What poet, songwriter, philosopher or writer has not pondered love, this powerful word and all it entails? Frankly, any definition of love we humans have attempted falls short of the dramatic biblical definition. In the Greek language, prior to the apostle Paul's day, there were primarily three words for love used:

- *eros,* meaning sexual desire
- *philos,* meaning relational love and tender affection
- *storge,* meaning familial love, as in a parent with a child

However, here in Galatians 5, as well as many other places in the New Testament, the apostle Paul uses a word that is not as commonly used in the classical Greek language—*agape* in its noun form and *agapao* in its verb form. In essence, he takes a word from the world of commerce and turns it into one of the most powerful words in all of the New Testament. It speaks of something more valuable than it really is because of the extreme price someone is willing to pay for it. Let me illustrate.

It was not too long ago a pair of Yubari King melons sold at auction for $23,000. No, they were not made of gold nor were they necessarily fit for a king. Actually, they looked like a couple of cantaloupes, worth less than a few dollars. Yet, these folks were convinced these rare melons were extra special and so did many others. The value of those melons at auction went up exponentially. Intrinsically, they were just cantaloupe-like melons and worth very little. But extrinsically they were worth whatever someone was willing pay to have them in their collection or in their mouths. The lesson is unmistakable. The more we value something, the more we will pay for it, regardless of its original worth. So it is with *agape* love.

How much are people really worth? If you melt us down we are really not worth much, perhaps no more than a few dollars-worth of chemicals. In some physical sense we are just garden fodder, glorified manure—a pile of those "ashes to ashes, dust to dust" (as stated in the English Burial Service, adapted from Genesis 3:19).

But how much are we worth to our family and friends? It is the same as asking how much they love us. The answer? We are worth whatever price they are willing to pay to have a relationship with us. And the level of our love is based on the level of our willingness to sacrifice for them. Thus the apostle Paul writes in Ephesians: "Husbands, love ["value," Greek verb: *agapao*] your wives as Christ loved [Greek verb: *agapao*] the church *and gave Himself up* for her . . ." (Ephesians 5:25, emphasis added).

How much are we worth to God? That is another way of asking how much He loves us. The answer? We are worth whatever price He was willing to pay to have a relationship with us. What price did He pay? How much did He *agapao* us? Reflect on two of the most popular passages in all of the Bible:

For God so loved [Greek verb: *agapao*] the world, that He gave His only begotten Son . . . (John 3:16).

Greater love [Greek noun: *agape*] has no one than this, that one lay down his life for his friends (John 15:13).

God valued us so much He made us his beloved—His Greatly Valued Ones [Greek: *agapetos*; cf. Romans 1:7; 9:26; 12:19]. The very same thing Our Heavenly Father said to Jesus, He declares is true of us: "This is My *beloved* Son, in whom I am well-pleased" (Matthew 3:17; cf. Matthew 12:18; 17:5; Mark 1:11; Luke 3:22, emphasis added).

I have had the joy of traveling to the Philippines some thirty times. On a number of occasions, I have visited the lush outdoor markets, watching folks buying fruit and vegetables and every sort of goods. As they barter with the vendor they will often complain about the high price. Speaking in Taglish, a mix of native Tagalog and English, we hear them exclaim, *"Mahal! Too costly! Much too expensive!"* But when they express love for their spouse, they use the exact same word, *"Mahal kita! I love you!"* Dear friends, I have found no clearer understanding of the true meaning of the

Greek word *agape* than in the national language of the Philippines. *Agape* love is costly. *Agape* love is expensive. *Agape* love is *mahal*.

This first-fruit of the Spirit—*agape* love—also speaks of the quality of self-sacrifice based on the worth God places on a person. Thus, *agape* love shows up in self-sacrificial actions and not just words. Of such we are often reminded in Scripture. Consider the popular Love Chapter, 1 Corinthians 13:

> Love is patient, love is kind, and is not jealous; love does not brag and is not arrogant, does not act unbecomingly; it does not seek its own, is not provoked, does not take into account a wrong suffered, does not rejoice in unrighteousness, but rejoices with the truth; bears all things, believes all things, hopes all things. Love never fails . . . (1 Corinthians 13:4-8).

I agree wholeheartedly with what the great American evangelist, D.L. Moody, said about this passage. "Some men occasionally take the journey into 1 Corinthians 13." He was implying few live there.

THE SUPREME EXAMPLE

Since the running analogy in this book is related to agriculture, perhaps I should try to create a definition of love related to passion fruit (*Passiflora edulus*). Hundreds of years ago the design of its flowers were used in South America as a teaching tool to illustrate the *agape* love of Christ, especially related to His sacrifice on the cross.

Agape love isn't hard to recognize. *Agape* love looks like Jesus. Concerning this first fruit of the Spirit, He is the supreme example—the *agape* love of God in the flesh! The apostle John reminds us: "We know love by this, that He [Jesus] laid down His life for us; and *we ought to lay down our lives for the brethren*" (1 John 3:16). He also wrote in that same epistle, "We [*agapao*] love, because He first [*agapao*] loved us" (1 John 4:19, emphasis added).

Read the Gospels. They are the historical accounts of both the life and love of Jesus. He valued equally sinners and saints, prostitutes and priests, down-and-outers and the rich and powerful. God loves and paid the ultimate price to have a relationship with common everyday sinners, just like us. It is worth repeating Paul's words: "But God demonstrates His own love [Greek: *agape*] toward us, in that while we were yet sinners, Christ died for us" (Romans 5:8).

THE SPECIFIC COMMANDS

The Peanuts cartoon character, Linus, summed up what many of us feel when he said, "I love mankind. It's people I can't stand." It is reasonable to expect God would give us, as His Greatly Valued Ones, a life-long mandate to value people as He values them. There are scores of biblical passages calling us, who are loved so much, to place that same worth on others. We who are the Beloved of God must take to heart the command Jesus gave: "A new commandment I give to you, that you love one another, even as I have loved you . . ." (John 13:34).

Agape love is more than an emotion. It is a decision of the will that results in self-sacrificial action. We may not feel like loving others, but we must esteem and serve them, simply because we are commanded to do so. It is as basic as that. In fact, the apostle Paul points out that it is this kind of love—the kind that imitates God's love for us—that is so aromatic: "Therefore be imitators of God, as beloved children; and walk in love, just as Christ also loved you, and gave Himself up for us, an offering and a sacrifice to God *as a fragrant aroma*" (Ephesians 5:1-2, emphasis added).

Even those who do not know Christ as Savior exercise some form of *agape* love. It is a love that comes from the image of God in them. Because of their sin nature, however, it is a flawed love. It is what I once heard called "*sloppy agape*." It is a conditional love that says:

"I will love you *if . . .*"
"I will love you *if* you love me back."
"I will love you *if* you give me what I want."
"I will love you *if* you always please me."

Every human being has the same capacity to exercise *agape* love; not just Christians. Jesus said it clearly:

. . . if you love those who love you, what credit is that to you? For even sinners love [Greek: *agapao*] those who love them . . . (Luke 6:32).

But God has a different standard of *agape* love for His born-again children: "But love [Greek verb: *agapao*] your enemies . . . and you will be sons of the Most High" (Luke 6:35). This kind of unconditional love looks even the most difficult people in the face and says, "I am a child of God. I will love you *in spite of* what you have done." It boldly declares, "Even if you hate me back or do things that displease me, I will value and place on you the worth God places on you. In fact, you cannot make me do anything less. I have only myself to blame if I choose not to love you with the love of the Lord."

THE SPIRITUAL SOURCE

So, where does this kind of unconditional love, this sacrificial love without a hook, come from? It certainly does not come from human nature. Consider with me its spiritual source. The apostle Paul said it clearly: "the [*agape*] love of God has been poured out within our hearts *through the Holy Spirit* who was given to us" (Romans 5:5, emphasis added).

Adding a different word for love and speaking of our relationship as brothers and sisters in Christ, the apostle Paul reminds us of where the ability to love one another comes from:

Now as to the love of the brethren [Greek: *philadelphia*], you have no need for anyone to write to you, for you yourselves are *taught by God* to love [*agapao*] one another; for indeed you do practice it toward all the brethren who are in all Macedonia. But we urge you, brethren, to excel still more (1 Thessalonians 4:9-10, emphasis added).

God is the ultimate source of *agape* love, as we are reminded in the little epistle of 1 John. Whereas 1 Corinthians 13 is "The Love Chapter;" 1 John is "The Love Book." Like a crate full of delicious apples, the whole epistle is jam-packed with passages related to loving one another. In 1 John 4:7-13, for example, the apostle John mentions *agape* love thirteen times in just seven verses. Do more than just count them; live them:

Beloved, let us LOVE one another, for LOVE is from God;
and everyone who LOVES is born of God and knows God.
The one who does not LOVE does not know God, for God is
LOVE. By this the LOVE of God was manifested in us, that
God has sent His only begotten Son into the world so that
we might live through Him. In this is LOVE, not that we
LOVED God, but that He LOVED us and sent His Son to
be the propitiation for our sins. Beloved, if God so LOVED
us, we also ought to LOVE one another. No one has seen God
at any time; if we LOVE one another, God abides in us, and
His LOVE is perfected in us. By this we know that we abide in
Him and He in us, because He has given us of His Spirit
(1 John 4:7-13, emphasis added).

We could go through all of 1 John, or for that matter, all of the
New Testament and be inundated with the importance of *agape*
love. I believe, however, all of the verses in the New Testament
calling us to love one another can be encapsulated in the simple
words of Galatians 5:22:

... the fruit of the Spirit is **love** ... (Galatians 5:22,
emphasis added).

THE SUBSTANTIAL IMPACT

Around the fourth century, Bishop Augustine was quoted as
saying:

"What does love look like? It has hands to help others, feet to
hasten to the poor and needy, eyes to see misery and want, ears
to hear the sighs and sorrows of men. That is what love looks
like" (Augustine, Bishop of Hippo).

Only the Holy Spirit who indwells us can teach us to value and
esteem others enough to self-sacrifice for them. He is crying out
within our regenerated hearts, "Love others as I have loved you."
Imagine what would happen if we did just that? Imagine the
substantial spiritual impact. Earlier, we spoke of the fruit of the
Spirit as attractive, even magnetic. What would be the impact on
the people around us if this first fruit of the Spirit-filled life—
agape love—were to take effect immediately?

I read somewhere, "When love is felt the message is heard." Unfortunately, the opposite is also true. No one will know we are His disciples if we do not have *agape* love for one another. Jesus reminded us of its evangelistic importance: "By this all men will know that you are My disciples, if you have love for one another" (John 13:35).

I recall reading one account of the infamous Spanish Inquisition, where an Inca chief in Central America was captured. His people had been brutally tortured into accepting the Christian faith. His captors asked him to become a Christian as well, assuring him of heaven if he did, but threatening him with immediate death and hell if he did not. He refused, declaring that he would rather go to hell with his people than go to heaven with people like them. Sadly, many of our non-Christian friends and family echo a similar reply when our lives are not consistent with what we say about God's love. Perhaps they are whispering even now, "I would rather stay the way I am than become an unloving Christian like you."

If we are going to touch the world we are going to need more *agape* love, the kind that only comes as a result of being indwelt with, and walking by, the Holy Spirit. Is Spirit-led *agape* risky? You bet it is. But, as Alfred Lord Tennyson famously said, "Tis better to have loved and lost, than never to have loved at all." Then again, "[*agape*] love never fails" (1 Corinthians 13:8).

The *agape* love God extends toward us even empowers us to love those who hate us. In the words of Jesus Himself: "But I say to you who hear, love [Greek: *agapao*] your enemies, do good to those who hate you" (Luke 6:27; cf. Matthew 5:44; Luke 6:35). I also like how Dr. Martin Luther King, Jr. put it, "I have decided to stick with love. Hate is too great a burden to bear."

THE SOLUTION TO OUR ANGER

What does Spirit-produced *agape* love have to do with dealing with life's frustrated expectations, unresolved hurts, and many expressions of repressed or expressed anger? Everything. Placing God's value on others is one of the most anger-stifling things we can do. Even when we disagree with them, we can place God's worth on them, because He loves us and them so very much.

One of our foster-daughters had a very hard time accepting loving correction of any kind. Her repeated response was to run, wrap herself in a blanket, and hide under the coffee table. On one occasion I took another blanket, wrapped myself and got under the table with her, without saying a word. As she peeked out the blanket, I whispered, "You can't make me stop loving you." She quickly covered herself. At the next peek, I could see from her sweet little eyes that she was softening and the anger was subsiding. *Agape* love truly does "blanket" a multitude of sinful anger (1 Peter 4:8)—theirs and ours—even when they want to cut us emotionally into a hundred pieces..

Apparently the banana tree is so resilient you can cut it into hundreds of pieces and it will survive. The only way it stops growing is when it is uprooted. So it is with us as we manage angry people and situations. As I read this I could not help but reflect on Paul's prayer for the ancient Colossians and for us today:

> For this reason I bow my knees before the Father, from whom every family in heaven and on earth derives its name, that He would grant you, according to the riches of His glory, to be strengthened with power *through His Spirit in the inner man*, so that Christ may dwell in your hearts   through faith; and that you, *being rooted and grounded in [agape] love*, may comprehend with all the saints what is the breadth and length and height and depth, and *to know the [agape] love of Christ* which surpasses knowledge, that you may be filled up to all the fullness of God (Ephesians 3:14-19, emphasis added).

INSPECTING THE FRUIT

1. Besides Jesus, who is the greatest example of love in your life?

2. What would be the impact on the people around you if an abundance of *agape* love were to take effect immediately in your life?

FURTHER ADVICE FROM THE MASTER GARDENER

1. Read 1 Corinthians 13: The Love Chapter, underlining all of the qualities and characteristics of *agape* love.

2. Read 1 John: The Love Book, underlining every use of the word love and the admonitions that follow.

CHAPTER SEVENTEEN

THE TASTY FRUIT OF
SPIRIT-FILLED JOY

When I was young, my father signed me up for a student work program for teens under fifteen. Apparently the program was designed to teach us responsible work habits. Little did I realize it would give me one of my greatest lessons in joy.

I was assigned the job of picking string beans in Watsonville, California for three cents a pound. I was intent on making a bundle of money. On my most productive day, however, I made a meager $9, having picked 300 pounds (just over 136 kilos). I was tired. I was angry. And from that day on, it showed on my miserable face. I grabbed those bean stalks, crushed the string beans and ripped them from the stalks. My friends were just as frustrated at how hard the work and how little the financial reward. They enticed me to join them in running through the rows, knocking as many bushes down as we could. It is no surprise the foreman fired us— all of us—on the spot. Yes, folks, I got fired from picking beans! Not quite a highlight on my resume. (I also got fired from my next job, working at a fast-food restaurant, but that is another story.)

Obviously, I had some growing up to do, not just in my work behavior but also in my general attitude. At the time, I really needed a crate full of joy, the kind I saw in so many of those farm workers who were just thankful for a job. To this day I wonder how some of them could laugh and sing as they carried their heavy crates to the scale.

I remember one girl, who was my age, challenged me to a contest to see which of us could pick more beans. She won! She cheered! She laughed! I will never forget her inexplicable joy in spite of having to do such backbreaking work. To this day, when I drive by workers, bent over in the produce fields, I often remember her countenance.

Where does anyone find that kind of joy for a lifetime? It was a fundamental question this pastor, once a teenage bean-picker, did not learn in college, seminary or doctoral studies. He learned it picking another kind of fruit—the fruit of the Spirit.

> But the fruit of the Spirit is . . . **joy** . . . (Galatians 5:22, emphasis added).

THE SCRIPTURAL DEFINITION

What exactly is joy? Again, we could go to what many people have written throughout the ages. Unfortunately, too many have equated joy with simple feelings of happiness, exuberance, even being a bouncy personality. Instead, let's look at the biblical definition. Unlike the unusual word the apostle Paul uses for love (*agape*), the Greek word he uses for joy is the very familiar Greek word *chara*. The word was so common in Greek culture it became one of the more popular girls names. (Today we have many we know who are named Kara). In fact, some form of the word joy or the related word rejoice is used over one hundred and thirty times in the New Testament. But what does it really mean?

Let's carefully read what the apostle Peter wrote in his first epistle. Before we do, we need to be reminded he wrote this to the people of God who were facing great persecution and suffering. In some cases, their loved ones were being crucified and their children were being torn apart by animals in the Roman arenas:

> In this you *greatly rejoice*, even though now for a little while, if necessary, you have been distressed by various trials, so that the proof of your faith, being more precious than gold which is perishable, even though tested by fire, may be found to result *in praise and glory and honor* at the revelation of Jesus Christ; and though you have not seen Him, you love Him, and though you do not see Him now, but believe in Him, you *greatly rejoice with joy inexpressible and full of glory* (1 Peter 1:6-8, emphasis added).

Here in this amazing text, especially considering the context in which it was written, we see a number of characteristics of Spirit-produced *chara* joy:

Quality #1: *Chara* joy is not dependent on circumstances.

In this you greatly rejoice, *even though* now for a little while, if necessary, you have been distressed by various trials . . . (1 Peter 1:6, emphasis added).

I shared with my congregation a quote I had heard, "If you don't think you have anything to be thankful for, look in a medical book at all the diseases you don't have." So true. Some of us, however, are nonetheless plagued with pain and sorrow—hardship beyond measure. But biblical joy says "even though . . ." Even though my body is hurting, in this I greatly rejoice. Even though my relationships are struggling, in this I have joy. Even though life is tough, in this I am filled with gratefulness to God. Thus the apostle Paul spoke of being "sorrowful yet always rejoicing" (2 Corinthians 6:10). He went on to speak of suffering Christians who, "in a great deal of affliction their abundance of joy overflowed" (2 Corinthians 8:2).

Quality #2: *Chara* joy is the supernatural response to our tested and proven faith in God.

We continue with the apostle Peter's words of comfort to these suffering Christians and to us: "In this (i.e. these various trials) you greatly rejoice so that the proof of your faith, being more precious than gold which is perishable, even though tested by fire, may be found to result in praise and glory and honor at the revelation of Jesus Christ" (1 Peter 1:6-7). Here the apostle Peter uses imagery from the world of metallurgy. Gold needed to be tested by fire to prove how genuine it was. The hotter the fire, the quicker the impurities, called dross, came to the surface and were able to be skimmed off. So it is with our lives, which are eternally more valuable to God than perishable gold. In the crucible of suffering we find the things of this world that do not matter are more easily skimmed off our lives (Colossians 3:1-4). In the midst of fiery trials we can lift up joyful praise and give glory and honor to the Soon-Coming Jesus. Biblical joy is the God-given ability to sing in any test of our faith, *It is well with my soul*. In the words of Jesus, "you will grieve, but your grief will be turned into joy" (John 16:20).

Quality #3: *Chara* joy cannot always be explained in words.

Some of us are naturally exuberant, outwardly expressive and extremely enthusiastic. We are amped! Pumped up! Is that what biblical joy is? Not necessarily. Sometimes biblical joy shows up in quiet ways—in a *chara* joy so deep there are no words to describe it. Thus the apostle Peter writes, "you greatly rejoice with *joy inexpressible*" (1 Peter 1:8, emphasis added). *Chara* joy is nothing less than an overwhelming gratitude for all God has done for us.

Quality #4: *Chara* joy is a characteristic of God.

The apostle Peter continues with the reminder that we can "greatly rejoice with joy inexpressible and *full of glory*" (1 Peter 1:8, emphasis added). *Chara* joy is joy that is full of the attributes of God. Biblical joy is God's joy in us. Sadly, some of us do not often think of God as joyful, but He is:

> The Lord your God is in your midst . . . . He will exult over you with joy. He will rejoice over you with shouts of joy ["triumphal singing," Hebrew: *rinnah*]" (Zephaniah 3:17).

When we walk in obedience to Him, God cheers our lives and we rejoice over His shouts of joy over us. In fact, our *chara* joy is one of the amazing proofs of the presence of God in our lives.

THE SUPREME EXAMPLE

Who can we look to for the kind of *chara* joy that lasts for a lifetime? The Lord Jesus Christ. Talk about One who had every reason to be joyless and miserable. Just a glance at the Gospel of John we find Jesus rejected by His countrymen (John 1:11) and His followers (John 6:66), betrayed by Judas (John 13:2), denied by Simon Peter (John 13:38), and deserted by His apostles (John 19:25-27). Even His own brothers did not believe in Him (John 7:5). Ultimately, He was crucified on a cruel Roman cross by the very people He came to save. And yet, even though all that happened, Jesus was able to look beyond the cross to the good it would bring to mankind and the glory it would bring to His Heavenly Father. It brought Him *chara* joy. I love what the writer to the Hebrews said of Jesus, "who for the joy set before Him endured the cross, despising the shame, and has sat down at the right hand of the   throne of God" (Hebrews 12:2).

THE SPECIFIC COMMANDS

The Man of Sorrows never lost His *chara* joy, no matter what happened! What an example to us. Thus, it stands to reason why the writers of Scripture are clear in presenting a long list of imperatives for us, as born-again believers who are indwelt by the Holy Spirit.

The shortest verse in the English Bible is John 11:35 "Jesus wept." The shortest verse in the Greek text, however, is the apostle Paul's timely command to believers of every age: "Rejoice always" (1 Thessalonians 5:16). The easiest verse in the Bible to memorize is not about Jesus crying, but about us rejoicing. Whisper it a few times, "Rejoice always." So easy to memorize; so hard to do, especially when we take to heart the all-encompassing words the apostle Paul wrote: "Rejoice in the Lord *always*; again I will say, rejoice! (Philippians 4:4, emphasis added). Christ-like *chara* joy is not optional.

THE SPIRITUAL SOURCE

How do we live a life always filled with *chara* joy—again and again? What is the ultimate source of lasting joy in our lives, even in the midst of life's challenges? It is a simple Sunday School question with a simple Sunday School answer. The source is God Himself.

I once saw a cartoon picturing a counselor with a box of tissue in one hand and with his other hand he is backhanding a client, shouting, "Snap out of it." The caption below read, "Single Session Therapy." Some of us have that view of God. We think He sees our misery and backhands us and says, "Snap out of it!" Not so. He wants us to experience His *chara* joy and He will take us through the process of spiritual growth that will get us there, if we let Him.

We begin by holding on to the life-sustaining counsel of Nehemiah: "Do not be grieved. *The joy of the Lord* is your strength" (Nehemiah 8:10, emphasis added). We also cling to the promise Jesus gave to His disciples: "These things I have spoken to you, so that *My joy* may be in you, and that *your joy* may be made full (John 15:11, emphasis added). Jesus is not merely talking about His joy, but about His <u>full</u> joy. He is saying, "My full joy can be your full joy."

How do we get His full joy in us? Can we find it in some "happy meal" to eat or some "joy brew" to drink? No! I love what the apostle Paul wrote in Romans 14:17: "the kingdom of God is not eating and drinking, but righteousness and peace and *joy in the Holy Spirit*" (Romans 14:17, emphasis added). Notice the phrase "joy *in* the Holy Spirit . . ." No matter how hard we try, we cannot make ourselves joyful. We cannot give ourselves a backhand and make ourselves snap out if it. The Holy Spirit of God who indwells us is the only One who can produce in us the full and lasting *chara* joy of the Lord. The apostle Paul is quick to point out to his beloved disciples: "You also became imitators of us and of the Lord, having received the word in much tribulation *with the joy of the Holy Spirit*" (1 Thessalonians 1:6, emphasis added).

THE SUBSTANTIAL IMPACT

What are the effects of Spirit-produced *chara* joy? Earlier I reminded us that biblical joy doesn't always show up in shouts and cheers. It can be an *inexpressible* joy, but it is never an *invisible* joy. *Chara* joy shows up—on our faces! In fact, a gloomy-faced Christian is a contradiction in terms.

One man said of the Christians he knew that they have managed to extract the bubbles from the champagne of life. Another complained that too many of his fellow Christians have preserved their doctrine in vinegar. The German philosopher, Friedrich Nietzsche, was one of the proponents of the "God is Dead Movement." He is known to have said of the Christians he knew that he would believe in their salvation if they looked a little more like people who have been saved. Charles Haddon Spurgeon is known to have said to his ministry students, "When you preach about heaven, smile. When you preach about hell, your everyday face will do." How very sad but how very true of too many of us.

I am told it takes seventeen muscles to smile and forty-three muscles to frown. Some of us have become muscle-bound frowners. The joy-filled words, "Praise the Lord" have turned to the sour laments, "Woe is me." Perhaps we need to look in a mirror and whisper to ourselves: *"If you are joyful, inform your face."*

When there is a moving of the Holy Spirit in our lives, it shows in our countenance! And it's contagious. After a revival, the former president of Wheaton College was quoted as saying, "We have never seen so many smiles per square face." I have always loved Walter Knight's classic definition of a joy that shows: "Joy is the flag that flies over the castle of our heart, announcing that the King is in residence today." Let the flag fly high today. Why today? Because *"This is the day which the Lord has made. Let us rejoice and be glad in it"* (Psalm 118:24, emphasis added). The familiar passage is calling us to stand up and joyfully cheer the day—today. Only the *chara* joy-producing, indwelling Holy Spirit can make that happen.

THE SOLUTION TO OUR ANGER

Consider the influence of this Spirit-produced *chara* joy we can exhibit the next time we are in conflict with someone. Imagine what kind of diffusing effect it would have when that person or situation does not rob us of our Christ-like joy. As is the case with all the fruit of the Spirit, no one steals our joy; we give it away.

We have a decision to make. The first is to consider how the Spirit of God who indwells us wants to stimulate us to *chara* joy, no matter what we are facing. The second is to do something about it by refusing to let people or circumstances take our joy from us. There is a third choice I hope we do not make. We can simply forget about what we have learned and go back to choosing to be miserable. When our lives are struggling with anger, bitterness and conflict, that is hardly worth the time spent. Bitterness is a costly choice.

One Christmas season I was standing in the checkout line at very busy department store. I could see the anger on people's faces, especially as rude people stepped in front of them. I, too, was getting frustrated. I was prompted by the Spirit to start singing to myself quietly, "Joy to the world, the Lord is come. Let earth receive her King. Let every heart prepare Him room. And heaven and nature sing . . ." To my surprise the lady behind me started singing with me. With her much better voice backing me, I sang louder. Surprisingly, the people around us joined in, many of them laughing at how silly we looked. Few of us knew all the words but our faces brightened as we sang together: "Repeat the sounding joy. Repeat the sounding joy. Repeat, repeat, the sounding joy."

I once read that joy is a vaccine. It certainly was that day. Joy shared was truly joy doubled and tripled—a few times over. Joy to the world, the Savior reigns. May there be an epidemic of contagious, Spirit-led *chara* joy and praise spreading in our midst!

INSPECTING THE FRUIT

1. What are the most difficult circumstances you are facing?

2. When was the last time you experienced *chara* joy, even in the midst of a challenging situation, that could not be put into words?

3. What does it mean for you to "Rejoice in the Lord always" (Philippians 4:4, 1 Thessalonians 5:16)?

4. If others were to measure your joy simply by the look on your face, what would those around you say?

5. Besides Jesus, who is the person in your life whose joy you desire to imitate?

6. Share about a time when your joy helped stimulate another person's joy.

FURTHER ADVICE FROM THE MASTER GARDENER

Read the following passages and comment as to why they had such joy:

Psalm 40:1-3	Luke 15:9-10
1 Chronicles 29:9	Acts 2:46-47
Nehemiah 8:9, 12	Acts 3:8
Luke 10:20	Acts 8:8

CHAPTER EIGHTEEN

THE TASTY FRUIT OF SPIRIT-FILLED PEACE

I am told the average American consumes about sixteen pounds (7.25 kilos) of fresh apples each year. They are second only to the banana as America's favorite fruit. We are blessed with so many types: Macintosh, Granny Smith, Pippin, and Red Delicious, to name a few. I especially love Golden Delicious apples. Such choices, however, have not always been available.

I was reading an article on historical pomology from the Smithsonian Institute's magazine regarding "heirloom apples"— varieties of apples that are now extinct or near extinction. As recently as a hundred years ago, there were some 14,000 varieties of apples flourishing nationwide. That's pretty incredible when we realize that when the first colonists arrived at Jamestown, Virginia, there were no cultivated apples in America. All that existed were a few wild and scattered crab apple trees.

Perhaps you are familiar with the name, James Chapman, also known as "Johnny Appleseed." He died in 1845, but not before he helped plant hundreds of apple orchards throughout Pennsylvania, Ohio and Indiana. Today, however, only fifteen varieties of apples make up ninety percent of the U.S. product.

We are here to discuss a variety of fruit that may be rare but will never be extinct—the very real cornucopia of fruit that flows from our lives when we are filled with the Holy Spirit and living under His daily influence and power. They are also the fruit that help us deal with the unrighteous fruit of anger in our lives. I remind us again of our key passage:

But the fruit of the Spirit is love, joy, peace, patience,
kindness, goodness, faithfulness, gentleness, self-control;
against such things there is no law (Galatians 5:22-23).

Many of us began the Christian life desiring to see all these fruit of the Spirit flourish in our lives, but as the seasons unfolded, we either lost interest or we went on to other endeavors. And yet, there are few things more fundamental to our health as Christians than what the apostle Paul writes here in Galatians 5:22-23. Who among us has not heard the expression: "An apple a day keeps the doctor away." Though it is certainly an overstatement, I can assure us, manifesting the fruit of the Spirit will definitely keep the flesh from producing its vile produce of sin. Even more so, it will attract others to the sweet aroma of the gospel of Jesus Christ.

We began in Part Two with *The Eight Principles of Spiritual Pomology.* We then embarked on a special study of the first two on the list of the nine fruit of the Spirit—*agape* love and *chara* joy. I invite us now to examine the next in our harvest of available fruit:

... the fruit of the Spirit is ... **peace** ... (Galatians 5:22, emphasis added).

THE SPIRITUAL DEFINITION

I once read a bizarre definition of peace suggesting it is the brief, glorious moment in history when everybody stands around reloading. That's not quite what the apostle Paul had in mind as he spoke of this lasting and abiding fruit of the Spirit-filled life. The common Greek word for peace is *eirene*. Some form of this word is used in every book of the New Testament, except 1 John, the epistle where we find, on the other hand, a basket full of references to the fruit of *agape* love. The word *eirene* was so popular in ancient Greece it became a name given to many girls. (We even get our modern name Irene from this same word.)

Take a journey through a timeline of human history. There hasn't been a single day when there has not been a feud going on in some family, tribe, town, or nation. As much as we strive for world peace, it has never happened. It never will until the Prince of Peace reigns as the King of Kings and Lord of Lords (Revelation 19:16).

As we examine the many verses in the New Testament we will not find *eirene* peace referring to the absence of conflict. Rather, *eirene* peace speaks of a deep-settled confidence that Almighty God is in control of the details of our lives, even in the midst of these problems. That is especially true when we are engulfed in hostile situations—internationally, nationally, corporately or personally.

In many respects the New Testament Greek word *eirene* is related to the Old Testament Hebrew word *shalom.* The word speaks of wholeness, accepting all God offers in its entirety. When we greet someone with *"Shalom!"* we are saying to them, *"May you accept God's wholeness—the fullness of His plan for your life."*

I once heard that peace is the deliberate adjustment of my life to the will of God. We desperately need to have the ability to understand, accept and adjust our lives to God's plans. To do so, we need a daily dose of Spirit-produced *eirene* peace. Sometimes we need a double dose.

I love the story of King Jehoshaphat, the king of Judah, found in 2 Chronicles 20. He woke up one morning, surrounded by a number of invading armies. His initial response is understandable: "Jehoshaphat was afraid and turned his attention to seek the LORD and proclaimed a fast throughout all Judah" (2 Chronicles 20:3). Like many of us might have done in the midst of struggle, he cried out to the LORD, "For we are powerless before this great multitude who are coming against us; nor do we know what to do, but our eyes are on You" (2 Chronicles 20:12).

When Jehoshaphat didn't know what to do, he prayed to the One whose name is *Yahweh Shalom*—"the LORD is Peace" (Judges 6:24). And through a prophet, the LORD of Peace tells the king exactly how to experience God's peace in the midst of this conflict. Take it to heart:

> . . . thus says the LORD to you, 'Do not fear or be dismayed because of this great multitude, for the battle is not yours but God's. Tomorrow go down against them. Behold, they will come . . . you will find them . . . . You need not fight in this battle; station yourselves, stand and see the salvation of the LORD on your behalf . . . . Do not fear or be dismayed; tomorrow go out to face them, for the LORD is with you.'
> Jehoshaphat bowed his head with his face to the ground, and all Judah and the inhabitants of Jerusalem fell down before the LORD, worshiping the LORD (2 Chronicles 20:15-18).

Then King Jehoshaphat spoke to anyone who would listen: "put your trust in the LORD your God and you will be established. Put your trust in His prophets and succeed" (2 Chronicles 20:20).

Simple counsel in the midst of chaos. Put your trust in God. Put your trust in those who teach you the Word of God. Expect to succeed.

The story continues. As the people began singing and praising God for His everlasting lovingkindness, the LORD Himself went to work on their behalf. He routed their adversaries without Jehoshaphat's army lifting a sword or spear. In fact, the enemies destroyed themselves! It is amazing how the story ends, "So the kingdom of Jehoshaphat was at peace ["tranquil, undisturbed," Hebrew: *shaqat*], for his God gave him rest ["a quiet, settled, well-placed confidence," Hebrew: *ruwach*] on all sides" (2 Chronicles 20:30). That is exactly what Holy Spirit-produced *eirene* peace does for us.

We may be surrounded by family conflicts to the north, work disputes to the south, strife and jealousy to the east and a host of other anger issues to the west. We might even be facing an invasion of inner turmoil right where we are standing. When we stand firm, with our faith in *Yahweh Shalom*, He gives us His peace—on all sides! We are surrounded by *eirene* peace and filled with a quiet, settled, well-placed *shalom*-confidence in Him.

THE SUPREME EXAMPLE

Where do we learn that kind of *eirene* peace? We learn it from the Lord Jesus Christ—the One whose name is the Prince of Peace (Isaiah 9:6). He is the epitome of one who accepted the Heavenly Father's will in every circumstance. Consider Jesus during His arrest, trial and crucifixion, knowing He had the power to destroy His captors and control His circumstances. Instead, He submitted to His Heavenly Father's will for His life and earthly ministry. Jesus cried out from the cruel cross, "Father, into Your hands I commit My Spirit" (Luke 23:46). It is not without significance that prior to that we find Jesus, the night of His arrest, on His knees, praying to His Heavenly Father, "My Father, if it is possible, let this cup pass from Me; yet not as I will, but as You will" (Matthew 26:39).

That is biblical peace. That is true *shalom* and genuine *eirene*. It is found in Jesus Christ and expected in all of us who are His followers. In a peace-destroying, conflict-producing world, we need to cry out daily: "Lord, not my will but Yours be done. Into Your hands I commit my life."

Just as it is Our Heavenly Father's desire for each of us to experience the *agape* love of God and the *chara* joy of the Holy Spirit, He also desires us to experience the *eirene* peace of Christ, the One who is the ultimate example of peace, the One who is the peace of *Yahweh Shalom* in the flesh. Daily, we need to rehearse, "For He Himself is our peace" (Ephesians 2:14).

THE SPECIFIC COMMANDS

I expect there are many of us facing some very tough times. Let the words of the apostle Paul be an encouragement to our restless hearts:

> Be anxious for nothing, but in everything by prayer and supplication with thanksgiving let your requests be made known to God. And *the peace of God*, which surpasses all comprehension, shall guard your hearts and your minds in Christ Jesus (Philippians 4:6-7, emphasis added).

Not only are we to *enjoy* His *eirene* peace *within* us, we are also commanded to *promote* His *eirene* peace *around* us. Just like Johnny Appleseed, we are to spread the seed of peace. In Ephesians 4:3 the apostle Paul spoke of "being diligent to preserve the unity of the Spirit in the bond of peace" (Ephesians 4:3).

In ancient Greece, villages had officials who were called "Keepers of the Public Peace." That's also our job as Christians. We are called to be peacemakers—*eirene* promoters—in our homes, workplaces, schools, churches and communities. In His Sermon on the Mount, Jesus presented His timeless kingdom principle: "Blessed are the peacemakers for they shall be called the sons of God" (Matthew 5:9). Perhaps I should issue each of us a badge, imprinted with *Peacemaker* or *Keeper of Peace*. I remind us of the first line of the now famous prayer of Francis of Assisi, "Lord, make me an instrument of Your peace." That needs to be our prayer, as well.

THE SPIRITUAL SOURCE

In 1847 Henderson Luelling cultivated a new kind of cherry. He wanted to give it a name that would reflect his desire to see a greater peace between the Chinese farmworkers and the white landowners. He named the heart-shaped cherries after his friend, a Chinese laborer. And today we enjoy delicious Bing cherries. The inventor wanted a fruit that brings peace. So did our Creator whose desire is for an even more lasting fruit— *eirene* peace.

Where does lasting *eirene* peace come from? It is impossible to create on our own. Consider with me what the Bible says about the scriptural source. In his epistle to the Philippians, the apostle Paul reminds us that the God of Peace will be with us (Philippians 4:9). How can that be? How is it possible for us, as sinners, to be at peace with Holy God, who hates sin? In his letter to the Romans, Paul tells us in no uncertain terms: "Therefore having been justified by faith, we have *peace* with God *through our Lord Jesus Christ*" (Romans 5:1, emphasis added). In other words, the God of Peace imparts His peace to us when we place our faith and confidence in the Lord Jesus Christ. Listen to Jesus' words on the matter: "*Peace* I leave with you; My *peace* I give to you; not as the world gives, do I give to you. Let not your heart be troubled, nor let it be fearful" (John 14:27, emphasis added). Later in the same Gospel he continues the thought:

These things I have spoken to you, that in Me you may have *peace*. In the world you have tribulation, but take courage; I have overcome the world (John 16:33, emphasis added).

The apostle Paul also reminds us that "the kingdom of God . . . is *peace* . . . in the Holy Spirit" (Romans 14:17, emphasis added). Want to say it simply? Then recite the familiar words:

. . . the fruit of the Spirit is . . . **peace** . . . (Galatians 5:22, emphasis added).

THE SUBSTANTIAL IMPACT

What would happen to the world around us if the Spirit-led fruit of *eirene* peace prevailed in our hearts, came out of our mouths and was seen in our actions? Consider the immense spiritual impact. I have.

As I mentioned earlier, our San Joaquin Valley is world famous for its agricultural abundance. In fact, it is one of the most fertile places on the planet. It is also considered one of the "Bible Belts" of America, with more churches per capita than most areas of the nation. Our prayer has been that we would not just be known for the produce from our fields, but the produce of peace in our hearts, our churches and, eventually in our community.

So far, after being here for twenty-five years, I am pleased to say we have a truly remarkable abundance of peace among our churches here in Fresno County. Notables like Billy Graham, Bruce Wilkinson, Luis Palau and Francis Chan have publicly commented about the amazing unity among the ministry leaders in this Valley. Then again, there is much more to do. The enemies of *eirene* peace are always mounting a campaign in our homes, our churches, our community, and especially in our hearts.

THE SOLUTION TO OUR ANGER

During the days when explorers like Columbus "sailed the ocean blue," the disease of scurvy took a high toll on the lives of sailors. The need for vitamin C found in citrus fruit like oranges, lemons, and limes, was desperate. That's where we are when it comes to this fruit of *eirene* peace. The world is plagued with a sort of spiritual and emotional scurvy. We are in desperate need to know *Yahweh Shalom* is in control of the details of our lives, especially when we are attacked by anger.

In dealing with the anger in my own life, I have come to learn *eirene* peace can only rule my bouts of conflict to the degree the *eirene* peace of Christ rules in my heart. I need a daily dose of personal and intimate time in the Word and prayer to the God of peace. Living with the constant temptation to over-react to people and control situations, I need the disease-destroying fruit of *eirene* peace. I need God's help to submit to His will and stop pretending to be General Manager of the Universe. I expect you do, too!

INSPECTING THE FRUIT

1. Would you speak of your upbringing as peace-filled? Explain briefly.

2. How about your life today? What feels the same? What feels different?

3. In what ways do you feel surrounded? Powerless?

4. In what areas are you having the hardest time submitting to the will of God, trusting He is in control of the details of your life?

5. Do you consider yourself a peace-maker?
   __at home?   __at work   __at school?
   __at church?   __in the community?

6. Name the people in your life who are examples of peace.

7. What would you expect to be the supernatural effects of *eirene* peace on your ungodly anger?

FURTHER ADVICE FROM THE MASTER GARDENER

Read the following passages and comment on the reason for their peace:

1 Kings 4:25

Matthew 10:34

John 14:27

John 20:25

CHAPTER NINETEEN

THE TASTY FRUIT OF
SPIRIT-FILLED PATIENCE

I have a friend who is a farmer from a long line of farmers. In my assessment, he even looks and acts like a farmer. He is pensive and speaks with a quietness I imagine a real farmer would speak. But when he talks about his grapes, he perks up with enthusiasm and gusto! His lessons on viticulture (the art of growing vines) stirred me to a greater understanding of John 15, regarding what it means to abide in Christ, the Vine and to be corrected by my Heavenly Father, the Vinedresser. (See my study outline of John 15:1-11 in the Appendix, titled *Connected to the Vine*).

One September, my farmer-friend invited me to join him for the harvest. As I walked down rows of grapevines, he explained the growth process, commenting on how this was such wonderful evidence of God's creative power. He smiled as he spoke, as if talking about his beloved grandchildren. In a sense, they are. These vines have been in his family for generations.

He mentioned he never knows from year to year what the crop will yield and what profit, if any, he will make. So much depends on . . . well . . . so much! Knowing him as I do, it is no surprise the character quality most commonly attributed to farmers is patience. I am drawn to the words of James:

Therefore be patient, brethren, until the coming of the Lord. The farmer waits for the precious produce of the soil, being patient about it, until it gets the early and late rains (James 5:7).

Drawing from that analogy, James also presents a vital life principle: "You too be patient; strengthen your hearts, for the coming of the Lord is near" (James 5:8).

THE SCRIPTURAL DEFINITION

Patience. It is what some call "the queen of virtues." But what is it? The world has many offerings of its own definitions:

> "Patience is something you admire in the driver behind you but not in the one ahead."

> "Patience is like a mosquito sitting on the bed of an anemic person who is waiting for a blood transfusion."

There is a better analogy from the world of agriculture and the words of Scripture:

> . . . the fruit of the Spirit is . . . **patience** . . . (Galatians 5:22, emphasis added).

The Greek word the apostle Paul uses here is *makrothumia*. I recall one commentator calling it "steadfastness of soul under provocation to change." That is good, but a little esoteric. Basically, the word means slow to wrath. In modern vernacular we might call it not being short-fused. Thus the King James Version of the Bible translated it "long-suffering." That's a good word, as well.

Biblical patience is a gentle tolerance, an ability to endure exasperating people and frustrating circumstances. It is the Holy Spirit-produced capability to keep our cool and our mouths shut. And yet, just because *makrothumia* patience is gentle does not mean it doesn't possess great power. I recall many years ago reading a biblical historian who made reference to the fact that it was by this *makrothumia* patience the Romans became masters of the world. They remained calm in battle. Thus he defined the word as "a conquering patience." I like that, too.

So putting this all together, *makrothumia* patience is a steadfastness of soul that makes us slow to wrath and not short-fused. It is a longsuffering, gentle tolerance that exhibits a conquering patience. I love the fullness of this word, don't you? I love the fullness it produces in our lives even more.

THE SUPREME EXAMPLE

Before we get to what this looks like on a personal level, let's consider the ultimate example. This special kind of *makrothumia* patience is first and foremost a characteristic of God, who is "slow to anger" (Psalm 86:15). In the midst of a particularly rebellious time in Israel's history, God speaks through the prophet:

> All My compassions are kindled.
> I will not execute My fierce anger;
> I will not destroy Ephraim again.
> For I am God and not man, the Holy One in your midst,
> And I will not come in wrath (Hosea 11:8-9).

All of us must admit we sinned this week, offending God in something we thought, said or did? If God were anything like us, He might have flown off the handle and struck us down with a conquering vengeance. As we may have heard before, "If God stamped out sin at midnight, who among us would be around at 12:01?"

The Scriptures are filled with references regarding the patience of God toward us as sinners (1 Peter 3:20; 2 Peter 3:15; Romans 9:22). One of my new favorites is in the tiny Old Testament book of Joel: "Now return to the Lord your God, for He is gracious and compassionate, slow to anger, abounding in lovingkindness, and relenting of evil" (Joel 2:13).

Of course, the embodiment of the patience of God is especially seen in Jesus Christ, the One who is the visible image of the invisible God and in whom all the fullness of deity dwells in bodily form (Colossians 1:15; 2:9). In other words, Jesus is the *makrothumia* patience of God personified.

I love the words of the apostle Paul regarding his own experience with the gentle tolerance of Jesus. He admitted he was a horrible sinner. He also admitted he was an object of Christ's gracious mercy and longsuffering:

> And yet for this reason I found mercy, in order that in me as
> the foremost, Jesus Christ might demonstrate His *perfect*
> *patience*, as an example for those who would believe in Him
> for eternal life (1 Timothy 1:16, emphasis added).

The apostle Paul was especially appreciative of the perfect patience of Christ, on two levels. First, he was the object of the perfect *makrothumia* patience of Christ extended toward him as "the foremost" of sinners" (1 Timothy 1:15). Secondly, the *makrothumia* patience of Christ towards him was the supreme example for every believer to follow, even though we all deserve to die in our sin (cf. Romans 6:23).

THE SPECIFIC COMMANDS

What parent has not put up with the question, "Are we there yet?"—to which we answer, "Soon." Our children are quick to respond, "When is soon?"—to which we give the standard parental response, no matter what amount of time is left in the journey, "Five more minutes! Now, just wait! Be patient!"

When it comes to showing Christ-like patience, the Bible has a whole list of imperatives from our Heavenly Father to His children. In essence, these commands are calling us to be like Jesus in extending the same kind of gentle tolerance and conquering patience toward others we have received from God. Look with me at just a couple of specific commands.

First, we are commanded not to disregard the *makrothumia* patience of God. In fact, it is what stimulates us to admit, confess and turn from our sin, such as our ungodly anger. Consider these words carefully: "Or do you think lightly of the riches of His kindness and forbearance and *patience*, not knowing that the kindness of God *leads you to repentance*?" (Romans 2:4, emphasis added). Secondly, we are commanded to be like Him in extending that kind of *makrothumia* patience toward others:

> And so, as those who have been chosen of God, holy and beloved, put on a heart of compassion, kindness, humility, gentleness and *patience* [Greek: *makrothumia*]; *bearing with one another*, and forgiving each other, whoever has a complaint against anyone; just as the Lord forgave you, so also should you (Colossians 3:12-13, emphasis added).

The apostle Paul's point is clear. We will never be patient with others until we more fully appreciate the patience of God toward us.

THE SPIRITUAL SOURCE

Don't we wish we could just take a "chill pill." But *makrothumia* patience, gentle tolerance, conquering patience, doesn't come in a pill—prescription, illegal or otherwise. We won't find it in a bottle—of beer, wine or whiskey. As is so true of *agape* love, *chara* joy, and *eirene* peace, God never commands us to have His *makrothumia* patience without providing the means for us to be successful. That is why we need to consider the spiritual source.

Many of us have short fuses. We admit we need God-given steadfastness of soul and Spirit-led patience of heart. We need gentle tolerance. And we need it right now! Where do we get the power to be patient? In his letter to the Colossians the apostle Paul points out that God strengthens us with His power so that we will be patient toward one another (Colossians 1:11). In other words, there is only one lasting source—the Holy Spirit of Power who indwells us. This brings us back to our key text:

> . . . the fruit of the Spirit is . . . **patience** . . . (Galatians 5:22-23, emphasis added).

As we submit to the power of the indwelling Holy Spirit, He gives us a conquering patience. He empowers us with the ability to be strong and to resist overreacting to exasperating people and frustrating circumstances.

THE SUBSTANTIAL IMPACT

What would be the supernatural results if this Christ-like *makrothumia* patience were to become more prevalent in our lives? The answer? Indescribable reward! Take to heart the assurance found in the New Testament letter to the Hebrews: "Therefore, do not throw away your confidence, which has a great reward. For you have need of endurance ["patience, steadfastness," Greek: *hupomone*], so that when you have done the will of God, you may receive what was promised" (Hebrews 10:35-36).

Don't miss the timeless words of King Solomon on this matter, as well: "A man's discretion makes him slow to anger, and *it is his glory* to overlook a transgression (Proverbs 19:11, emphasis added). The Hebrew word here translated *glory* is *tipharah*. It is a word used in other places regarding the glorious beauty of a king's garments and crown as well as the glory and honor they represent. What is King Solomon talking about here?

I trust we have witnessed someone demonstrate the kind of *makrothumia* patience we know only comes from God. It is a crown of Christ-like beauty, reflecting the divine majesty of our merciful and patient Heavenly Father. Frankly, it might just be the one fruit of the Spirit those who know us have been waiting to see, in order to truly believe God is who He said He is. Now, that's some tasty and attractive fruit!

As appealing as these qualities of biblical patience would be to anyone, especially those who might suffer our wrath, I remind us where ultimately these come from. There is only one way for lasting *makrothumia* patience to happen in our lives. We have to be right with God through faith alone in Jesus Christ. We also have to walk in the power of the indwelling Holy Spirit through daily submission to His will. Any of our human attempts at producing the divine fruit of patience will fail every time. Let's consider that the next time we are tempted to explode and blow off some scorching steam! Perhaps we would do well by beginning our day with a simple prayer: "Lord, make me like a patient farmer. Strengthen my heart with a Christ-like, conquering patience and gentle tolerance."

THE SOLUTION TO OUR ANGER

I once read, "He who smiles rather than rages is always stronger." This became dramatically clear when, as a newlywed college student, I was working in the photo department of a popular drugstore. An older lady was well known among my fellow workers as a grump. In our minds, she was the mother of all grumps! Regularly she would come to the photo counter and loudly complain about the quality of her pictures we had developed. She blamed the camera. She blamed the processing. She screamed at us. She was horrible! Honestly, she was horrible. It was tempting to usher her out the door.

At the time I was a new Christian, still working things out regarding my typical impatience with these kinds of people. One memorable day, I decided to do things differently. I left her for a moment and prayed God would miraculously change this obviously bitter woman. Instead, as I would soon discover, He decided to change me.

I came back to the counter and looked her in the eyes, "I am so very sorry you are having trouble. Here is your money back. Now, let me see if I can help you take better pictures." I patiently walked her through the steps. In those moments of special attention, she melted. She even smiled, something none of us had ever seen. My Spirit-produced *makrothumia* patience and my soft answer had turned away her wrath—and mine! After that day, she came to see me weekly, insisting only I wait on her. My fellow workers were still happy to hand her off to me. Her pictures were still horrible, but her countenance brightened my day.

I will always be grateful for how God used this grumpy lady to provide me with one of many lessons on gracious mercy and gentle tolerance and steadfastness of soul. Even though I was working at a drugstore, I can assure you, those minutes of conquering patience didn't come in a pill. They came as a gift from the indwelling Holy Spirit to my receptive heart. I wish I could tell you I only needed this one lesson. Over the years, more life-lessons on *makrothumia* patience have been far too necessary.

INSPECTING THE FRUIT

1. Who are the people with whom you have the greatest problem showing patience?

2. What are the situations about which you have the greatest struggle being more tolerant?

3. What word best describes you when you are being impatient?

    short-fused__   intolerant__   other:_____

4. What words best describe you when you are exhibiting Christ-like patience?

    longsuffering__   gentle tolerance__   conquering patience__

    other:_____

FURTHER ADVICE FROM THE MASTER GARDENER

1. Read Psalm 40:1-3 and then list the eight results of waiting patiently for the Lord:

"I waited patiently for the Lord. And He . . ."

    1._____(40:1)

    2._____ (40:1)

    3._____ (40:2)

    4._____ (40:2)

    5._____ (40:3)

    6._____ (40:3)

    7._____ (40:3)

    8. _____ (40:3)

2. Read Psalm 37. Mark down the verses related to patience.

CHAPTER TWENTY

THE TASTY FRUIT OF
SPIRIT-FILLED KINDNESS

I have another friend who grows pomegranates. It is such a strange-looking fruit, with its deep red outer skin that feels as hard as a rock. Some thirty times the Bible mentions the pomegranate as one of the most popular fruit in Israel's history. Apparently, in Old Testament times, it was right up there with figs and dates. We even find them embroidered on the bottom fringe of the High Priest's robe. During the Exodus, when the wandering people of God were complaining about what they missed back in Egypt, pomegranates were on the list, along with fresh water and meat (Numbers 20:5). God assured them the Promised Land would be an abundant land "of vines and fig trees and *pomegranates*" (Deuteronomy 8:8, emphasis added).

I wish I could express the same appreciation for this tough-skinned fruit, but frankly I am not crazy about them. First, I think they are ugly, especially on the inside. They are also a hassle to eat. The juice stains my hands, the seeds are difficult to get to and the pulp is bitter. Even when I do get to the tasty part of the fruit (called arils), they make the inside of my mouth feel strange. Even the name doesn't sound very appealing—*pom*, meaning apple, plus *granate*, which, although it is spelled differently, sounds to me like granite, the rock. The actual Latin name is *Punica granatum*. Rather unpleasant name, if you ask me. This doesn't mean pomegranates are not good for us. They are quite nutritious, filled with anti-oxidants and all kinds of other good stuff this city boy can't explain.

We are considering the fruit of the Spirit-filled life—the basket full of Christ-like attributes the indwelling Holy Spirit of God is wanting to produce in us daily. I have noticed that what is true of pomegranates is also true of the nine spiritual fruit. They will most likely get our hands dirty. They are sometimes difficult to swallow and they will cause some reaction. But they are also all very good for us and for the people around us. Again, we recite our key text. Hopefully, by now, we know it by heart:

> But the fruit of the Spirit is love, joy, peace, patience, kindness, goodness, faithfulness, gentleness, self-control; against such things there is no law (Galatians 5:22-23).

Let's also review our definition:

The fruit of the Spirit is the abundant harvest of Christ-like qualities the indwelling Holy Spirit produces in the regenerated and obedient heart.

Besides looking at "The Eight Principles of Spiritual Pomology," we have covered the first four of the nine fruit of the Spirit: *agape* love, *chara* joy, *eirene* peace and *makrothumia* patience. We come now to the fifth fruit of the Spirit-filled life:

> . . . the fruit of the Spirit is . . . **kindness** . . . (Galatians 5: 22- 23, emphasis added). (The King James Version calls it "gentleness").

THE SCRIPTURAL DEFINITION

As was the case in our study of love, joy, peace and patience, man's understanding of kindness certainly falls far short of God's. We tend to see kindness as doing nice things for people—being tender, courteous and affectionate. Sometimes it gets translated into real life as being good to our brothers and sisters or giving to the poor and needy. Those certainly are important qualities but this fruit of the Spirit involves so much more. Let's look carefully at the biblical definition.

The word the apostle Paul uses here is the Greek word *chrestotes*. It speaks of a sweetness of character that shrinks from inflicting pain and a tenderness of heart that endeavors to deal with people graciously. It is not primarily referring to doing kind deeds but more so about treating people as important. Quite specifically, it shows up in real life as not using, abusing or misusing others.

In some sense, kindness is one of the outward expressions of *agape* love that values people the way God values them. Therefore, it stands to reason why the apostle Paul wrote as he did: "Love [Greek: *agape*] is kind [Greek: *chresteuomai*—a form of *chrestotes* in which one shows himself useful to others] . . . ." (1 Corinthians 13:4).

The early Christians were sometimes called *Chrestotai*. It means "The Kind Ones." One wonders if we would still be called that today. Instead of being the *Chrestotai*, maybe we deserve to be called the *Grumpotai*—my term for "The Grumpy Ones." Too many of my fellow believers are like cactus fruit (prickly pears). Because the Holy Spirit indwells them, they are delicious on the inside but thorny and vicious on the outside.

By the way, the word *chrestotes*, translated kindness, is related to another Greek word *chrestos*, translated kind. The word is used in the Gospels by Matthew and Luke, as well by the apostles Peter and Paul in some of their epistles. In its basic meaning *chrestos* refers to something that doesn't chafe, that isn't too rough and is easy to be near. In fact, it is "kind to the back." Thus Jesus said, "For My yoke is easy [Greek: *chrestos*]" (Matthew 11:30). The word *chrestos* also speaks of being mellow, like wine that is kind to the palate: "And no one, after drinking old wine wishes for new; for he says, 'The old is good.' [Greek: *chrestos*]" (Luke 5:39).

Because I have never hitched an animal to a yoke nor do I like wine, when I think of *chrestotes* kindness, I think of America's favorite fruit—the banana. Frankly, it is also my favorite. There's something wonderfully mellow and smooth (*chrestotes*) about a succulent banana. Not too sweet; not too tart. So easy to eat. Dip it into a little melted peanut butter and I think I have a little taste of heaven on earth.

I was reading a while ago that, according to nutritionists, the banana is considered to be the most completely nutritious food on the planet. The article went on to say that in an emergency a human could survive on bananas longer than any other single food. By the way, very few people are allergic to bananas. I guess we could say bananas are kind to us. They are *chrestos*. They don't chafe.

Putting it all together, we find the spiritual fruit of *chrestotes* kindness is a sweetness of character that shrinks from inflicting pain, a lifestyle that endeavors to graciously deal with people, and a heart that desires not to chafe. It isn't too rough and it is kind to a person's back. It is a spirit that chooses to mellow like a smooth glass of wine, or, in my thinking, a perfectly ripe banana. That's quite a word, isn't it? Certainly it is a much-needed fruit of the Spirit, the kind we all need to survive in this cruel world.

THE SUPREME EXAMPLE

From whom then do we learn this kind of biblical kindness? We certainly could spend much time talking about the kindness of Almighty God, even to those who rebel against Him. The Bible says, "for He Himself is kind [Greek: *chrestos*] to ungrateful and evil men" (Luke 6:35). We especially see evidence of *chrestotes* kindness in the person of Christ. The apostle Paul speaks of Jesus Christ and the kindness of God as one and the same: "But when the kindness of God our Savior and His love for mankind appeared He saved us . . ." (Titus 3:4-5). The apostle Paul is saying Jesus was the very kindness of God incarnate. He was God's *chrestotes* in the flesh. There are many examples of this. Even though surrounded by sinners, Jesus was never harsh to those who were repentant. He hated their sin but He was kind to the sinner. He loathed the offense but loved the offender. He was kind to their back. He didn't chafe!

Remember the gospel account of the woman caught in adultery and the now famous words of Jesus: "He who is without sin among you, let him be the first to throw a stone at her" (John 8:7). Jesus wasn't condoning the adulterous woman's sin. He was just extending *chrestotes* kindness to this needy woman. We are specifically commanded to follow His example.

THE SPECIFIC COMMANDS

Look carefully at what the apostle Paul wrote in his letter to the folks in the Church of Ephesus: "And be kind [*chrestos*] to one another, tender-hearted, forgiving each other, just as God in Christ [*Christos*] also has forgiven you" (Ephesians 4:32). This is a play on words. The Greek word for being kind is *chrestos*; the Greek word for Christ is *Christos*. Paul is telling us all to "Be *chrestos* like *Christos*." In other words, be kind like Christ.

I remind us of the popular words found in the little book of Micah, where we are commanded to "do justice, to love kindness, and to walk humbly" with our God (Micah 6:8). Sadly, some of us do justice far more than we love kindness. We can be harsh, condemning, punitive and merciless, all in the name of justice. Our humble prayer needs to be: "Lord, teach me to exercise godly judgment bathed in the fruit of kindness." Want to say it some other ways?:

• "Dear Lord, teach me not to chafe!"

• "Heavenly Father, teach me to get off other people's backs."

• "Oh God, help me to mellow out and not be so intense."

THE SPIRITUAL SOURCE

Although I hate shopping here in the U.S.A., when I am in a foreign country I love to go to the outdoor markets. There is something about seeing row upon row of different kinds of local fruit and produce. I want us to imagine all the deliciously kind things God has done for us over the years. Imagine them as fruit placed before us, row by row. Hear God's Holy Spirit prompting us to savor them over and over again because we have "tasted the kindness of the Lord (1 Peter 2:3). In the simple words of King David, "O taste and see that the Lord is good . . ." (Psalm 34:8).

If we are going to learn how to exercise the delicious fruit of kindness, we must first reflect on the delicious *chrestotes* kindness of God toward us. The apostle Paul reminded us just how much God's kindness leads to brokenness: "Or do you think lightly of the riches of His kindness [*chrestotes*] and forbearance and patience, not knowing that the kindness [*chrestotes*] of God leads you to repentance?" (Romans 2:4).

After we have spent some time reflecting on the kindness of God toward us, we then draw upon the power of the indwelling Holy Spirit to exercise this same kindness toward others. Want to say it more succinctly?

. . . the fruit of the Spirit is . . . **kindness** . . . (Galatians 5:22-23, emphasis added).

THE SUBSTANTIAL IMPACT

What would happen if this Spirit-produced fruit of *chrestotes* kindness were fully produced in our lives? What would be the spiritual impact? I once read about a professor who had a sign in his office that read, "Kindness Spoken Here." The Holy Spirit wants to post that sign on the doorpost of our hearts. He wants His *chrestote* kindness toward us to come out in acts of kindness toward others. I love the words of John Wesley: "Do all the good you can do, in all the ways you can, to all the souls you can, at all the times you can, with all the zeal you can, as long as ever you can." Imagine the fruit if these words were truly our life's testimony.

THE SOLUTION TO ANGER

One of the rewards of *chrestotes* kindness is how contagious it is. The ancient philosopher Sophocles once said, "Kindness gives birth to kindness." Our Spirit-empowered acts of *chrestotes* kindness really can be the catalyst for change in an angry family, a hostile workplace or in any angry situation. In fact, it can spread to our families, neighborhoods, churches, communities and to our world. Perhaps some of us *Grumpotai*—my made-up word for "Grumpy Ones"—might even come to a place where we are considered one of the *Chrestotai*—"The Kind Ones."

This became remarkably illustrated one frustrating night as I was stranded in an airplane on the runway at Denver International Airport. The ground crews were completely unprepared for an early snowstorm that caused such long delays our plane needed to be de-iced twice. Since our take-off was expected at any time, we were told we could not leave our seats. Hours passed and people were obviously upset. Some were shouting that they were thirsty and hungry, about which the flight attendants could do nothing. Captains orders!

Suddenly a passenger in the front shouted, "Hey, I have some snacks. Anybody want some?" She passed a box to the seat behind her. It was empty by the time it got to my seat. Then another passenger in the back shouted, "I've got some cookies and crackers." He passed them forward. Soon snacks and fruit of all kinds were being passed everywhere. One of the flight attendants decided to sneak out of her seat and let the passengers serve each other bottled water. As we feasted, the atmosphere of the plane became like a party. This one woman's kindness started it rolling. The story didn't end there.

After a few hours, they cancelled the flight and we were ushered off the plane. It was now 2 a.m. We were told all area hotels were filled and all the food outlets were closed. We were given blankets and invited to sleep in the waiting area. As we took turns sleeping, mostly on the carpet, my fellow passengers extended even more kindness, as they watched each other's luggage and helped parents with small children. One woman's kindness on an airplane turned an angry situation into a memorable experience. That is the lasting fruit of *chrestotes* kindness. The little poem by an anonymous writer says it well:

I have wept in the night
For shortness of sight
That to somebody's need made me blind.
But I never have yet
Felt a twinge of regret
For being a little too kind.

INSPECTING THE FRUIT

1. Reflect on the *chrestotes* kindness of God over your lifetime. Mark some specific years when it was especially demonstrated on this timeline. (Use a separate piece of paper, if necessary.)

Year of your birth   Today

How do these reminders encourage your heart and stimulate kindness in your life?

2. Consider a recent incident where you were unkind, harsh, condemning, punitive, abusive, inflicted pain in a merciless way or when you did not deal graciously with someone. How would walking by the power of the indwelling Holy Spirit have helped the situation?

3. Who are the best human examples of *chrestotes* kindness in your life?

FURTHER ADVICE FROM THE MASTER GARDENER

Read the following Bible passages and comment on the kindness exhibited:

Rebekah to Abraham's servant (Genesis 24:18-20)

Rahab to the spies in Jericho (Joshua 2:6, 18)

David to Mephibosheth (2 Samuel 9:7)

Barzillai to David (2 Samuel 17:28-29)

Boaz to Ruth (Ruth 2:8-9)

The Good Samaritan to the Injured Man (Luke 10:25-37)

Cornelius, a Gentile to the Jews (Acts 10:2)

The disciples in Antioch to the brethren in Judea (Acts 11:29)

The natives at Malta to Paul and the shipwrecked crew (Acts 28:2, 7)

CHAPTER TWENTY-ONE

THE TASTY FRUIT OF
SPIRIT-FILLED GOODNESS

While living on the Central Coast of California, my wife enjoyed taking our children on excursions to pick berries—blackberries, raspberries, boysenberries and olallieberries. As far as our kids were concerned, the fun part of the trip was eating the berries as they were picking them. In their thinking, these soft-skinned berries were made to be consumed on the spot. Nature's candy! We will see that God has provided another fruit as good on the outside as it is on the inside. Before we do, let's remember our definition:

The fruit of the Spirit is the abundant harvest of Christ-like qualities the indwelling Holy Spirit produces in the regenerated and obedient heart.

Now on to our sixth fruit of the Spirit-filled life:

... the fruit of the Spirit is ... **goodness** ... (Galatians 5:22, emphasis added).

THE SCRIPTURAL DEFINITION

Let me hasten to say that the world's idea of goodness is far different from the scriptural definition. The word the apostle Paul uses is the Greek word *agathosune* from the root word *agathos*. *Agathosune* is used only four times in all of the New Testament, every time by the apostle Paul. This word was not commonly used in the ancient Greek culture. It is, therefore, a rather difficult word to define, though we are certainly familiar with the concept.

Its basic meaning has to do with doing what is right, regardless of the consequences. William Penn is known to have said, "Right is right, even if everyone is against it; and wrong is wrong even if everyone is for it." In the New Testament context, it points to a willingness to stand alone for righteousness with a Spirit-led passion for truth. *Agathosune* goodness balances *chrestotes* kindness, so we will stand up for the truth and confront sin. Whereas, the fruit of kindness shows mercy, the fruit of goodness shows justice. Both are much needed. Again we consider the words of Micah in the Old Testament: "He has told you, O man, what is good; and what does the Lord require of you but to do justice, to love kindness, and to walk humbly with your God?" (Micah 6:8).

In New Testament terms, when we walk in obedience to the indwelling Holy Spirit, He produces *chrestotes* kindness that moves us to show mercy and *agathosune* goodness that motivates us to show justice. The fruit of goodness involves an uprightness that not only confronts evil in the world but hates the sin in our own hearts. Thus, we need to take to heart the words of James:

> Or do you think that the Scripture speaks to no purpose: "He jealously desires the Spirit which He has made to dwell in us"? But He gives a greater grace. Therefore *it* says, "GOD IS OPPOSED TO THE PROUD, BUT GIVES GRACE TO THE HUMBLE." Submit therefore to God. Resist the devil and he will flee from you. Draw near to God and He will draw near to you. Cleanse your hands, you sinners; and purify your hearts, you double-minded. Be miserable and mourn and weep; let your laughter be turned into mourning and your joy to gloom. Humble yourselves in the presence of the Lord, and He will exalt you (James 4:5-10).

THE SUPREME EXAMPLE

As in all the fruit of the Spirit we have our greatest illustration in Jesus, the One who is the supreme example of this Spirit-produced fruit. Jesus is the *agathosune* goodness of God in the flesh. In the Gospel of Mark, Jesus is called "Good Teacher" (Mark 10:17, using the word *agathos*). In the Gospel of John, Jesus declared Himself to be the "good Shepherd" (John 10:11, again using the word *agathos*). Although we spoke of Jesus' *chrestotes* kindness toward the repentant woman caught in adultery (John 8:1-11), we must also see His *agathosune* goodness exemplified in His dealing with the rebellious moneychangers in the Temple:

And Jesus entered the temple and cast out all those who were buying and selling in the temple, and overturned the tables of the moneychangers and the seats of those who were selling doves. And He said to them, "It is written, 'My house shall be called a house of prayer'; but you are making it a robbers' den" (Matthew 21:12-13).

THE SPECIFIC COMMANDS

On the one hand, Jesus knew when to exercise *chrestotes* kindness without being harsh. He also knew when to let his passion for *agathosune* goodness prevail and deal head on with sin. We are ordered by God to do the same, as we stand up for the truth and expose error:

> Therefore do not be partakers with them, for you were formerly darkness, but now you are light in the Lord; walk as children of light (for the fruit of the light consists in all *goodness* and righteousness and truth), trying to learn what is pleasing to the Lord. And do not participate in the unfruitful deeds of darkness, but instead even expose them; for it is disgraceful even to speak of the things which are done by them in secret. But all things become visible when they are exposed by the light, for everything that becomes visible is light (Ephesians 5:7-13, emphasis added).

At this point, I think it would be helpful for us to consider a few of over a hundred uses of the word *agathos*, forming the root of *agathosune* goodness. These present clear instructions and the prerequisites for engaging in effective *agathosune* goodness:

- We are to love what is good (Titus 1:8).

- We are to engage in good deeds (Matthew 5:16; 12:35; Ephesians 2:10; 2 Timothy 3:17; Titus 2:7; 3:14).

- We are to do good to all men, especially to the household of faith (Galatians 6:10).

- We are to do good, even to those who hate us (Luke 6:33, 35).

- We are not to lose heart or grow weary in doing good (Galatians 6:9; 2 Thessalonians 3:13).

- We are to stimulate one another to good deeds (Hebrews 10:21).

- We are to bear good fruit and not grow weary (Matthew 7:17-19; Luke 6:43, 45; Colossians 1:10; James 3:17).

- We are to hold fast to and cling to what is good (Romans 12:19; 1 Thessalonians 5:21).

THE SPIRITUAL SOURCE

What parent hasn't confronted a child's sin with the words, "Be good!" That is not an easy command to follow. Even the great apostle Paul gave personal testimony of his own struggle with the tug of war between his sinful flesh and the indwelling Holy Spirit:

> For I know that nothing *good* dwells in me, that is, in my flesh;
> for the willing is present in me, but the doing of the *good is* not.
> For the *good* that I want, I do not do, but I practice the very evil
> that I do not want. But if I am doing the very thing I do not want,
> I am no longer the one doing it, but sin which dwells in me. I
> find then the principle that evil is present in me, the one who
> wants to do *good* (Romans 7:18-21, emphasis added).

It was obvious to Paul, as it should be to all of us, young and old. We need divine help in being *agathos* good and exercising the fruit of *agathosune* goodness.

In his letter to the Christians at Rome the apostle Paul expressed his powerful prayer for them and for us:

> Now may the God of hope fill you with all joy and peace in
> believing, that you may abound in hope by the power of the
> Holy Spirit. And concerning you, my brethren, I myself also am
> convinced that you yourselves are *full of goodness*, filled
> with all knowledge, and *able also to admonish one another*
> (Romans 15:13-14, emphasis added).

He went on to write in his letter to the Galatians: "the fruit of the Light consists in all goodness and righteousness and truth (Ephesians 5:9). His point is clear. Being full of Spirit-produced *agathosune* goodness means having a knowledge of biblical truth that becomes our fuel for being able to admonish and warn others. There are scores of other passages we could examine. Let me summarize all of them in the simple words of Galatians 5:

> But the fruit of the Spirit is . . . **goodness** . . . (Galatians 5:22, emphasis added).

THE SUBSTANTIAL IMPACT

Imagine what would happen if we were to have our lives filled with this kind of *agathosune* goodness. Consider the spiritual impact. I encourage us to view the apostle Paul's prayer for the Thessalonians as his prayer for us:

> To this end also we pray for you always that our God may count you worthy of your calling, and fulfill *every desire for goodness* and the work of faith with power; so that the name of our Lord Jesus may be glorified in you, and you in Him, according to the grace of our God and the Lord Jesus Christ (2 Thessalonians 1:11-12, emphasis added).

That is not to say those we confront will initially appreciate our rebuke. Sometimes goodness is also expressed in a quiet willingness to be despised for doing what is right, rather than suffer God's chastening for doing what is wrong (1 Peter 3:13-17).

It is not as if God has left us alone. Almighty God not only desires us to have this kind of *agathosune* goodness in our hearts, He also makes it possible. In the words of the apostle Peter: "seeing that His divine power has granted to us everything pertaining to life and godliness, through the true knowledge of Him who called us by His own glory and excellence" (2 Peter 1:3). I love the ancient proverb as it presents a hopeful result of exercising Spirit-led goodness: "The evil will bow down before the good, and the wicked at the gates of the righteous" (Proverbs 14:19).

THE SOLUTION TO ANGER

What does this have to do with dealing with our everyday conflict and managing our anger? Try dealing with conflict anywhere without a generous serving of *agathosune* goodness, along with *chrestotes* kindness. Like an evening snack of apples and bananas, both fruit go so very well together. One tastes like justice; the other tastes like mercy. Let's pray we and the people around us will taste them both. And when it does, something amazing happens. We experience the promise of those famous words in the Shepherd's Psalm: "surely goodness and mercy shall follow me all the days of my life . . ." (Psalm 23:6). Imagine a life like that!

As parents, foster-parents, and now grandparents to over a dozen children (They keep coming!), we have had our share of temper-tantrums—mostly theirs! When I am tempted to over-react to something one of them has done wrong, my wife is quick to remind me of what we have established as our personal code of conduct: "Regardless of their reaction, we will do the right thing because it is the right thing to do. We must refuse to let their attitudes or behaviors reduce us to sin."

That's the *agathosune* goodness and the *agathos* fruit we pray our children and our children's children will learn to pick daily.

INSPECTING THE FRUIT

1. Describe the last time you had to directly confront sin.

2. As you recall how you approached the situation, do you feel you exercised both Christ-like kindness and Spirit-led goodness?

3. Reflect on this quote from John Wesley:

"Do all the good you can do, in all the ways you can, to all the souls you can, at all the times you can, with all the zeal you can, as long as ever you can."

4. Name the people in your life who exude goodness.

5. What would you expect would be the effects of goodness on your anger if it were prevalent in your life?

FURTHER ADVICE FROM THE MASTER GARDENER

Read the following New Testament passages related to those who stood against sin and for truth. What was the outcome?

Ephesians 5:6-14

Matthew 18:15-20

CHAPTER TWENTY-TWO

THE TASTY FRUIT OF
SPIRIT-FILLED FAITHFULNESS

There has always been a special appreciation on the part of God's people for "the fruit of the vine," especially grapes. Most churches that partake of communion will use some form of grape juice as a reminder of the Last Supper, the final Passover meal, where Jesus served His disciples. During the Seder Feast the one presiding over the meal normally recites the following blessing over the cup: *"Baruch atah, Adonai Eloheinu, Melech ha Olam, borei p'ri hagafen."* In English: *"Blessed are You, Oh Lord, Our God, King of the Universe, who brings forth the fruit of the vine."*

There is another kind of fruit that comes from the hand of the Lord, our God, King of the Universe. It is a kind of fruit one does not eat or drink, but is even more desirable and delectable than grapes. I am speaking of the godly qualities that come from the harvest of the regenerated and obedient heart, indwelt by the Holy Spirit of God and submitting to the lordship of Jesus Christ. They are called the fruit of the Spirit-filled life and could easily be called *"The Ingredients of Christ-like Godliness."* By now you should have them memorized:

> But the fruit of the Spirit is love, joy, peace, patience,
> kindness, goodness, faithfulness, gentleness, self-control;
> against such things there is no law (Galatians 5:22-23).

Before we move on to our personal inspection of the next fruit on the list, I want us to take a moment and reflect on a prayer I once wrote, based on the classic Hebrew prayer just cited:

> Blessed are you, Oh Lord, Our God, King of the Universe,
> who brings forth not just the fruit of the vine but the fruit of the

Holy Spirit. Make us more like Your Son, Jesus the Messiah. May this harvest of the heart be the center of our focus. May these ingredients of godliness be the foundation by which we manage our lives in the midst of earthly chaos. In the mighty name of Yeshua, ha Mashiach—Jesus, the Messiah. Amen.

Now on to our next fruit on the list:

". . . the fruit of the Spirit . . . **faithfulness** . . . (Galatians 5:22, emphasis added). (The King James Version simply calls it "faith.")

THE SCRIPTURAL DEFINITION

What comes to our minds when we hear the word faithfulness? Some might rush to the root word *faith*. Others might look further to the word faithful. But what does it really mean?

About every two hours, in Yellowstone National Park, the historic geyser, Old Faithful, blows thousands of gallons of boiling water and subterranean steam well over a hundred feet into the sky. You can count on it. I would like to think biblical faithfulness is more than just being known for blowing off steam. Yet, there is something to be said about regularity and dependability.

In the Old Testament the Hebrew word for faithfulness is *emunah*. In its root form this Hebrew word speaks of firmness and stability, like a firm piece of fruit. It is found in Psalm 37 where we are called to "dwell in the land and cultivate faithfulness [Hebrew: *emunah*]" (Psalm 37:3). Throughout the Old Testament we are reminded that God is faithful. He is firm in His positions and stable in His character. In other words, He is unlike the fickle pagan gods. Nothing about Him is untrustworthy.

When we come to its use in the New Testament we find the common Greek words *pistis* and *pistos*. Both mean a secure belief, a stable confidence, and an unbending trust. They also speak of being firm in one's resolve, dependable and trustworthy. In its verb form [*pisteuo*], it means to place our trust in something or someone. In essence, faithfulness says, "I believe . . . so much so I will act on that belief." Many of you remember the old saying, "God said it. I believe it. That's good enough for me." Actually, true faithfulness says, "God said it. It's true whether I believe it or not. I will trust and obey, no matter what!" (cf. James 2:14, 17).

The Holy Spirit desires to produce in us this fruit of *pistis* faithfulness. He wants to make us people who are full of faith— people who believe in God, take Him at His Word and, as a result, become trustworthy and dependable people who can be taken at our word.

There used to be a day when a man's word was his bond. We made binding contracts with a word and a handshake. Now we live in a world where it is difficult to trust what people say. They are quick to make promises and just as quick to break them. Now we need contracts, courts and lots of expensive lawyers to enforce them. Faithfulness has been replaced by fickleness and flakiness, even in the family of God. Too many of us unfaithful humans have made promises, even to God, and have not kept them: "Lord, I promise to do this . . . do that . . . give this . . . go there . . . . Oh well, God, it didn't work out. Maybe next time." And, of course, the ever-popular: "Heavenly Father, if you get me out of this mess, I will . . . . (Then after God saves you, you respond.) Now that You have delivered me, Lord, can I reconsider my promise to You?"

The root word for faithfulness is the word faith. Our English word comes from the Anglo-Saxon word *feyth*, which means to cling. I really like that. It wasn't that long ago I came to know the difference between a cling peach and a free stone peach. With cling peaches, the fruit clings to the center pit. In a very real sense that is what this fruit of faithfulness is. It is the Spirit-led ability to cling to God and His Word as the center stone of our lives. As a result people cling to us.

Throughout sacred history we have seen many examples of this kind of faithfulness. If we had the time we could reflect on Hebrews, Chapter 11, which could be rightly called *Portraits of Faithfulness*. Hopefully, you have been encouraged by the life-stories of these heroes of the faith:

• Abel	• Enoch	• Noah	• Abraham
• Sarah	• Isaac	• Jacob	• Joseph
• Moses	• Rahab	• Gideon	• Barak
• Samson	• Jephthah	• David	• Samuel
• The Prophets	• Faithful Women		

All of these folks trusted God and we, therefore, can trust what they say about the faithfulness of God. That's *pistis* faithfulness.

THE SUPREME EXAMPLE

I cannot venture a guess as to what kind of worship music will be around in coming generations. No matter what genre is prevalent, I expect true believers will be singing some form of the beloved hymn of the faith, *Great is Thy Faithfulness*. It was written by Thomas Chisholm around the turn of the twentieth century. Thomas became a Christian at twenty-seven and entered the ministry a year later. Sadly, poor health forced him to retire soon after and he began a career of selling insurance. During that time he wrote some twelve hundred poems and the words for several hymns. None were more well-known than these (Sing them if you know the tune):

Great is Thy faithfulness, O God my Father;
There is no shadow of turning with Thee;
Thou changest not, Thy compassions, they fail not;
As Thou hast been, Thou forever will be.

The lyrics continue with the chorus:

Great is Thy faithfulness!
Great is Thy faithfulness!
Morning by morning new mercies I see.
All I have needed Thy hand hath provided;
Great is Thy faithfulness, Lord, unto me!

Another stanza moves our hearts even further:

Pardon for sin and a peace that endureth
Thine own dear presence to cheer and to guide;
Strength for today and bright hope for tomorrow,
Blessings all mine, with ten thousand beside!

The song ends with the repeated reminder:

Great is Thy faithfulness.
Great is Thy faithfulness
Great is Thy faithfulness, Lord unto me!

That, my friends, is the testimony of the ages: "Know therefore that the Lord your God, He is God, *the faithful God*, who keeps His covenant and His lovingkindness to a thousandth generation with those who love Him and keep His commandments." (Deuteronomy 7:9, emphasis added).

God isn't fickle or flakey! Isn't that great news? Without His faithfulness we would have no real assurance of the forgiveness of our many sins: "If we confess our sins, *He is faithful* [Greek: *pistos*] and righteous to forgive us our sins and to cleanse us from all unrighteousness (1 John 1:9, emphasis added)

Since Jesus is the visible image of the invisible God, in whom all the fullness of God's attributes dwell in bodily form (Colossians 1:15; 2:9), it is right for us to look at His earthly life, as well. In the four gospels we clearly find Jesus Christ demonstrating His perfect faithfulness. For example, consider how Jesus trusted His Heavenly Father as He cried out in His High Priestly prayer, "Thy word is truth . . ." (John 17:17). The gospels are filled with numerous examples of Jesus saying He not only believed His Father, but was willing to obey His Father at all costs. Throughout His time on earth He came to do the will of His Father—nothing more, nothing less, and nothing else (John 5:30; 6:38; Matthew 26:39; Luke 22:42;). That is *pistis* faithfulness!

Being faithful is so much a part of Jesus' character that in Revelation 19:11 He is simply called "The Faithful and True Witness." It seems obvious why the Bible clearly commands us to be like Christ in this area of faithfulness. He is truly the One to copy.

THE SPECIFIC COMMANDS

There is no more fundamental passage regarding our call to faithfulness than the apostle Paul's familiar words in 1 Corinthians 4:2: "In this case, moreover, it is required of stewards that one be found trustworthy ["faithful," Greek: *pistos*]" (1 Corinthians 4:2). We servants of God who have trusted and believed [*pisteuo*] in Christ, have as a primary objective, to be faithful [*pistos*] to God. That means to trust Him and be trustworthy, to believe Him and be believed. It is a mandate to take Him at His Word so we can be taken at ours. In fact, we have been called to be "faithful until death" (Revelation 2:10).

Let me illustrate this with an Old Testament story. If we were asked to retell in our own words the biblical story of King David, many of us could probably share something about David and Goliath, David and Saul, David and Jonathan, or David and

Bathsheba. But what about the story of David and Ittai? Ittai was one of King David's mighty men, a true hero (2 Samuel 23:29). His commitment to faithfulness is remarkable: "But Ittai answered the king and said, 'As the Lord lives, and as my lord the king lives, surely wherever my lord the king may be, whether for *death or for life*, there also your servant will be'" (2 Samuel 15:21, emphasis added). Here was a man who clung to the king no matter what the threat. He was faithful until death. Can that be truly said of us now? What about when our earthly lives are completed?

- Are we committed to be faithful to our spouse until death?

- Are we committed to be faithful parents for as long as we live, striving to be heroes of the faith in the eyes of our children?

- Are we committed to be mighty men and women of God in Christ's Church until He comes for us?

- Are we committed to fulfilling our calling as servants of God on earth until such time we begin our time in heaven, serving Him for eternity?

- Are we committed to be faithful until death, even in the little things?

THE SPIRITUAL SOURCE

How does one develop this kind of biblical faithfulness? It is definitely not automatic in the life of the believer. When I received my seminary diploma and later my ordination, I was not suddenly filled with the fruit of *pistis* faithfulness. This is not to say it cannot be learned. The real classroom is the human heart, indwelt by the Spirit of a faithful God and motivated by a heart of trust and obedience.

Like all the fruit of the Spirit, *pistis* faithfulness has a spiritual source. Consider what the apostle Paul wrote to his child in the faith, Timothy, just months before Paul, faithful to the end, was ultimately executed for his faith: "Now flee from youthful lusts, and *pursue* righteousness, *faith,* love and peace, with those who call on the Lord from a pure heart" (2 Timothy 2:22, emphasis added). Notice the word pursue. It is the Greek word *dioko*, meaning to chase someone or something with great effort. Paul was calling Timothy and us to chase after faithfulness, regardless of how difficult it is. Look again at Psalm 37: "Trust in the Lord, and do good; dwell in the land and *cultivate faithfulness*" (Psalm 37:3, emphasis added). David, the Psalmist, is also calling us to till the soil of faithfulness in our own lives. The word cultivate [Hebrew: *ra'ah*] is really a command for us to keep company with and regularly associate with faithfulness. Literally, it can be translated, "companion with faithfulness". Run after it. Befriend it. Hang around it. Feed on it for a lifetime, as it nourishes our souls.

We start by regularly associating with and keeping company with Our Faithful God. Call it what you will: *Standing on the Promises* or living a lifestyle that chooses to *Trust and Obey*. Daily we must talk to God in prayer and listen to Him from His Word. When we do, we will watch *pistis* faithfulness grow in our lives, even in the smallest of tasks.

I once read the real test of a big person is their ability to occupy a small place in a great way. A life of *pistis* faithfulness starts with obeying God in the little things. Doing what we are asked to do. Finishing a job well. And never giving up! So said Jesus: "He who is faithful *in a very little thing* is faithful also in much . . ." (Luke 16:10, emphasis added).

THE SUBSTANTIAL IMPACT

What would happen to us if this fruit of *pistis* faithfulness was a consistent part of our lives? Certainly we would see tremendous results in our relationships, as people came to trust us more. Few things in life can take its place. Faithfulness—to trust and be trustworthy in all matters large and small—is one of the greatest virtues, far surpassing popularity, brilliance, fame, or fortune.

THE SOLUTION TO ANGER

Faith honors God. God also honors faith. Ponder the results in our anger-infused lives if we endeavored to walk in Holy Spirit-produced *pistis* faithfulness in the midst of every conflict. We would surely run from our sinful passions that push us to lash out. We would, instead, chase after the faith to believe God has a better plan. Great occasions for serving God rarely come. Sometimes they show up as little opportunities to respond correctly to other people.

In the Parable of the Talents in Matthew 25:14-30, Jesus expresses the real value of a life filled with the fruit of *pistis* faithfulness. As we walk in faithful obedience to the Lord, investing our time, talent and treasures in things that count for eternity, we can expect to hear these words from *Melech ha Olam*—King of the Universe: "Well done, good and faithful slave; you were faithful [Greek: *pistos*] with a few things, I will put you in charge of many things, *enter into the joy of your master*" (Matthew 25:21, emphasis added). May that be one of the driving passions of our lives!

INSPECTING THE FRUIT

1. What specifically is your plan to increase your personal pursuit of faithfulness?

2. How might this affect those who are close to you?

3. What are some of "the little things" in which you can exhibit faithfulness?

FURTHER ADVICE FROM THE MASTER GARDENER

Read the Parable of the Talents in Matthew 25:14-30. Write down a summary of what Jesus taught about the fruit of faithfulness in each of the following verses:

Matthew 25:21

Matthew 25:23

Matthew 25:29

CHAPTER TWENTY-THREE

THE TASTY FRUIT OF
SPIRIT-FILLED GENTLENESS

I love blueberries. There are few snacks more refreshing than frozen blueberries on a hot summer day. As they melt in my mouth, the gentle skins peel off and stick to my teeth, providing a few more seconds of flavor. Sheer pleasure! We come now to another tasty fruit of the Spirit:

> . . . the fruit of the Spirit is. . . **gentleness** . . . (Galatians 5:23, emphasis added).

THE SCRIPTURAL DEFINITION

You would think gentleness would be easy to define. Yet, philosophers and theologians throughout the ages have stumbled over this word. In ancient Greece, Aristotle wrote, "Gentleness lies somewhere between excessive anger and no anger at all." How is that for definitive? Other Greek writers, like Plato and Plutarch, wrote that gentleness is an "indescribable mildness." That doesn't help much, either. In the sixteenth century, Martin Luther defined gentleness as the quality of not being easily provoked to anger. Some in his day called it "grace for the soul."

Finally, by the time the seventeenth century rolled around, the translators of the King James Version of the Bible chose to translate the word as *meekness*. Frankly, that's a great word in the beautiful but archaic language of the 1600s. Unfortunately, today the word meek can mean being a wimp of the lowest order. Is gentleness just another word for acting like a weak, cowardly, namby-pamby, pantywaist? Hardly!

If we are going to have this fruit of gentleness pour out of our lives, we best get on with the biblical definition. The Greek word the apostle Paul uses here for gentleness is *prautes*, which has as its root in the word *praus*, meaning a mildness of disposition, the opposite of self-assertion and self-interest. Like many of the Greek words in the apostle Paul's list of the fruit of the Spirit, *prautes* is an especially difficult word to translate into one word. The word was used to speak of a wild animal that had become tamed and brought under a master's control. Although the animal is mild-mannered, it is nonetheless strong and quite capable of exhibiting great power. The word *prautes*, translated here in Galatians as gentleness, came to refer to strength or power under control. Biblically-speaking, *prautes* people were well-managed gentle giants.

With all this imagery in mind, let me give you my definition, hopefully more helpful than "Gentleness is like a frozen blueberry, melting on your tongue." Biblical gentleness is the God-given ability to respond to a difficult person or a challenging circumstance with a strength that is under the control of the indwelling Holy Spirit.

Gentleness is the quality of not over-reacting, of not abusing our power or position. It is the Spirit-led ability to not bully people or push them around. It is the opposite of self-assertion. It chooses to back off when offended, to love rather than retaliate. I recently heard a speaker call it a "sweet reasonableness."

Let's be honest. Some of us have a hard time being gentle. We over-react. We assert our authority. We abuse our power. I was sent this cute poem by email that expresses how some of us less gentle people view life. It is called *The Little Birdie*:

I woke early one morning,
The earth lay cool and still
When suddenly a tiny bird
Perched on my window sill,
He sang a song so lovely
So carefree and so gay,
That slowly all my troubles
Began to slip away.
He sang of far off places
Of laughter and of fun,
It seemed his very trilling,
Brought up the morning sun.
I stirred beneath the covers
Crept slowly out of bed,
Then gently shut the window
And crushed his little head. (Author unknown)

Obviously, this guy was just not a morning person! He was also not one to be too keen on manifesting the fruit of *prautes* gentleness. We, however, have plenty of biblical examples of those who were. Consider the life of Saul of Tarsus, who became the great apostle Paul. Here was the once fiery zealot and ardent persecutor of Christians, now gloriously converted to a saving knowledge of Jesus Christ. But, in his early days of ministry, after his conversion to Christ, we find him still struggling with gentleness. (Remember our lesson on spiritual pomology where we learned that the fruit of the Spirit are not automatic nor fully developed when we are young in the Lord).

Initially, Paul was hardly the epitome of *prautes* gentleness. We find him in the Book of Acts, aggressively arguing with Barnabas over John Mark (Acts 15:37-39). As Paul's life became more and more controlled by the power of the indwelling Holy Spirit, the fruit of *prautes* gentleness grew to greater fruition. As he matured he was also able to deal honestly with the lack of gentleness he saw in others. Take to heart what Paul writes to the fleshly Corinthian Christians, who certainly were cause for Paul's righteous anger: "Shall I come to you with a rod or with love and a spirit of gentleness" (1 Corinthians 4:21).

Every parent knows this tension. As we read First and Second Corinthians, we find that Paul certainly rebuked people, but he did so with a strength that was under control, the fruit of *prautes* gentleness in his life. This was something very much needed by the apostle and by all of us, as well.

THE SUPREME EXAMPLE

Once again, as is the case with all the fruit of the Spirit, we have our best example of gentleness in Jesus Christ. He is the *prautes* gentleness of God in full view. That is one of the reasons the Incarnate Son of God came. Thus, the prophecies concerning the Messiah presented Him not just as the powerful Lord but as the gentle king: "Behold your King is coming to you, *gentle* . . ." (Matthew 21:5, emphasis added). Talk about true meekness and incredible power under divine control. Jesus said of Himself: "Take My yoke upon you, and learn from Me, *for I am gentle* and humble in heart; and you shall find rest for your souls" (Matthew 11:29, emphasis added).

We find that kind of gentleness throughout the earthly life of Jesus. Normally we think of the stories of the gentle way He treated the children or the woman caught in adultery or even his patience with His disciples. But, in my opinion, one of the greatest evidences of His meekness, His gentleness and strength under control, is exhibited during His arrest, trials and crucifixion.

When Jesus was being arrested He was quick to remind His disciples He could have called for the help of twelve legions of angels (Matthew 26:53). A Roman legion contained six thousand soldiers. Do the math. Jesus could have called on seventy-two thousand angelic warriors to deliver Him from that crowd. Remember, in the Old Testament, one angel was responsible for tens of thousands of people dying. Imagine a myriad of the heavenly host fighting on your side. (I would have called them all.) But Jesus refused to exercise all of His power. He refused to over-react, even when taunted (Luke 23:35). That is biblical gentleness. That is true *prautes* meekness. That is strength under control. That is being the gentle giant God has called all of us to be.

We have so much to learn from Jesus regarding this kind of gentleness. Even the apostle Paul admitted this: "Now I, Paul, myself urge you by the meekness and *gentleness* of Christ . . ." (2 Corinthians 10:1, emphasis added). The apostle Peter adds this description of the gentleness of Christ: "while being reviled, He [Christ] did not revile in return; while suffering, He uttered no threats, but kept entrusting Himself to Him who judges righteously" (1 Peter 2:23).

THE SPECIFIC COMMANDS

The world calls us to wield our power and make our strength known. It calls us to shout out, "Don't mess with me!" The Bible, however, commands every born-again believer to pursue gentleness. Consider the challenge the apostle Paul gave to Timothy: "But flee from these things, you man of God; and *pursue* righteousness, godliness, faith, love, perseverance and *gentleness*" (1Timothy 6:11, emphasis added). Again, this word pursue Paul used [Greek: *dioko*] also speaks of running eagerly after something or someone. In other passages, it refers to a believer being persecuted or chased. Think about this. We are to eagerly chase after *prautes* gentleness as if we were running for our lives, as if our lives depended on it. They do!

190

Once we have pursued it, the Bible calls us to *put on* gentleness so that we are clothed with it every day: "And so, as those who have been chosen of God, holy and beloved, *put on* a heart of . . . gentleness [Greek: *prautes*]" (Colossians 3:12, emphasis added). Once we have pursued it and put it on, we are to demonstrate our transformed hearts to others "with all humility and *gentleness*, with patience, showing forbearance to one another in love . . ." (Ephesians 4:2, emphasis added). That's quite a wardrobe—one worth parading in public!

I was surprised to look online and view the many varieties of necklaces. Some even had real fruit. Spirit-filled *prautes* is the ornament hanging around the neck of a gentle spirit. Sometimes that kind of gentleness is demonstrated in a Spirit-led quietness. Like holding our tongue. Like refusing to retaliate when we have the ability and the power to do so. That's a beautiful accessory in our spiritual wardrobe!

I remind you of what the apostle Peter wrote to wives who have the tough job of responding to a disobedient and unloving husband. With an inner strength God's Holy Spirit provides, He calls them to exhibit: "the hidden person of the heart, with the imperishable quality of a [*prautes*] gentle and quiet ["tranquil, peaceable," Greek: *hesuchios*] spirit, which is precious in the sight of God (1 Peter 3:4).

THE SPIRITUAL SOURCE

Where does one even begin to discover this "grace of the soul?" Like all the other fruit, biblical gentleness has a supernatural source. Again, we look at this simply-stated passage in Galatians, where the context reminds us *prautes* gentleness is the fruit of walking in the power of the indwelling Holy Spirit:

> . . . the fruit of the Spirit is . . . **gentleness** . . . (Galatians 5:22-23, emphasis added).

THE SUBSTANTIAL IMPACT

What would happen if this strength under control became a regular part of our lives? Besides being a little easier to live with, let's consider the spiritual impact. There is nothing so strong as gentleness; nothing so gentle as real strength under Holy Spirit control. I remind us again of what Jesus said: "Take My yoke upon you, and learn from Me, for I am gentle and humble in heart; and *you shall find rest* ["intermission, recreation," Greek: *anapausis*] *for your souls*" (Matthew 11:29, emphasis added).

We must daily practice imitating our <u>Gentle</u> Savior and, in so doing, find rest for our souls! Many of us really need some soul-rest—a spiritual intermission— today. In fact, it would do us well if we, by God's power, put on a heart of gentleness right now, along with a heart of love, joy, peace, patience, kindness, goodness, faithfulness and self-control. In the words of the old McDonald's commercial: "You deserve a break today."

When would you think we would need the fruit of *prautes* gentleness the most? Let me ask it this way. When are we most prone to over-react or abuse our power or position? When we are correcting people, of course. And the Bible has many references calling us to exercise Spirit-led *prautes* gentleness in those times:

> . . . with *gentleness* correcting those who are in opposition, if perhaps God may grant them repentance leading to the knowledge of the truth . . . (2 Timothy 2:25, emphasis added).

> Brethren, even if a man is caught in any trespass, you who are spiritual, restore such a one in *a spirit of gentleness*; each one looking to yourself, lest you too be tempted (Galatians 6:1, emphasis added).

> . . . but sanctify Christ as Lord in your hearts, always being ready to make a defense to everyone who asks you to give an account for the hope that is in you, yet with *gentleness* and reverence . . . (1 Peter 3:15, emphasis added).

Take a moment to reflect on the apostle Paul's very personal admonition. It serves as the foundation upon which we prepare to correct others, even in the most serious of situations and conflict: "Now I, Paul, myself *urge you by the meekness and gentleness of Christ*—I who am *meek* when face to face with you, but bold toward you when absent!" (2 Corinthians 10:1 emphasis added). It takes the Spirit-led *prautes* gentleness of Christ Himself to correct those who oppose God, restore those who sin against the Lord and defend the faith to those who are seeking answers. It also takes *prautes* gentleness to discipline and disciple others, especially our children. That is a Christ-like quality that does not come naturally for anyone.

THE SOLUTION TO ANGER

How does *prautes* gentleness help us with managing our everyday conflicts? Imagine the response if we were to take "the gentle approach" to resolving angry situations. I do not have to imagine. I am a living witness.

One day, while sitting in my living room, my young daughter and a couple of her friends rushed frantically in the front door. My daughter screamed, "Dad, there's a group of men next door and they are whistling at us and calling us foul names." I flew out of my chair and, in my stocking-covered feet, ran out the door and confronted them as a group, "How dare you mess with those little girls. They are children. What's the matter with you guys?" The three men got very quiet. They knew I was speaking as a protective father and I meant business. To my surprise, it was a strength under control, a *prautes* gentleness. Though I was indignant, I had no desire to do them harm. They were quick to apologize. I shook their hands and returned to my home.

I have since reflected on what might have happened if my foolish and sinful anger would have been unleashed. Besides getting beat up by these much larger and stronger construction workers, it would have been a terrible example to those kids. How can I lead them to a peaceful life if I showed them I could not lead myself? Instead of us now laughing at the memory of me standing up to these big men, they might have been placing flowers on my grave. *Prautes* gentleness can also be a lifesaver. Ponder that the next time reason turns to rage.

INSPECTING THE FRUIT

1. Who are the people you tend to overpower?

2. Reflect on a recent conflict where you were less than gentle. How might the fruit of gentleness have changed what you said and did?

3. How might it have changed the outcome?

4. Who is the greatest human example of gentleness you know? What is different about them?

FURTHER ADVICE FROM THE MASTER GARDENER

Read 1 Peter, Chapter 2. Comment on the gentleness of Christ, especially in the midst of persecution.

Read 1 Peter, Chapter 3. Comment on the gentleness we are to exhibit in the midst of suffering.

Read Acts 6:8-60 regarding the martyrdom of Stephen. Compare his gentleness to that of Saul of Tarsus in Acts 8:1-3.

CHAPTER TWENTY-FOUR

THE TASTY FRUIT OF SPIRIT-FILLED SELF-CONTROL

There is something about a fruitcake that brings all kinds of reactions, good and bad, from "Boy, is that tasty!" to "Hey, what are those little green things in there?" Just what are the ingredients in a fruitcake? Inquiring minds want to know. The best answer I've heard: "Don't ask!"

We are not here to identify the mysterious ingredients that make up a fruitcake. We are here to talk about the kind of spiritual fruit that are the understandable ingredients of a Spirit-filled life—an abundance of Christ-like qualities the indwelling Holy Spirit wants to see flow from our regenerated and obedient hearts. We can rightly refer to these as the *Cornucopia of Christ-likeness* and the *Harvest of the Heart*. The apostle Paul calls them the fruit of the Spirit-filled life. Let me remind us of our key text. By now, it should be indelibly imprinted in our brains. Hopefully, it has also been written on the tablet of our hearts:

> But the fruit of the Spirit is love, joy, peace, patience,
> kindness, goodness, faithfulness, gentleness, self-control;
> against such things there is no law (Galatians 5:22-23).

We have already examined "The Eight Principles of Spiritual Pomology." Let's do a brief review:

Principle #1: The fruit of the Spirit is not automatic.

Principle #2: The fruit of the Spirit is not limited.

Principle #3: The fruit of the Spirit is not fully produced in us immediately.

Principle #4: The fruit of the Spirit is all one harvest of the heart.

Principle #5: The fruit of the Spirit represents the life of Christ in us.

Principle #6: The fruit of the Spirit is a sweet harvest.

Principle #7: The fruit of the Spirit attracts others to Christ.

Principle #8: The fruit of the Spirit is evidence of victory over sin.

In previous chapters we did a fairly thorough fruit inspection of *agape* love, *chara* joy, *eirene* peace, *makrothumia* patience, *chrestotes* kindness, *agathasune* goodness, *pistis* faithfulness and *prautes* gentleness. Now we come to the last specific fruit on Paul's list:

> . . . the fruit of the Spirit is . . . **self-control** . . . (Galatians 5:23, emphasis added).

THE SCRIPTURAL DEFINITION

Next to love, this is probably the fruit of the Spirit most preached about by my fellow ministers. But what exactly is the apostle Paul talking about when he speaks of self-control? Is he talking about the opposite of over-indulgence, as Plato put it, or "temperance" as the King James Bible translates it? Does he mean "sobriety in the whole life of the man" as Martin Luther called it? Is he addressing the need for inner strength, self-restraint or even intestinal fortitude, referred to as such by some in our day? Consider with me the biblical definition.

Suppose we were called to a stage and asked to attempt to juggle some apples and oranges. In order to succeed we would need to hold on firmly to each fruit. When we throw them we would need to keep them from getting away from us. In other words, juggling requires keeping a number of things from getting out from under our control. That is a simple explanation of this Greek word *egkrateia* (properly pronounced *enkrateia*). Thus it gets translated in classical Greek as self-control, self-restraint, even abstinence from excess. It also refers to the ability to master our desires and subdue our cravings so things don't get out of control.

Fundamentally, the apostle Paul is addressing the basic need for every believer to have Spirit-empowered victory over fleshly desires. In order to do so, the Holy Spirit wants to bring us through a life-long process of maturity. In simpler terms, He wants us to grow up! Let me give my four-part operational definition of maturity, the principles I have tried to teach my children on what it really means to grow in maturity:

1. Growing in maturity requires weighing consequences.

Immaturity says, "Who cares what happens tomorrow?"
Maturity says, "I will reap tomorrow what I sow today."

2. Growing in maturity requires delaying gratification.

Immaturity says, "I want it and I want it now."
Maturity says, "I may want it now but it is better to wait."

3. Growing in maturity requires developing godly qualities.

Immaturity says, "Be all the world says I can be."
Maturity says, "Be what God has called me to be."

4. Growing in maturity requires exercising self-control.

Immaturity says, "Do what pleases me."
Maturity says, "Do what pleases God."

The indwelling Holy Spirit desires to daily produce in us the kind of *enkrateia* self-control that bears fruit and produces life-long maturity in every arena of life: physically, emotionally, spiritually, relationally, sexually, and financially. And the list goes on.

The apostle Paul spoke of exercising self-control "in all things" (1 Corinthians 9:25). He even spoke of the need for *enkrateia* self-control, not just in what we are doing but even in what we are thinking. He wrote concerning the importance of "taking *every thought* captive to the obedience of Christ." (2 Corinthians 10:5, emphasis added).

Do I even need to go into detail as to how much this fruit of the Spirit is needed in our lives? I once read a quote from the British statesman, Edmund Burke, in which he observed we are only qualified for liberty to the degree we can put "moral chains" on our ungodly appetites. Our lack of self-control keeps us in bondage. We need a controlling power within us, even for the little things.

In the days of wooden ships more vessels were destroyed by small worms than by large cannons. For many of us, the worms of immaturity are eating away at our effectiveness as Christ-followers. We need self-control, especially as we come nearer to the return of Christ and people's behaviors show an even greater lack of self-restraint:

> But realize this, that in the last days difficult times will come.
> For men will be lovers of self, lovers of money, boastful,
> arrogant, revilers, disobedient to parents, ungrateful, unholy,
> unloving, irreconcilable, malicious gossips, *without self-control*,
> brutal, haters of good, treacherous, reckless, conceited, lovers
> of pleasure rather than lovers of God... (2 Timothy 3:1-4,
> emphasis added).

THE SUPREME EXAMPLE

Having said all of this, it would be especially helpful if we had a good example of self-control. We do. Again, like all other eight fruit of the Spirit, Jesus Christ is the embodiment of *enkrateia* self-control.

The Son of Man, who had left His glory in Heaven, could have made His earthly life so much easier. With just a word, He could have gathered all the world's riches for Himself. Instead, the Son of Man had no place to lay His head (Matthew 8:20). With just a word, He could have delivered Himself from that cruel Roman cross (Matthew 26:53). Instead, He looked at His executioners and prayed, "Father, forgive them; for they do not know what they are doing" (Luke 23:34). Jesus was completely undeserving of the harsh criticism when the people in His day called Him a glutton and a drunkard (Matthew 11:19). He was, instead, a bastion of self-control. And God wants us to be just like Him.

THE SPECIFIC COMMANDS

We live in a "Do your own thing" culture and an "It's my life and I will do what I want" world. But the indwelling Holy Spirit desires our thoughts and behaviors be under His complete control, even concerning those things others may feel free to think and do.

- The apostle Paul presents the PRINCIPLE:

> All things are lawful for me, but not all things are profitable. All things are lawful for me, but I will not be mastered by anything (1 Corinthians 6:12).

- The apostle Peter presents the PROCESS:

> . . . in your knowledge, add *self-control*, and in your *self-control*, perseverance, and in your perseverance, godliness . . . (2 Peter 1:6, emphasis added).

- The apostle Paul then presents the PRIZE:

> Everyone who competes in the games exercises *self-control* in all things. They then do it to receive a perishable wreath, but we an imperishable (1 Corinthians 9:25, emphasis added).

- The apostle Paul even presents self-control as a primary qualification for those in leadership POSITIONS:

> For the overseer must be above reproach as God's steward, not self-willed, not quick-tempered, not addicted to wine, not pugnacious, not fond of sordid gain, but hospitable, loving what is good, sensible, just, devout, *self-controlled* . . . (Titus 1:7-8, emphasis added).

THE SPIRITUAL SOURCE

Although the word in Galatians gets translated as <u>self</u>-control, I believe it has more to do with <u>Spirit</u>-control. Ultimately, He is the supernatural source; the only real power that can control our excesses. History bears this out.

During the period from 1920 to 1933, Americans experienced a period of supposed restraint. The Eighteenth Amendment of the Constitution established the prohibition of alcoholic beverages. Some willingly participated, even promoting total abstinence. Most did not. In fact, during those Roaring Twenties and beyond, rum-running and organized crime had its heyday. The city of Chicago became a haven for prohibition-dodgers. Less than fifteen years after it was instituted, the Eighteenth Amendment was repealed. The "noble experiment" had become a failed attempt.

History revealed what we already knew. Creating laws against drinking alcohol just made people want to drink more. Joining organized programs without a sincere change of heart proved powerless to produce lasting change. Three thousand years ago, Proverbs described human nature as it really is: "Stolen water is sweet; and bread eaten in secret is pleasant" (Proverbs 9:17).

Today we have a number of community-wide and faith-based abstinence programs, encouraging personal accountability. As much as I appreciate the efforts of such programs, they do not work if the people who sign up are not learning self-control. We may be able to encourage their temporary abstinence but we cannot program their life-long temperance. Lasting *enkrateia* self-control is something that has to come from a regenerated and obedient heart, indwelt by the Holy Spirit of God. The apostle Paul said it simply, but said it best:

> . . . the fruit of the SPIRIT is . . . **self-control** . . . (Galatians 5:23, emphasis added).

THE SUBSTANTIAL IMPACT

In some ancient cultures a lack of self-control was considered a sign of personal freedom, as people declared, "I am not bound by rules. I can do what I please." Such was the case in ancient Israel: "With our tongue we will prevail; our lips are our own; who is lord over us?" (Psalm 12:4). King Solomon opposed such a notion: "He who is slow to anger is better than the mighty, and *he who rules his spirit*, than he who captures a city" (Proverbs 16:32, emphasis added).

There is great earthly reward that comes when we rule our spirit and when our fleshly and foolish desires are in check. Self-controlled people go further in life; unrestrained people do not. Most people will testify that self-control is a fundamental quality needed to be a good student, worker, spouse, parent, employee and citizen. There are great earthly rewards awaiting the self-controlled person. For the born-again believer, who is walking in the Spirit and manifesting the fruit of *enkrateia* self-control, there are even greater eternal awards: "And everyone who competes in the games exercises *self-control in all things*. They then do it to receive a perishable wreath, but we an imperishable" (1 Corinthians 9:25, emphasis added).

THE SOLUTION TO ANGER

One rainy night, when I was a teenager, I was alone on the night shift at a fast-food restaurant. A customer rushed in and asked to use our restroom. I politely informed him we were not permitted to allow the public to use it and that he would have to go to the nearby gas station. He became indignant, cussing at me as if I were to blame for my boss's rules and his discomfort. As he was leaving, he shouted in anger, "I'll be right back. Make me a cheeseburger."

This man had just insulted me and I was furious. But I was also at work. What could I do? I did what many immature, self-absorbed, uncontrolled sinners who lacked self-control would do. I got even! As I grabbed a raw hamburger patty, I noticed two dead flies on the window sill. I scooped those dried carcasses up and shoved them deep in the meat. After grilling the burger perfectly, I added an abundance of cheese, lettuce and tomatoes. My generosity was quite literally a cover-up for my quiet revenge. The man returned. I accepted his money and smiled, as I watched him eat every morsel of that tainted food. As he left, I said, "Have a nice evening, sir!"

I have often reflected on that night, some fifty years ago. (I wonder what the statute of limitations is?). On that drizzly night, this foolish young man missed an opportunity to grow up. Although my actions were probably not fatal, I can still remember how pleasantly wicked my actions felt. I accept, in a very personal way, the words God spoke to Cain: "Sin is crouching at the door, and its desire is for you, *but you must master it*. (Genesis 4:7, emphasis added). I didn't!

What has Spirit-produced *enkrateia* self-control have to do with dealing with our anger? Anyone who has exploded or even quietly lashed out to hurt others doesn't need to ask. And anyone who has experienced the consequences of our lack of self-control could also easily testify. We don't need to put dead flies in a hamburger to prove it. Our lack of *enkrateia* self-control shows up in a host of other ways. In fact, sin is always crouching at our door. It's time to master it before it masters us!

PUTTING THEM ALL TOGETHER IN ONE BASKET

One of the most common reactions we have heard from our many foster-children usually follows their first look at the basket full of fresh fruit regularly in our kitchen. "Wow! Can I have some?" Our response is, "Of course. They are all there for you to enjoy."

We observe these nine fruit of the Spirit-filled life and we ask, "Lord, can we have some?" and God answers, "Of course." So we come to His banquet table and look over the abundant choices:

- The tasty fruit of Spirit-filled *agape* **love**—which is the supernatural ability to value myself and others with the worth God places on me and them.

- The tasty fruit of Spirit-filled *chara* **joy**—which is the supernatural ability to be sincerely grateful to God, regardless of circumstances.

- The tasty fruit of Spirit-filled *eirene* **peace**—which is the supernatural ability to have a deep-settled confidence that God is in control of the details of my life.

- The tasty fruit of Spirit-filled *makrothumia* **patience**—which is the supernatural ability to demonstrate a gentle tolerance with exasperating people and frustrating situations.

- The tasty fruit of Spirit-filled *chrestotes* **kindness**—which is the supernatural ability to shrink from inflicting pain and deal with people with grace and mercy.

- The tasty fruit of Spirit-filled *agathosune* **goodness**—which is the supernatural ability to stand up for what is right in the eyes of God and, if necessary, expose and confront sin.

- The tasty fruit of Spirit-filled *pistis* **faithfulness**—which is the supernatural ability to take God at His Word and, as a result, become trustworthy and taken at our word.

- The tasty fruit of Spirit-filled *prautes* **gentleness**—which is the supernatural ability to respond, without over-reacting, with a strength that is under divine control.

- The tasty fruit of Spirit-filled *enkrateia* **self-control**—which is the supernatural ability to master our desires and subdue our cravings before things get out of control.

Then we hear God say, "Don't just pick one. Enjoy them all! But, look carefully. There's room for more fruit in the basket. Let Me show you..."

THE FRUIT OF THE SPIRIT-FILLED LIFE IS "SUCH THINGS"

I always thought fruit on the ground was off-limits. My ignorance fed my assumption that it was rotten. Quite the contrary. Farmers often refer to this as windfall fruit. If collected before the insects invade, it can be quite tasty fruit. In fact, windfall fruit can be an unexpected blessing.

So far we have inspected nine of the fruit of the Spirit-filled life. Love. Joy. Peace. Patience. Kindness. Goodness. Faithfulness. Gentleness. Self-control. In Galatians 5:23, we find a tenth kind of fruit mentioned—windfall fruit—an unexpected blessing:

But the fruit of the Spirit is love, joy, peace, patience, kindness, goodness, faithfulness, gentleness, self-control; against *such things* there is no law (Galatians 5:22-23, emphasis added).

The phrase "such things" really refers to classes of things. Remember, the fruit of the Spirit is not limited to this list in Galatians. The fruit of the Spirit is not only love, joy, peace, patience . . . okay . . . you know them!

Engage in any study of pneumatology (a study of things related to the Holy Spirit) and we will conclude that the fruit of the Holy Spirit's ministry in our lives is much broader.

Let's take a brief look at another list of more fruit of the Spirit, taken from other passages in the New Testament:

OTHER WINDFALL FRUIT OF THE HOLY SPIRIT

Windfall Fruit #1: The Holy Spirit convicts us of sin. (John 16:8-9)

He convicts the world of sin and unrighteousness, stirring the conscience of the vilest of people. We also have a keener awareness of how believers fall short of God's holy standards for His beloved children. He leads us to true repentance (Matthew 3:8).

Windfall Fruit #2: The Holy Spirit regenerates us. (Titus 3:5; 1 Corinthians 6:11)

He makes it possible for us to respond to the Gospel of grace and be made right with God through faith alone in Christ. He creates our truth-seeking hearts, drawing us to the Father (John 6:44).

Windfall Fruit #3: The Holy Spirit enables us to enjoy the abundant and eternal life the Risen Lord gives. (John 10:10; Romans 8:11)

He constantly reminds us that we are truly alive in Christ. It is both a present reality and a future promise.

Windfall Fruit #4: The Holy Spirit indwells us. (1 John 3:24; Romans 8:9; John 14:16-17; John 16:12)

He is not only with us; He is in us, permanently indwelling our hearts. We cannot run from Him and He will never leave us.

Windfall Fruit #5: The Holy Spirit transforms us. (2 Corinthians 3:18)

He is striving to make us like Jesus Christ in His glorious attributes, one day at a time and over a lifetime.

Windfall Fruit #6: The Holy Spirit seals us. (Ephesians 1:13; 4:30; 2 Corinthians 1:22; 5:5)

He is the Holy Spirit of Promise who eternally secures us in our relationship with God, our Heavenly Father.

Windfall Fruit #7: The Holy Spirit fills us.
(Ephesians 5:18)

He doesn't leave us empty. He fills us, making it possible to praise Him and submit to one another because of our reverence for Christ.

Windfall Fruit #8: The Holy Spirit comforts us.
(John 14:26; Galatians 5:5)

He is our Paraclete Helper, our Indwelling Counselor, the One who comes alongside of us and encourages our hearts to remain steadfast.

Windfall Fruit #9: The Holy Spirit teaches us.
(John 14:26; 16:13; 1 Corinthians 2:13-14)

He is the one who illumines the Scriptures, helping us to understand and apply them to our lives.

Windfall Fruit #10: The Holy Spirit baptizes us.
(1 Corinthians 12:13)

He has made every born-again believer a part of the one Body of Christ: the Church, the forever family of God.

Windfall Fruit #11: The Holy Spirit unites us.
(Ephesians 2:22; Philippians 1:27; Ephesians 4:3)

He has made us one with Christ and all of His disciples. He drives us to unity of spirit and purpose.

Windfall Fruit #12: The Holy Spirit quickens us.
(John 4:24; Ephesians 2:18; Ephesians 6:18)

He makes it possible for us to pray and worship God in spirit and in truth. He stirs our cold and indifferent hearts.

Windfall Fruit #13: The Holy Spirit equips us.
(Romans 12:4-8; Ephesians 4:11-12)

He is preparing every believer to build up the Body of Christ, using their unique talents and the spiritual gifts with which He has endowed us.

Windfall Fruit #14: The Holy Spirit empowers us.
(Acts 1:8; 1 Thessalonians 1:5)

He is enabling us to reach out with His power to our family, neighborhood, workplace, school, city, state, nation and the world.

Windfall Fruit #15: The Holy Spirit leads us.
(Romans 8:14; Galatians 5:18)

He is constantly giving us His specific guidance, as we walk this side of heaven. He is the Internal Guide leading us.

Windfall Fruit #16: The Holy Spirit anoints us.
(2 Corinthians 1:21-22; 1 John 2:22, 27)

He covers us with His presence and enables us with His power to minister in His strength and not our own.

Windfall Fruit #17: The Holy Spirit helps us bear fruit that glorifies God.
(John 15:8; Colossians 1:10; Titus 3:14)

He produces in us and through us the fruit of:

- enduring hope
- sacrificial mercy
- global evangelism
- persevering prayer
- ceaseless praise
- intimate fellowship
- lasting endurance
- effective discipleship
- sincere repentance
- and so much more

What a basket full of unexpected blessings!

Let us return to what the apostle Paul writes in the last part of our key text:

> ... against **such things** there is no law (Galatians 5:23, emphasis added).

The apostle Paul wants us to understand that against such things—these nine fruit of the Spirit (love, joy, peace…) and these many other windfall ministries of the Holy Spirit—there is no law. In other words, we do not need an external list of man-made rules for Christian living. We have an indwelling Holy Spirit to lead and guide us from the inside out (Galatians 5:16, 18, 25). Instead, the Christian life flows freely from the cornucopia of our Spirit-filled hearts. The harvest of these fruit of the Spirit and windfall fruit is peace with God, peace with others and peace with ourselves (Philippians 4:7; Colossians 3:15). In fact, the only thing restraining me from growing to be more like Christ is . . . well . . . ME! Simply stated, it all adds up to becoming like Jesus—one fruit at a time.

After teaching on the fruit of the Spirit, Dave Parsons, who at the time was the senior pastor of Bethel Baptist Church in Santa Rosa, California, wrote the following prayer. It's appropriately titled:

"Christ-likeness"

Lord, help me . . .
> *To love, not lust,*
> *To labor, not loaf,*
> *To praise, not pout,*
> *To depend, not doubt,*
> *To pardon, not punish,*
> *To serve, not be selfish,*
> *To commend, not criticize,*
> *To be courageous, not cower,*
> *To be gracious, not grouchy,*
> *To be caring, not calloused,*
> *To be assured, not anxious,*
> *To be humble, not haughty,*
> *To be peaceable, not petty,*
> *To be giving, not greedy,*
> *To be content, not covet,*
> *To be faithful, not false .*
> *Lord, help me to be just like You.* (Used by permission)

INSPECTING THE FRUIT

1. In what areas do you have the least self-control?

2. Measure your maturity in each of the following areas:

   • Weighing consequences before I do something
   Mature   Immature
   10 9 8 7 6 5 4 3 2 1

   • Delaying gratification
   Mature   Immature
   10 9 8 7 6 5 4 3 2 1

   • Developing godly qualities in my life
   Mature   Immature
   10 9 8 7 6 5 4 3 2 1

   • Exercising self-control
   Mature   Immature
   10 9 8 7 6 5 4 3 2 1

FURTHER ADVICE FROM THE MASTER GARDENER

1. Read the following passages and comment on what they teach about self-control: Proverbs 23:1-2; Luke 9:23-24; 1 Corinthians 8:13; 9:27

2. Read the list of Windfall Fruit of the Holy Spirit. Pick out three and comment about their influence on dealing with your anger.

   a. Windfall Fruit #____: _____
      Comment:

   b. Windfall Fruit #___: _____
      Comment:

   c. Windfall Fruit #___: _____
      Comment:

CHAPTER TWENTY-FIVE

A TALE OF TWO ORCHARDS

Considering all we have discussed concerning destroying the rotten fruit of anger and, instead, harvesting the tasty fruit of the Spirit, I invite you to a journey of the soul—a parable of the heart.

We are walking together down a country road on a cool autumn day. As we look to the right and to the left we notice two very different fruit orchards. We stop to examine both. To our right we see a sign in front of rows of healthy trees:

The Godly Anger Orchard
Owned by the Master Gardener
Under the Management of the Holy Spirit

To our left, we see a rotting wooden sign in front of forest of decaying trees:

The Ungodly Anger Orchard
Owned by Our Sinful Flesh
In Partnership with the Devil and the World

Our eyes are first drawn to the left. We walk nearer and catch the rotting stench of ungodly anger—emotionally, socially, physically and spiritually. We understand that, if left alone, a forest of future generations of unrighteous anger trees is expected. Oh, how these trees need immediate pruning for their sake and the sake of those that follow. Even then, we are not hopeful, unless emergency care is given.

We single out one tree, sadly typical of the rest in this Ungodly Anger Orchard. We look at its dying leaves and see the all-too-familiar rotting fruit of the flesh—*echthra* enmities, *eris* strife, *zelos* jealousy, *thumos* outbursts of anger, *eritheia* disputes, *dichostasia* dissensions, *hairesis* factions, and *phthonos* envying. Looking closer, we see other very similar fruit growing on the tree—*orge* anger, *kakia* malice, *blasphemia* slander, *aischrologia* abusive speech, *krauge* clamor, and *pikria* bitterness. It troubles our hearts as we observe the destruction of what might have once been a healthy tree.

We are now focused on the major branches, spreading out from the trunk. We recognize them as the anger branches: picking on the innocent victim (scapegoating), building up and blowing up (stamp saving), getting sick (stress illness), running outwardly, retreating inwardly (withdrawal) and getting even (passive-aggression). We also see more of the weak limbs, representing the many ways of expressing anger, as they beat against each other. All of these anger branches are entangled, as scapegoating branches try to crowd out stamp saving branches, as stress illness limbs try to push away those runaway branches, and as the passive-aggressive branches eventually get even with those mean, expressive limbs. This poor tree is being strangled by wrath.

How did all this happen to make this such an ungodly anger tree? We search for answers as we examine the trunk. We are somehow enabled to sense its plant hormones signaling to nearby trees, as it reacts to the trials that come from just being a tree. Like all fruit trees in all of the fruit orchards of the Master Gardener, this tree had experienced the typical storms, droughts, and insect attacks. In this case, however, this tree was so diseased in its core that it was not able to withstand the challenges. Left improperly dealt with, and infected with disease from the other nearby trees, this tree had turned into an ungodly anger tree of its own. In fact, it was so uncontrolled, selfish and destructive it also affected the whole orchard.

There is no easy explanation of what we have observed. Looking down the disease-ridden and cracked trunk, we notice a long list of unbiblical and misplaced expectations, etched deeply into the trunk. The carvings are partially scarred over and filled with insect larvae.

We now look at the dry soil below the tree. It is full of decaying, insect-infested fruit. We see a portion of three major roots crowning above the surface of the parched ground. We recognize they represent our basic needs, physically, emotionally and spiritually. We look closer and see a small weathered poster, attached to the trunk. Its printed words have obviously been ignored:

My God will supply all your needs.
(Philippians 4:19)

Why were there so many rotting trees in this Ungodly Anger Orchard? The disease of sinful anger had sapped the life from this orchard. These rows of ungodly anger trees now stand, waiting for the Divine Pruner and the Heavenly Harvester. Their future remains to be seen.

Our eyes are now diverted to the orchard to the right—the Godly Anger Orchard, filled with lush green trees as far as our eyes can see. It is so very pleasing and the smell of fresh fruit wafts in the breeze. Springing forth from every godly anger tree we see fruiting branches. The *shalom* of God can be felt in the healthy soil around them and the sheen of the Spirit of God can be seen on their trunks. It is obvious to us these trees have been well-connected, well-pruned and well-nurtured. The expectation is that there will continue to be generations of the same to follow. We are hopeful.

We focus on one of the trees. In the midst of a canopy of green leaves we find an abundance of healthy limbs and branches, bearing a variety of the abundant fruit of the Spirit-filled life: *agape* love, *chara* joy, *eirene* peace, *makrothumia* patience, *chrestotes* kindness, *agathosune* goodness, *pistis* faithfulness, *prautes* gentleness, and *enkrateia* self-control. It makes our mouths water for a taste of each one.

We are enabled to sense its chemical signals communicating with nearby trees. Unlike the distressed outcry of the ungodly anger tree, we feel the joyful praise, as if this tree is proclaiming:

Let it be known. Even in the midst of the attacks from the inside and the storms, droughts and disease from the outside, with the help of the Master Gardener, I have withstood the challenge.

As our gaze moves downward we find a list of biblical expectations gently written on its sturdy trunk. Under them we find the words:

Walking in the Spirit
Submitting to His Will
Trusting in His Promises

It is the indelible reminder of what keeps this godly anger tree healthy and free of infestation.

On the ground we also see a windfall of other fruit, fresh enough to eat: the fruit of conviction, transformation, comfort, instruction, equipping, empowerment and leading. We reach for a piece and, while doing so, we find it easy to dig into the perfectly moist ground. We marvel at the roots and are reminded of its basic needs Our Master Gardener—Our Heavenly Farmer—promised to meet. We notice a poster, with easy-to-view letters, gently attached to the tree. It reads:

> *Your Father knows what you need before you ask Him.*
> *(Matthew 6:8)*

There is no question. This is a firmly planted, healthy tree, inside and out. So are the other trees around it. The Master Gardener is pleased. And so are we.

As we leave the area, we ask ourselves: "Why is this Godly Anger Orchard so different? Does not the Master desire all of His trees to produce a healthy and abundant harvest of peace that pleases Him and blesses future generations?" We know the answer. Before any one of us was planted here on *terra firma*, Our Master Gardener made a decision:

> *"I will give them a choice to decide what kind of tree they want to be. They will reap the harvest they sow, as will the generations of trees that follow. If they choose to be godly trees, I will also give them the ability to walk by My power and manifest the fruit of My Spirit. In so doing, they will be enabled and equipped to deal daily with the fruit of the flesh, over a lifetime. I will prune, water and nourish them as they allow Me to. In so doing, they will enjoy a rich harvest of the fruit of My Holy Spirit. And when I, the Heavenly Harvester, come, I will recognize they have fulfilled My purpose."*

May the words of the Psalmist be reflected in the generational harvest of our lives:

> **The righteous man will flourish like the palm tree,**
> **He will grow like a cedar in Lebanon.**
> **Planted in the house of the LORD,**
> **They will flourish in the courts of our God.**
> **They will still yield fruit in old age;**
> **They shall be full of sap and very green**
>
> **(Psalm 92:12-14)**

INSPECTING THE FRUIT

1. Describe the anger orchard of your life.

2. What do you hope for the generations to follow?

FURTHER ADVICE FROM THE MASTER GARDENER

Read in the Appendix, *Connected to the Vine: A Study Outline of John 15:1-11.*

APPENDIX

SMALL GROUP AND PERSONAL STUDY GUIDE

Regarding Personal Study

For personal study, go at your own pace, but be sure to do all the assignments at the end of each chapter. We also encourage you to do this with your spouse, or a friend.

Regarding Group Study

In each chapter do all of the *Inspecting the Fruit* assignments. Decide, in advance, whether your group will also do the readings in each chapter titled *Further Advice from the Master Gardener*.

Four Week Program:
(See the instructions above regarding Group Study)

Week 1: Read Preface, Intro and Chapters 1 to 7   Date due:_____

Week 2: Read Chapters 8 to 13   Date due:_____

Week 3: Read Chapters 14 to 18   Date due:_____

Week 4: Read Chapters 19 to 25 + Appendix   Date due:_____

Six Week Program:
(See the instructions above regarding Group Study)

Week 1: Read Preface, Intro and Chapters 1 to 5   Date due:_____

Week 2: Read Chapters 6 to 9   Date due:_____

Week 3: Read Chapters 10 to 13   Date due:_____

Week 4: Read Chapters 14 to 16   Date due:_____

Week 5: Read Chapters 17 to 20   Date due:_____

Week 6: Read Chapters 21 to 25 + Appendix   Date due:_____

Eight Week Program
(See the instructions above regarding Group Study)

Week 1: Read Preface, Intro and Chapters 1 to 4   Date due:_____

Week 2: Read Chapters 5 to 8   Date due:_____

Week 3: Read Chapters 9 to 11   Date due:_____

Week 4: Read Chapters 12 to 14   Date due:_____

Week 5: Read Chapters 15 to 17   Date due:_____

Week 6: Read Chapters 18 to 20   Date due:_____

Week 7: Read Chapters 21 to 23   Date due:_____

Week 8: Read Chapters 24 and 25 + Appendix   Date due:_____

Twelve Week Program
(See the instructions above regarding Group Study)

Week 1: Read Preface, Intro and Chapters 1 to 3   Date due:_____

Week 2: Read Chapters 4 to 6   Date due:_____

Week 3: Read Chapters 7 and 8   Date due:_____

Week 4: Read Chapters 9 and 10   Date due:_____

Week 5: Read Chapters 11 and 12   Date due:_____

Week 6: Read Chapters 13 and 14   Date due:_____

Week 7: Read Chapters 15 and 16   Date due:_____

Week 8: Read Chapters 17 and 18   Date due:_____

Week 9: Read Chapters 19 to 21   Date due:_____

Week 10: Read Chapters 22 and 23   Date due:_____

Week 11: Read Chapters 24 and 25   Date due:_____

Week 12: Read Appendix   Date due:_____

ANCIENT WISDOM RELATED TO ANGER

The Book of Proverbs contains many passages related to the nature of conflict and provides abundant wisdom on how to understand and deal with our anger, as well as learn to deal with the anger of others. (Note: For easy reference, all the following passages are written out under Section VII)

I. The Many Faces of Unrighteous Anger

The Book of Proverbs presents a wide variety of words describing a number of types of angry people. Circle the ones that most reflect your personality.

• The Contentious One (Hebrew: *madown*)

This is the most common word for strife and contention. It speaks of a hot-tempered person who stirs up strife, discord and disagreements in others. (Proverbs 15:18; 16:28; 17:14; 18:18; 19:13; 21:9, 19; 22:10; 23:29; 25:24; 26:20-21; 27:15; 28:25; 29:22).

• The Divisive One (Hebrew: *medan*)

Related to the Contentious One (Hebrew: *madown*), this word focuses on the quarrelsome person who loves to sow discord and division, especially by bearing false reports about others (Proverbs 6:19; 10:12).

• The Snorting Fool (Hebrew: *aph*)

This is the quick-tempered person whose anger is quite visible (e.g. nose-snorting and rapid breathing). It is used to refer to a someone filled with anger, wrath and a nasty temper. Proverbs call this person to learn to become slow to anger (Proverbs 14:17, 29; 15:1, 18; 16:32; 19:11; 21:14; 22:24; 24:18; 27:4; 29:8, 22; 30:33).

• The Frustrated One (Hebrew: *ka'as*)

This is the extremely frustrated and grieving person whose sadness and disappointment provokes him or her to anger (Proverbs 12:16; 17:25; 21:9; 27:3).

• The Offended Rebel (Hebrew: *pasha*)

This is the person who is living in rebellion and breaking away from any authority. His or her revolts come in numerous forms of transgression (Proverbs 18:19).

- **The Backbiting Critic** (Hebrew: *za'am*)

This is the indignant person whose anger is often expressed in a torrent of biting and critical words directly to the person or behind their back. The anger, however, shows on his or her face (Proverbs 25:23).

- **The Explosive One** (Hebrew: *ebrah*)

This person's wrath is expressed in outbursts of excessive and overflowing anger, fury and wrath (Proverbs 11:4, 23; 14:35; 22:8).

- **The Trembling One** (Hebrew: *ragaz*)

The image is that of people who are so moved by anger they physically tremble and shake, like an earthquake (Proverbs 29:9; cf. 30:21)

- **The Roaring Lion** (Hebrew: *za'aph*)

Related to the Snorting Fool (Hebrew: *aph*), this person's consuming wrath has become as fierce as an enraged wild animal, breaking into a camp (Proverbs 19:12).

- **The Hot-Tempered Snake** (Hebrew: *chemah*)

This kind of venomous anger resembles the strike of a poisonous viper whose bite causes fever and death (Proverbs 6:34; 15:1; 15:18; 16:14; 19:19; 21:14; 22:24; 27:4; 29:22).

- **The Noisy Brawler** (Hebrew: *hamah*)

This is the person whose anger is expressed like a boisterous and drunken person, howling loudly and ready to fight with anyone in his or her way (Proverbs 1:21; 7:11; 9:13; 20:1; cf. 23:29-30).

- **The Mouthy Scoffer** (Hebrew: *luts*)

The root of the word presents the image of a mouth that is spilling out criticism. It refers to one who boastfully derides and mocks others and pushes them to respond in anger (Proverbs 1:22; 3:34; 9:7-8, 12; 14:6; 15:12; 19:25, 28-29; 20:1; 21:24; 22:10; 24:9).

- **The Harsh One** (Hebrew: *etseb*)

This is the person whose offensive anger has a primary objective to cause pain and sorrow (Proverbs 15:1).

• **The Argumentative One** (Hebrew: *riyb*)

Although sometimes this word can be used to speak of a man pleading his case; it is also used of a person who finds any reason to argue. He or she loves a good fight! (Proverbs 15:18; 17:1, 14; 18:6, 17; 20:3; 26:17; 30:33).

• **The Short-Fused One** (Hebrew: *qatser*)

This is the quick-tempered person who is easily angered and, instead of pursuing understanding, engages in any hasty scheme to get his or her own way (Proverbs 14:17, 29).

• **The Broken Spirited One** (Hebrew: *naka*)

This is the one who has been smitten and wounded over and over again and it affects his or her attitudes and actions toward others. Sometimes, in the midst of the pain, this person lashes out to hurt others (Proverbs 15:13; 17:22; 18:14).

• **The Hardened One** (Hebrew: *qashah*)

This is the one who, after a series of disappointments, has become stiff-necked and hard-headed. He or she is stubborn and quite difficult (Proverbs 28:14; 29:1).

A Further Observation:

Typical of Hebrew wisdom literature there is much overlap of these many faces of unrighteous anger. Sometimes more than one of these images is used in the same passage. For example:

> Proverbs 15:1 "A gentle answer turns away wrath ["venomous anger," Hebrew: *chemah*], but a harsh word stirs up anger ["rapid breathing, snorting," Hebrew: *aph*]."

> Proverbs 15:18 "A hot-tempered man ["with venomous anger," Hebrew: *chemah*] stirs up strife ["division, false reports," Hebrew: *madown*], but the slow to anger [slow to "rapid breathing, snorting," Hebrew: *aph*] calms a dispute ["an argument," Hebrew: *riyb*]."

> Proverbs 21:14 "A gift in secret subdues anger ["rapid breathing, snorting," Hebrew: *aph*], and a bribe in the bosom, strong wrath ["venomous anger," Hebrew: *chemah*]."

II. The Causes of Anger

According to the Book of Proverbs, the source of anger can be:

__ jealousy (6:34; 27:4)
__ hatred (10:12; 14:17)
__ intolerance of those who offend us (10:12)
__ unresolved bitterness (14:10)
__ over-reaction and emotional outbursts (14:17; 14:29; 15:18)
__ letting disagreements get out of hand (17:14)
__ failure to overlook sins of others (19:11)
__ alcohol, drugs, etc. (20:1)
__ pride and arrogance (21:24; 28:25)
__ hardened heart toward the Lord (28:14)

III. The Characteristics of the Quick-Tempered Person

According to the Book of Proverbs, the quick-tempered person:

__ chooses to be angry (11:23)
__ knows his own bitterness (14:10)
__ is arrogant and proud (14:16)
__ acts foolishly (14:17; 20:3; 27:3)
__ exalts folly (14:29)
__ speaks harshly (15:1)
__ stirs up and spreads strife (15:18; 16:28; 29:22; 30:33)
__ is hard to live with (17:1; 21:9; 25:24)
__ is deeply affected physically, emotionally and spiritually (17:22)
__ shall suffer as a result of his temper (19:19)
__ is repeatedly short-tempered (19:19)
__ has fierce wrath and anger "like a flood" (27:4)
__ can set a city "aflame" with his wrath (29:8)
__ over-reacts in anger during conversations with wise men (29:9)
__ always loses his temper (29:11)
__ often abounds in sin (29:22)
__ is forceful in his wrath (30:33)

IV. The Characteristics of the Person Who Is Slow to Anger

According to the Book of Proverbs, the one who is slow to anger:

__ loves even those who offend him/her (10:12)
__ shows great understanding (14:29)
__ speaks softly and gently (15:1)

__ pacifies contention and appeases strife (15:18)
__ doesn't stir up and spread strife (15:18; 16:28; 29:22; 30:33)
__ shows strength and self-control (16:32)
__ is pleasant to live with (17:1; 21:9; 25:24)
__ stops a disagreement before it gets out of control (17:14)
__ is healthier physically, emotionally and spiritually (17:22; 18:14
__ doesn't provoke others to anger (20:2)
__ minds his own business (26:17)
__ doesn't get involved in others' disputes (26:17)
__ is trusting the Lord (28:14, 26)
__ doesn't over-react in anger (29:9)
__ holds back his temper (29:11)
__ is less apt to sin than the quick-tempered man (29:22)

V. How to Control My Anger

According to the Book of Proverbs, I must:

__ learn to love those that sin against me (10:12)
__ learn to be more understanding of others (14:29)
__ realize that my anger is contagious (15:1; 22:24-25)
__ learn to lower my voice when upset or angry (15:1)
__ stop the quarrel before it gets out of hand (17:14)
__ overlook small offenses and don't over-react (19:11)
__ realize my inability to control my own anger (19:19)
__ realize that acting in anger is much easier than self-control (20:3)
__ stay away from others who are easily angered (20:3; 21:9; 22:24-25)
__ learn self-control (25:28)
__ not get involved in other's disputes (26:17)
__ trust in the Lord to keep from being angry (28:26)
__ seek wisdom to turn away from wrath (29:8)

VI. How to Deal with Others Who Are Angry

According to the Book of Proverbs, in order to deal with others who are angry, I must:

__ love them (10:12; 21:14)
__ speak gently and softly to them (15:1)
__ acknowledge that some situations take time to heal (18:19)
__ not provoke them by doing what I know angers them (20:2)
__ stay away from them, as best I can (20:3; 21:9; 22:24-25)
__ give gifts to them (love in action!) (21:14)
__ drive them out if anger persists and no repentance is evident (22:10)

___ leave them alone until they have had time to cool off (22:24-25)
___ not meddle in a dispute or call others to take sides (26:17)
___ not talk behind their backs about them or the incident (26:20)
___ seek wisdom to turn away their wrath (29:8)

VII. Ancient Wisdom Related to Anger

As you read through each one of these gems from the Book of Proverbs, put an **X** next to those that are of particular help to you as you learn to deal with your anger on a daily basis. Put an **M** next to the ones you would like to memorize.

___ Proverbs 1:21-22

At the head of the noisy *streets* she cries out; at the entrance of the gates in the city she utters her sayings: "How long, O naive ones, will you love being simple-minded? And scoffers delight themselves in scoffing and fools hate knowledge?

___ Proverbs 3:34

Though He scoffs at the scoffers, yet He gives grace to the afflicted.

___ Proverbs 6:12, 14-15

A worthless person, a wicked man, is the one who . . . walks with a perverse mouth . . . who with perversity in his heart continually devises evil, who spreads strife. Therefore his calamity will come suddenly. Instantly he will be broken and there will be no healing.

___ Proverbs 6:16-19

There are six things which the Lord hates. Yes, seven which are an abomination to Him: Haughty eyes, a lying tongue, and hands that shed innocent blood, a heart that devises wicked plans, feet that run rapidly to evil, a false witness who utters lies, and one who spreads strife among brothers.

___ Proverbs 6:34

For jealousy enrages a man, and he will not spare in the day of vengeance.

__ Proverbs 7:11

She is boisterous and rebellious, her feet do not remain at home.

__ Proverbs 9:7-8

He who corrects a scoffer gets dishonor for himself, and he who reproves a wicked man gets insults for himself. Do not reprove a scoffer, or he will hate you, Reprove a wise man and he will love you.

__ Proverbs 9:12

If you are wise, you are wise for yourself, and if you scoff, you alone will bear it.

__ Proverbs 9:13

The woman of folly is boisterous. She is naive and knows nothing.

__ Proverbs 10:12

Hatred stirs up strife, but love covers all transgressions.

__ Proverbs 11:4

Riches do not profit in the day of wrath, but righteousness delivers from death.

__ Proverbs 11:23

The desire of the righteous is only good, but the expectation of the wicked is wrath.

__ Proverbs 12:16

A fool's anger is known at once, but a prudent man conceals dishonor.

__ Proverbs 12:25

Anxiety in a man's heart weighs it down, but a good word makes it glad.

__ Proverbs 13:10

Through insolence comes nothing but strife, but wisdom is with those who receive counsel.

__ Proverbs 14:6

A scoffer seeks wisdom and finds none, but knowledge is easy to one who has understanding.

__ Proverbs 14:10

The heart knows its own bitterness, and a stranger does not share its joy.

__ Proverbs 14:16-17

A wise man is cautious and turns away from evil, but a fool is arrogant and careless. A quick-tempered man acts foolishly, and a man of evil devices is hated.

__ Proverbs 14:29

He who is slow to anger has great understanding, but he who is quick-tempered exalts folly.

__ Proverbs 14:35

The king's favor is toward a servant who acts wisely, but his anger is toward him who acts shamefully.

__ Proverbs 15:1

A gentle answer turns away wrath, but a harsh word stirs up anger.

__ Proverbs 15:12

A scoffer does not love one who reproves him. He will not go to the wise.

__ Proverbs 15:13

A joyful heart makes a cheerful face, but when the heart is sad, the spirit is broken.

__ Proverbs 15:18

A hot-tempered man stirs up strife, but the slow to anger calms a dispute.

__ Proverbs 16:14

The fury of a king is like messengers of death, but a wise man will appease it.

__ Proverbs 16:28

A perverse man spreads strife, and a slanderer separates intimate friends.

__ Proverbs 16:32

He who is slow to anger is better than the mighty, and he who rules his spirit, than he who captures a city.

__ Proverbs 17:1

Better is a dry morsel and quietness with it than a house full of feasting with strife.

__ Proverbs 17:14

The beginning of strife is like letting out water, so abandon the quarrel before it breaks out.

__ Proverbs 17:19

He who loves transgression loves strife; he who raises his door seeks destruction.

— Proverbs 17:22

A joyful heart is good medicine, but a broken spirit dries up the bones.

— Proverbs 17:25

A foolish son is a grief to his father and bitterness to her who bore him.

__ Proverbs 18:1

He who separates himself seeks his own desire, he quarrels against all sound wisdom.

__ Proverbs 18:6

A fool's lips bring strife, and his mouth calls for blows.

__ Proverbs 18:14

The spirit of a man can endure his sickness, but as for a broken spirit who can bear it?

— Proverbs 18:17-19

The first to plead his case seems right, until another comes and examines him. The cast lot puts an end to strife and decides between the mighty ones. A brother offended is harder to be won than a strong city, and contentions are like the bars of a citadel.

— Proverbs 19:3

The foolishness of man ruins his way, and his heart rages against the Lord.

__ Proverbs 19:11-13

A man's discretion makes him slow to anger, and it is his glory to overlook a transgression. The king's wrath is like the roaring of a lion, but his favor is like dew on the grass. A foolish son is destruction to his father, and the contentions of a wife are a constant dripping.

__ Proverbs 19:19

A man of great anger will bear the penalty, for if you rescue him, you will only have to do it again.

__ Proverbs 19:25

Strike a scoffer and the naive may become shrewd, but reprove one who has understanding and he will gain knowledge.

__ Proverbs 19:28-29

A rascally witness makes a mockery of justice, and the mouth of the wicked spreads iniquity. Judgments are prepared for scoffers, and blows for the back of fools.

__ Proverbs 20:1

Wine is a mocker, strong drink a brawler, and whoever is intoxicated by it is not wise.

__ Proverbs 20:2-3

The terror of a king is like the growling of a lion; he who provokes him to anger forfeits his own life. Keeping away from strife is an honor for a man, but any fool will quarrel.

__ Proverbs 21:9

It is better to live in a corner of a roof than in a house shared with a contentious woman.

__ Proverbs 21:14

A gift in secret subdues anger, and a bribe in the bosom, strong wrath.

__ Proverbs 21:19

It is better to live in a desert land than with a contentious and vexing woman.

__ Proverbs 21:24

"Proud," "Haughty," "Scoffer," are his names, who acts with insolent pride.

__ Proverbs 22:8

He who sows iniquity will reap vanity, and the rod of his fury will perish.

__ Proverbs 22:10

Drive out the scoffer, and contention will go out, even strife and dishonor will cease.

__ Proverbs 22:24-25

Do not associate with a man *given* to anger; or go with a hot-tempered man, or you will learn his ways and find a snare for yourself.

__ Proverbs 23:29-30

Who has woe? Who has sorrow? Who has contentions? Who has complaining? Who has wounds without cause? Who has redness of eyes? Those who linger long over wine, those who go to taste mixed wine.

__ Proverbs 24:9

The devising of folly is sin, and the scoffer is an abomination to men.

__ Proverbs 24:17-18

Do not rejoice when your enemy falls, and do not let your heart be glad when he stumbles; or the Lord will see it and be displeased, and turn His anger away from him.

__ Proverbs 25:20

Like one who takes off a garment on a cold day, or like vinegar on soda, is he who sings songs to a troubled heart.

__ Proverbs 25:23

The north wind brings forth rain, and a backbiting tongue, an angry countenance.

__ Proverbs 25:24

It is better to live in a corner of the roof than in a house shared with a contentious woman.

__ Proverbs 25:28

Like a city that is broken into and without walls is a man who has no control over his spirit.

__ Proverbs 26:17

Like one who takes a dog by the ears is he who passes by and meddles with strife not belonging to him.

__ Proverbs 26:20-21

For lack of wood the fire goes out, and where there is no whisperer, contention quiets down. Like charcoal to hot embers and wood to fire, so is a contentious man to kindle strife.

__ Proverbs 27:3-4

A stone is heavy and the sand weighty, but the provocation of a fool is heavier than both of them. Wrath is fierce and anger is a flood, but who can stand before jealousy?

__ Proverbs 27:15

A constant dripping on a day of steady rain and a contentious woman are alike.

__ Proverbs 28:14

How blessed is the man who fears always, but he who hardens his heart will fall into calamity.

__ Proverbs 28:25-26

An arrogant man stirs up strife, but he who trusts in the Lord will prosper. He who trusts in his own heart is a fool, but he who walks wisely will be delivered.

— Proverbs 29:1

A man who hardens his neck after much reproof will suddenly be broken beyond remedy.

__ Proverbs 29:8-9

Scorners set a city aflame, but wise men turn away anger. When a wise man has a controversy with a foolish man, the foolish man either rages or laughs, and there is no rest.

___ Proverbs 29:11

A fool always loses his temper, but a wise man holds it back.

___ Proverbs 29:22

An angry man stirs up strife, and a hot-tempered man abounds in transgression.

___ Proverbs 30:33

For the churning of milk produces butter, and pressing the nose brings forth blood; so the churning of anger produces strife.

For Further Study:

Wise Living in a Foolish Age: Studies in the Book of Proverbs

(Available through JARON Ministries International, Inc. www.jaron.org)

A LIFE SKILLS OUTLINE
FOR GETTING ALONG WITH OTHERS

A BIBLICAL GUIDE TO
LIVING IN PEACE WITH OTHERS

1 Peter 3:8-12 "To sum up, let all be harmonious, sympathetic, brotherly, kindhearted, and humble in spirit; not returning evil for evil, or insult for insult, but giving a blessing instead; for you were called for the very purpose that you might inherit a blessing. For, "Let him who means to love life and see good days refrain his tongue from evil and his lips from speaking guile." And let him turn away from evil and do good; Let him seek peace and pursue it. "For the eyes of the Lord are upon the righteous, and His ears attend to their prayer, but the face of the Lord is against those who do evil."

I. The Magnitude of the Need for Getting Along With Others

1 Peter 3:8 "To sum up, let all be harmonious, sympathetic, brotherly, kindhearted, and humble in spirit . . ."

II. The Method for Getting Along With Others (Part One)

Principle #1: Look for common ground.

1 Peter 3:8 "let all be harmonious . . ."

Principle #2: Enter into the world of their feelings.

1 Peter 3:8 "let all be . . . .sympathetic . . . "

Principle #3: Treat all people as important.

1 Peter 3:8 "let all be . . . brotherly . . ."

Principle #4: Be gutsy enough to forgive.

1 Peter 3:8 "let all be . . . kindhearted . . ."

Principle #5: Stop looking out for number one.

1 Peter 3:8 "let all be . . . humble in spirit . . ."

Principle #6: Don't bite back.

1 Peter 3:9 "not returning evil for evil, or insult for insult . . ."

Principle #7: Retaliate with a blessing.

1 Peter 3:9 "but giving a blessing instead . . ."

III. The Motivation for Getting Along With Others (Part One)

Motivation #1: Getting along with others is the natural response to God's supernatural blessing in my life.

1 Peter 3:9 "for you were called for the very purpose that you might inherit a blessing." (cf. Psalm 34:12-17)

Motivation #2: Getting along with others is my ticket to a long and happy life.

1 Peter 3:10 For, "Let him who means to love life and see good days refrain his tongue from evil and his lips from speaking guile . . . " (cf. Ecclesiastes 2:17-18)

IV. The Method for Getting Along With Others (Part Two)

We now continue from Section II with five more principles:

Principle #8: Muzzle my mouth.

1 Peter 3:10 "Let him who means to love life and see good days refrain his tongue from evil and his lips from speaking guile." (cf. Proverbs 18:4, 7, 21; James 3:8; Psalm 39:1; Psalm 141:3)

Principle #9: Swerve to avoid a collision.

1 Peter 3:11 "And let him turn away from evil . . ." (cf. Proverbs 20:3; 17:14)

Principle #10: Do the right thing.

1 Peter 3:11 "And let him turn away from evil and do good . . ." (cf. James 4:17; Galatians 6:9)

Principle #11: Be a peace-chaser.

1 Peter 3:11b "Let him seek peace and pursue it." (cf. Matthew 5:9; Hebrews 12:14)

V. The Motivation for Getting Along With Others (Part Two)

1 Peter 3:12 "For the eyes of the Lord are upon the righteous, and His ears attend to their prayer, but the face of the Lord is against those who do evil."

We now continue from Section III with three more motivations:

Motivation #3: God's loving eyes are watching us.

1 Peter 3:12 "For the eyes of the Lord are upon the righteous . . ."

Motivation #4: God's attentive ears are listening to us.

1 Peter 3:12 "His ears attend to their prayer . . ." (cf. Psalm 34:15; 102:1)

Motivation #5: God's angry face is set against those who do evil.

1 Peter 3:12 "but the face of the Lord is against those who do evil."

Your Assignment:

1. Which of the eleven principles for getting along with others most applies to you?

   Principle # ___. _____

   Principle # ___. _____

   Principle # ___. _____

2. Which of the five motivations most challenge you to get along with others?

   Motivation # ___. _____

   Motivation # ___. _____

(Continued on next page)

3. With this outline in mind, read 1 Peter 3:8-12 in three different Bible translations.

4. Pick a version you most like and read 1 Peter 3:8-12 five more times.

For Further Study:

Getting Along With People (message series available at www.jaron.org)

THE TASTE TEST
FOR GODLY SPEECH

Ephesians 4:29 "Let no unwholesome word proceed from your mouth, but only such a word as is good for edification according to the need of the moment, so that it will give grace to those who hear."

Before you enter a conversation, ask yourself the following questions:

Question #1: Is what I am about to say good for edification?

1. Is what I am about to say intended to build up or destroy?
2. Is it intended to lash out and hurt or to restore?
3. Is it good for their emotional and spiritual progress?
4. Am I about to attack the person or the problem?
5. Does what I am about to say bring hope for resolution?
6. Will these words feed or starve the soul? (Proverbs 10:21)
7. Am I about to use "loaded" words? (Galatians 5:15)
8. Am I just "digging up the dirt?" (Proverbs 16:27)

Question #2: Is what I am about to say according to the need of the moment?

1. Is what I'm about to say fitting for the occasion? Is it timely?
2. Does it really need to be said?
3. Should this be said at another time?
4. Is there a better way to say it? (Proverbs 12:18; Matthew 12:36-37)

Question #3: Will what I am about to say give grace to those who hear?

1. Does the way I'm communicating "minister grace" to others?
2. Does what I am saying benefit those who listen?
3. Are my words a well-packaged grace-gift?

For Further Study:

Taming the Tongue (message series available at www.jaron.org)

A WORKSHEET FOR RESOLVING CONFLICT

Ten Rules for Fighting Fair

Quickly review this list. (A more detailed discussion is found in Chapter Thirteen, titled *Gardening Tips for Dealing with Anger Daily* and Chapter Fourteen, titled *More Gardening Tips for Dealing with Anger*).

Rule #1: Be more tolerant of other shortcomings. "Lighten up!" (Proverbs 19:11; 1 Peter 4:8)

Rule #2: Don't provoke others to anger. "Don't push each other's button!" (Proverbs 20:2; Ephesians 6:4)

Rule #3: Don't knowingly put yourself in a situation where you know you'll get angry. "Don't grab the dog by the ear!" (Proverbs 20:3; 22:24-25; 26:17)

Rule #4: Stop a quarrel before it gets out of control. "Don't let the water out of the dam!" (Proverbs 17:14)

Rule #5: Don't talk behind another's back. "Don't rally troops!" (Proverbs 26:20)

Rule #6: Think before you talk. "Engage your brain before opening your mouth!" (Ephesians 4:29)

Rule #7: Lower your voice. "Talk to the others as if you are talking to God!" (Proverbs 15:1)

Rule #8: Forgive and seek forgiveness. "Be the first to ask forgiveness!" (Matthew 5:21-24; Ephesians 4:31-32)

Rule #9: Consider other's needs as more important than your own. "Let others have it their way!" (Philippians 2:3-4)

Rule #10: Love in word and deed. "Soothe the other person with a gift in secret!" (Proverbs 10:12; 21:14)

Now, continue on with the following worksheet for resolving conflict.

1. Describe briefly the specific nature of the conflict:

2. Which of the above rules for fighting fair do you feel you violated?

3. Which do you feel were violated by the other person with whom you are in conflict?

Read thoughtfully through the following list of "one another" statements:

3. Place an **X** next to those which you feel the other person has done toward you. Put an **O** next to those which you feel you have violated in your conflict with the other person. Where applicable, in the space between each point write a few words of personal application to your present conflict.

What God Wants Us <u>To Do</u>

__ Abound in love for one another (1 Thessalonians 3:12; John 13:34-35; 15: 12, 17).

__ Accept, receive and welcome one another (Romans 15:7).

__ Admonish (warn) one another (Romans 15:14).

__ Be at peace with one another (1 Thessalonians 5:13; cf. Mark 9:50).

__ Be devoted to one another in brotherly love (Romans 12:10).

__ Be hospitable to one another (Mark 9:50; 1 Peter 4:9; Romans 12:13).

__ Be kind to one another (Ephesians 4:32).

__ Be of the same mind toward one another (Roman 12:16; 15:5; Philippians 2:2-4).

__ Bear one another's burdens (Galatians 6:2).

__ Be sincere in your genuine love for one another (1 Peter 1:23).

__ Be tender-hearted towards one another (Ephesians 4:32).

__ Be willing to be wronged by one another (1 Corinthians 6:7).

__ Bear with one another (Colossians 3:13).

__ Build up (edify) one another (Romans 14:19).

__ Clothe yourself with humility toward one another (1 Peter 5:5).

__ Come together and wait for one another (1 Corinthians 11:33).

__ Comfort one another (1 Thessalonians 4:18).

__ Confess your faults to one another (James 5:16).

__ Contribute to the (financial) needs of one another (Romans 12:13).

__ Encourage (come alongside) one another (1 Thessalonians 5:11; Hebrews 3:13; 10:25).

__ Fellowship with one another (1 John 1:7).

__ Forgive one another, just as you have been forgiven by God (Colossians 3:13; Ephesians 4:32).

__ Give preference to one another (Romans 12:10).

__ Greet one another (Romans 16:16; 1 Peter 4:10; 5:14; 1 Corinthians 16:20).

__ Love (value and self-sacrifice for) one another (Romans 12:9-10; 1 Peter 4:8; John 13:34; 15:12-17; 1 John 3:11, 23; 4:7, 11-12; 2 John 1:5).

__ Pray for one another (James 5:16).

__ Pursue peace with one another (Romans 14:19).

__ Rebuke one another (Luke 17:3).

__ Recognize that God is actively teaching us how to love one another (1 Thessalonians 4:9).

__ Regard one another as more important than yourself (Philippians 2:3).

__ Restore one another (Galatians 6:1).

__ Seek after that which is good for one another (1 Thessalonians 5:15).

__ Serve one another (Galatians 5:13).

__ Show patience toward one another (Ephesians 4:2).

— Speak to one another as if it were a song or a prayer to the Lord (Ephesians 5:19).

__ Speak truth to one another (Ephesians 5:25).

__ Stimulate one another to love and good deeds (Hebrews 10:24).

__ Submit to one another (Ephesians 5:21; 1 Peter 5:5).

__ Teach and exhort one another (Colossians 3:13,16; Hebrews 3:13).

__ Treat one another as part of God's family (Romans 12:5).

__ Use your God-given gifts to serve one another (1 Peter 4:10; Galatians 5:13).

__ Wash one another's feet (i.e. be a Christ-like servant toward the other) (John 13:14).

What God Wants Us **Not** To Do

__ Don't allow division between one another (1 Corinthians 12:25).

__ Don't assume you are wiser than the other person (Romans 12:16).

__ Don't bite and devour one another (Galatians 5:15).

__ Don't cause one another to stumble (to sin) (Romans 14:13; 1 Corinthians 12:25).

__ Don't challenge one another (Galatians 5:26).

__ Don't complain against one another (James 5:9).

__ Don't deprive one another (sexually-speaking, for married couples) (1 Corinthians 7:5).

___ Don't do anything to one another from a heart of selfishness or empty conceit (Philippians 2:3).

___ Don't envy one another (Galatians 5:26).

___ Don't examine one another without first examining yourself (Galatians 6:4).

___ Don't harden one another by the deceitfulness of sin (Hebrews 3:13).

___ Don't hate one another (Titus 3:3).

___ Don't hold a grudge against one another (1 Peter 4:8).

___ Don't injure one another (Acts 7:26).

___ Don't judge one another (Matthew 7:1; Romans 14:13; James 4:11).

___ Don't let pride keep you from one another (1 Peter 5:5).

___ Don't let the day end being angry at one another (Galatians 5:26).

___ Don't lie to one another (Colossians 3:9).

___ Don't make it a habit to be separate from one another (in church, fellowship, etc.) (Hebrews 10:25).

___ Don't provoke one another (Galatians 5:26).

___ Don't repay one another with evil for evil (1 Thessalonians 5:15).

___ Don't revert to the evil you used to do (Titus 3:3).

___ Don't speak evil against one another (James 4:11).

— Don't turn your freedom into an opportunity to sin against one another (Galatians 5:13).

Now go to that person today and do what you know God wants you to do!

> James 1:19-22 "This you know, my beloved brethren. But everyone must be quick to hear, slow to speak and slow to anger; for the anger of man does not achieve the righteousness of God. Therefore, putting aside all filthiness and all that remains of wickedness, in humility receive the word implanted, which is able to save your

souls. But prove yourselves doers of the word, and not merely hearers who delude themselves."

James 4:1-3 "What is the source of quarrels and conflicts among you? Is not the source your pleasures that wage war in your members? You lust and do not have; so you commit murder. You are envious and cannot obtain; so you fight and quarrel. You do not have because you do not ask. You ask and do not receive, because you ask with wrong motives, so that you may spend it on your pleasures."

Ephesians 4:26-27 "Be angry, and yet do not sin; do not let the sun go down on your anger, and do not give the devil an opportunity.

Write a summary of what you will do next to resolve this conflict:

_____

_____

_____

_____

_____

_____

_____

_____

_____

_____

_____

_____

CONNECTED TO THE VINE

A Study Outline of John 15:1-11

The Parable of the Vineyard

Ancient Israel is often pictured in the Bible as a vine and a vineyard (cf. Psalm 80:8-19; Jeremiah 2:21-22; Ezekiel 15:1-8; Isaiah 5:1-7). When the relationship between the tribes of Israel and God, the Vinedresser, was healthy Israel was a fruitful vine. When it was unhealthy, the nation of Israel shriveled up and became fruitless.

Isaiah 5:1-7

> *Let me sing now for my well-beloved*
> *A song of my beloved concerning His vineyard.*
> *My well-beloved had a vineyard on a fertile hill.*
> *He dug it all around, removed its stones,*
> *And planted it with the choicest vine.*
> *And He built a tower in the middle of it*
> *And also hewed out a wine vat in it;*
> *Then He expected it to produce good grapes,*
> *But it produced only worthless ones.*
> *And now, O inhabitants of Jerusalem and men of Judah,*
> *Judge between Me and My vineyard.*
> *What more was there to do for My vineyard that I have not done in it?*
> *Why, when I expected it to produce good grapes did it produce worthless ones?*
> *So now let Me tell you what I am going to do to My vineyard:*
> *I will remove its hedge and it will be consumed;*
> *I will break down its wall and it will become trampled ground.*
> *I will lay it waste;*
> *It will not be pruned or hoed,*
> *But briars and thorns will come up.*
> *I will also charge the clouds to rain no rain on it.*
> *For the vineyard of the LORD of hosts is the house of Israel*
> *And the men of Judah His delightful plant.*
> *Thus He looked for justice, but behold, bloodshed;*
> *For righteousness, but behold, a cry of distress.*

The Allegory of the Vine, the Vinedresser and the Branches

John 15:1-11

> *I am the true vine, and My Father is the vinedresser. Every branch in Me that does not bear fruit, He takes away; and every branch that bears fruit, He prunes it so that it may bear more fruit. You are already clean because of the word which I have spoken to you. Abide in Me, and I in you. As the branch cannot bear fruit of itself unless it abides in the vine, so neither can you unless you abide in Me. I am the vine, you are the branches; he who abides in Me and I in him, he bears much fruit, for apart from Me you can do nothing. If anyone does not abide in Me, he is thrown away as a branch and dries up; and they gather them, and cast them into the fire and they are burned. If you abide in Me, and My words abide in you, ask whatever you wish, and it will be done for you. My Father is glorified by this, that you bear much fruit, and so prove to be My disciples. Just as the Father has loved Me, I have also loved you; abide in My love. If you keep My commandments, you will abide in My love; just as I have kept My Father's commandments and abide in His love. These things I have spoken to you so that My joy may be in you, and that your joy may be made full*

I. Connected to the Vine: God, the Son (John 15:1)

John 15:1 "**I AM** the true vine . . . " (emphasis added)

Some of us have attached ourselves to the wrong vine.

> Colossians 2:6-7 "Therefore as you have received Christ Jesus the Lord, so walk in Him, having been firmly rooted and now being built up in Him and established in your faith, just as you were instructed, and overflowing with gratitude."

A. The True Vine: Jesus the Messiah (*Yeshua ha Mashiach*)

John 15:1 "I am the true vine . . ."

To attach to anything or anyone else in order to be fruitful human beings is futile and empty.

B. The Right Connection: Putting Our Faith in Jesus Christ Alone

C. The Visible Fruit: Our Good Deeds That Glorify God

The healthy Christian produces:
1. The fruit of good works (Titus 3:14; Colossians 1:10)
2. The fruit of repentance (Matthew 3:8)
3. The fruit of the Spirit (Galatians 5:22-23)
4. The fruit of evangelism (1 Corinthians 16:15)
5. The fruit of praise (Hebrews 13:15)
6. The fruit of righteousness (Hebrews 12:11)
7. The kind of fruit that glorifies God (John 15:8)

John 15:8 "My Father is glorified by this, that you bear much fruit, and so prove to be My disciples."

II. Corrected by the Vinedresser: God, the Father (John 15:1)

A. The Skilled Farmer: Our Heavenly Father

1. His Role: To Take Care of the Vineyard

John 15:1 "My Father is the vinedresser" [Greek: *georgos*, meaning "one who tills the soil."]

The Vinedresser had three primary responsibilities:
• To make sure the branches are rightly connected to a healthy vine.
• To regularly feed and water the vines.
• To prune (clean) the vine as necessary.

2. His Process: Pruning the Branches

There is no fruitful correction by the Father unless there is eternal connection to the Father, through faith in Jesus Christ.

III. Condition of the Branches: Kinds of Disciples (John 15:2-3)

A. Dead Branches That Bear No Fruit

John 15:2 "Every branch in Me that does not bear fruit, He takes away ["cuts off, lifts up," Greek: *airo*]..."

> **View #1:** The fruitless branches are true believers who lose their salvation. The Vinedresser cuts them off.
>> **The problem:** John 10:28 – No one can pluck a true believer out of the Father's hand (cf. John 15:6)

246

View #2: The fruitless branches are true believers who are "lifted up" [Greek: *airo*] and encouraged to bear fruit.

> **The problem:** John 15:6—They (not their fruit) are gathered, cast into the fire and burned.

View #3: The fruitless branches are non-abiding unbelievers (Judas-like disciples) who will be cast in the Lake of Fire. This view holds that a "fruitless Christian" is a contradiction.

John 13:10 ". . . you are clean but not all of you . . ." (referring to Judas, the Betrayer).

John 15:4 "Abide in Me, and I in you. As the branch cannot bear fruit of itself unless it abides in the vine, so neither can you unless you abide in Me."

John 15:4 ". . . the branch cannot bear fruit by itself . . ."

John 15:6 "If anyone does not abide in Me, he is thrown away as a [lit. the] branch [like Judas] and dries up; and they gather them, and cast them into the fire [the Lake of Fire] and they are burned."

John 15:8 "My Father is glorified by this, that you bear much fruit, *and so prove to be My disciples*" (cf. 1 John 2:19; 2 Corinthians 13:5; Romans 8:16, emphasis added).

Note: The word disciple [Greek: *mathetes*] can refer to a learner or even follower but not necessarily a true believer (John 6:66; 12:4; 13:10;15:2-3; cf. Romans 11:16-24; Ephesians 3:10; James 2:17; Matthew 7:17, 20).

> **The problem:** Some teach that the phrase "in me" (John 15:4-7) refers to refers to true believers; not unbelievers.

(In my opinion, View #2 or View #3 are the best options, biblically and theologically)

B. Living Branches That Bear Fruit

John 15:2-3 ". . . and every branch that bears fruit, He prunes it so that it may bear more fruit. You are already clean because of the word which I have spoken to you."

The Four Kinds of Living Branches (Disciples)

1. Those that bear <u>some</u> fruit
2. Those that bear <u>more</u> fruit
3. Those that bear <u>much</u> fruit
4. Those that bear <u>lasting</u> fruit

The Vinedresser (God the Father) cuts off [Greek: *airo*] fruitless disciples and prunes [Greek: *kathareo*] fruitful disciples.

Pruning the Living Branches

1. The Purpose of Pruning

The Vinedresser (God the Father) prunes us in order to...

. . . direct our spiritual growth in the right direction
. . . bring our lopsided lives into balance
. . . prevent the weight of our sin from breaking other branches
. . . keep us small, humble and fruitful
. . . rejuvenate our lives when we become old and sapless trees
. . . allow more of the Son's light to nourish us
. . . correct or repair the damage sin has caused us
. . . remove diseased branches (the phony disciples) from our midst
. . . increase our spiritual productivity and fruitfulness
. . . keep us healthy and free of disease

2. The Practice of Pruning

a. His Pruning Tool: The Word of God

The Vinedresser (God, the Father) prunes genuine disciples of the True Vine by driving them to the Word of God.

John 15:3 "You are already clean [lit. pruned] because of the word which I have spoken to you."

b. His Pruning Methods

> • God often uses trials to drive us to His Word for pruning (James 1:2-4).

> • God also uses other believers to drive us to His Word for pruning. (Hebrews 10:24-25).

> • God uses anything and everything in our lives to drive us to His Word which trims away the things that destroy our ability to bear fruit. (Hebrews 12:10-11).

"Prune my life, Lord. In the name of Jesus Christ: the True Vine in whom I am eternally connected and for whom I will be lovingly corrected."

IV. Abiding in the Vine: Jesus Christ (John 15:4-8)

A. The Nature of Abiding (John 15:4)

Jesus is calling us to rightly connect to Him and, once rightly connected, to continually abide in Him.

John 15:4 "Abide in Me, and I in you. As the branch cannot bear fruit of itself unless it abides in the vine, so neither can you unless you abide [Greek: *meno*, meaning live, abide, remain, persevere] in Me."

Abiding Principle #1: Abiding in Christ is a choice.

John 15:4 "Abide in me . . ."

"Lord, I *choose* to abide in You."

Abiding Principle #2: Abiding in Christ is reciprocal.

John 15:4 "Abide in Me, and I in you."

James 4:8 "Draw near to God and He will draw near to you."

"Lord, *close* the gap between You and me today."

Abiding in Christ is choosing to continually walk in joyful intimacy with Him, so that Christ's life flows through me in fruitful living.

Abiding Principle #3: I am abiding in Christ when I am in intimate fellowship with Him.

John 6:56 "He who (continually) eats my flesh and (continually) drinks my blood abides in Me and I in him." Simply stated, this is a call to an abiding and lifelong personal and intimate relationship with Jesus.

Abiding Principle #4: I am abiding in Christ when I am walking as Christ walked.

1 John 2:6 "The one who says he abides in Him ought himself to walk in the same manner as He walked."

"Lord Jesus, no matter what I face I want to do what You Jesus would do."

B. The Result Of Abiding (John 15:5-8)

John 15:5 "for apart from Me you can do nothing." (cf. Hosea 14:8 "From Me comes your fruit.")

The goal of the Christian life is abiding; the result is fruit.

The Ten Results of Abiding Intimately In Christ

Result #1: We will see the fruit of good works.

cf. Colossians 1:9-10 regarding bearing fruit "in every good work."

James 2:14 "Faith without works is dead . . . being by itself."

Abiding in Christ shows!

Result #2: We will see the fruit of repentance.

Matthew 3:8 "Therefore bear fruit in keeping with repentance..."

- True repentance involves admitting we have sinned.

- True repentance involves confessing and agreeing with God.

- True repentance involves returning to God from sin.

Result #3: We will see the fruit of the Spirit.

Galatians 5:22-23 "The fruit of the Spirit is love, joy, peace, patience, kindness, goodness, faithfulness, gentleness, and self-control . . ."

Result #4: We will see the fruit of evangelism.

We will see new converts. (cf. John 4:31-36 and 1 Corinthians 16:15 regarding the "first-fruits of Achaia").

Result #5: We will see the fruit of praise.

Hebrews 13:15 speaks of "the sacrifice of praise to God, that is, the fruit of the lips that give thanks to His name."

Result #6: We will see the fruit of righteousness.

Hebrews 12:11 "All discipline for the moment seems not to be joyful, but sorrowful; yet to those who have been trained by it, afterwards it yields the peaceful fruit of righteousness."

Result #7: We will see the fruit of giving.

When we abide in the Vine, one of the results is a greater desire to contribute (cf. Romans 15:28 where generosity is called "this fruit").

Result #8: We will see more answered prayer.

John 15:7 "If you abide in Me, and My words abide in you, ask whatever you wish, and it will be done for you." (cf. James 5:16)

The impact of our prayer lives is directly related to the depth of our abiding.

Result #9: We will see the kind of fruit that glorifies God.

John 15:8 "My Father is glorified by this, that you bear much fruit, and so prove to be My disciples."

Fruit is any thought, attitude or action God values and brings glory to Him.

> 1. The glory of God was Jesus' reason for being on earth (John 17:4).

2. The glory of God is our reason for being here on earth, as well. (Matthew 5:16; 1 Peter 2:12).

Result #10: We will see the evidence we are truly disciples of Christ.

John 15:8 "My Father is glorified by this, that you bear much fruit, and so prove to be My disciples."

What do I see in our my life I can legitimately call the "fruit of abiding"?

John 15:2 ". . . every branch that bears fruit, He prunes it, that it may bear more fruit."

John 15:8 "By this is My Father glorified that you bear much fruit . . ."

V. Abiding in His Love (John 15:9-11)

Abiding in Christ is choosing to continually walk in joyful intimacy with Him, so that Christ's life flows through us in fruitful living.

A. Accepting His Love

John 15:9 "Just as the Father has loved Me, I have also loved you; abide in My love . . . ."

John 15:12 "This is My commandment, that you love one another, just as I have loved you."

1 John 4:16 "We have *come to know* and *have believed* the love which God has for us. God is love, and the one who abides in love abides in God, and God abides in him" (emphasis added).

1 John 3:1 "See how great a love the Father has bestowed on us, that we would be called children of God; and such we are . . . ."

Romans 8:38-39 "For I am convinced that neither death, nor life, nor angels, nor principalities, nor things present, nor things to come, nor powers, nor height, nor depth, nor any other created thing, will be able to separate us from the love of God, which is in Christ Jesus our Lord."

B. Obeying His Commands

John 15:10 "If you keep My commandments, you will abide in My love; just as I have kept My Father's commandments, and abide in His love."

John 14:15 "If you love Me you will keep my commandments."

John 15:14 "You are My friends, if you do what I command you."

1 John 2:4-5 "The one who says, 'I have come to know Him,' and does not keep His commandments, is a liar, and the truth is not in him; but whoever keeps His word, in him the love of God has truly been perfected. By this we know that we are in Him . . ."

C. Experiencing His Joy

John 15:11 "These things I have spoken to you, that My joy may be in you, and that your joy may be made full."

Joy is the deep settled confidence that God is in control of the details of my life.

1. We Experience His Joy in Us.

John 16:20-24 "Truly, truly, I say to you, that you will weep and lament, but the world will rejoice; you will grieve, but your grief will be turned into joy. Whenever a woman is in labor she has pain, because her hour has come; but when she gives birth to the child, she no longer remembers the anguish because of the joy that a child has been born into the world. Therefore you too have grief now; but I will see you again, and your heart will rejoice, and no one will take your joy away from you. In that day you will not question Me about anything. Truly, truly, I say to you, if you ask the Father for anything in My name, He will give it to you. Until now you have asked for nothing in My name; ask and you will receive, so that your joy may be made full." (cf. Hebrews 12:2)

2. We Experience our Joy Made Full.

John 15:11b ". . . that your joy may be made full."

1 Thessalonians 5:11b "Rejoice always."

"Joy is the flag which is flown from the castle of the heart when the King is in residence there" (Walter Knight).

ABOUT THE AUTHOR

James Michael Cecy was born in Toronto, Canada, and moved to California when he was eleven years old. He entered the U.S. Navy in 1969 and served on the aircraft carrier, USS Kitty Hawk, during the Vietnam War. On November 17, 1971, the day he was discharged from active naval duty, God stirred his heart and Jim trusted in Jesus Christ alone for his salvation. He quickly became an avid student of the Bible.

Jim was called to pastoral ministry in 1975, serving churches in California for over forty years. He has served as the Senior Pastor-Teacher at Campus Bible Church of Fresno (formerly Campus Baptist Church) since 1995. He is known for his commitment to Scripture, his enthusiastic expositional teaching, and his passion to equip God's people locally and globally.

Pastor Jim has a Bachelor of Arts degree in Speech-Communication from San Jose State University (1975). He earned his Master of Divinity degree in Bible Exposition from Talbot Theological Seminary (1978). In 1992 Jim received his Doctor of Ministry degree from Western Seminary (San Jose Campus).

Dr. Cecy is the founder and president of JARON Ministries International, a training ministry that equips pastors, missionaries, chaplains, and Christian leaders around the world. It is based in Fresno, California. In addition to his domestic ministry in North America, Jim has traveled extensively in numerous countries. His training seminars have reached hundreds of thousands of people on five continents. Jim has produced a variety of written, audio and video materials on a wide variety of subjects, which are available in a number of languages through JARON Ministries International (www.jaron.org) and his personal website (www.puritywar.com). His weekly expository sermons and messages are also available at www.campusbiblechurch.com

Jim and his wife Karon were married in 1973. They raised three daughters and, since 1987, have cared for twenty-three foster-children. Two, even as adults, remain a part of the family. Jim and Karon are abundantly blessed with an increasing number of grandchildren.

ABOUT JARON MINISTRIES INTERNATIONAL

JARON stands for *Jesus' Ambassadors Reaching Out to Nations.*

JARON exists to:

• Build a team of Ambassadors of Jesus Christ (pastors, missionaries, chaplains and Christian leaders) who will teach, disciple, and encourage Christian leaders in the United States and abroad.

• Serve as a ministry of instruction and motivation to local churches and Christian organizations through pulpit supply, classroom instruction, conferences, seminars, retreats, short-term ministries, and special services.

• Produce and provide biblically sound and currently relevant written, audio and video training materials.

• Provide biblical, Christ-centered counseling to those in need.

JARON is a registered non-profit organization (501c3) in the State of California. For further information about materials or seminars, please contact:

JARON Ministries International, Inc.,
4710 N. Maple Avenue, Fresno, CA. 93726
559-227-7997 www.jaron.org

OTHER MATERIALS BY DR. JIM CECY

- Abiding in Christ

- A.C.T. of Repentance

- Battling Believers; Scuffling Saints

- Beginning a Generation: Building a Legacy

- Communication in Marriage

- Family in Order

- Fruit of the Spirit-Filled Life

- Getting Along With People

- Marks of a Healthy Family

- Mastering My Habits

- Mastering the Scriptures: A Self-Study Course in Effective Bible Study

- Patience: The Quiet Virtue

- Profile of a Fearful Christian

- Profile of a Godly Family

- Profile of an Angry Christian

- Taming the Tongue

- The Emotions: God Energizers

- The Marriage Mission

- The Purity War: A Biblical Guide to Living in an Immoral World

- Wise Living in a Foolish Age: Studies in the Book of Proverbs

A number of other study materials by Dr. Cecy are available at www.jaron.org or www.campusbiblechurch.com or www.puritywar.com

SCRIPTURE INDEX

OLD TESTAMENT

FOREIGN WORD INDEX

Some words are presented as used in the biblical text and not in their root forms. Author also took some liberty and diverted from classic transliteration for easier pronunciation.

Agricultural Terms	Meaning
agronomist	*expert in field crop production*
botanist	*expert in the study of plant-life*
conks	*mushroom-like growths*
Codling Moth	*Cydia pomonella (See note)*
Cydia pomonella	*the Codling Moth*
D.O.V.	*fruit that is dried on the vine*
Durio zibethinus	*durian*
entomologist	*a scientist who studies insects*
fruticulture	*the science of fruit-growing*
ganoderma	*incurable wood rot fungus*
mummies	*dead fruit that houses insects*
Passiflora edulus	*passion fruit*
pheromones	*a secreted chemical that triggers*
	a hormonal response in the same species
pomology	*the study of fruit*
Punica granatum	*pomegranate*
refractometer	*instrument for measuring fruit sugar*
viticulture	*the science of grape-growing*

Anglo-Saxon	Meaning
feyth	*faith*

Filipino (Tagalog)	Meaning
mahal	*love, beloved, valuable, costly, expensive*
mahal kita	*"I love you."*

Greek	Meaning
aganaktesis	*great irritation*
agape	*love, value (noun)*
agapao	*love/value (verb)*
agapetos	*beloved*
agathos	*good*
agathosune	*goodness*
airo	*take away, cut off, lift or raise up*

aischrologia	*abusive, filthy speech*
anapausis	*rest, intermission, recreation*
asotia	*excessive and riotous*
athumeo	*dispirit, dishearten*
blasphemia	*slander, abusive language*
chara	*joy, delight*
chole	*gall, bile*
cholao	*be bitter angry, resentful*
chresteuomai	*show oneself useful*
chrestos	*kind, useful*
chrestotes	*kindness*
Chrestotai	*Kind Ones (title used in Church history to refer to Christians)*
Christos	*Christ, Anointed One*
dichostasia	*dissention*
didote	*"Do not give (a place to the devil)"*
doxa	*attribute, quality, glory*
echthra	*enmities*
eclipso	*black out, fail*
eirene	*peace*
ekdikesis	*vengeance*
ekdikeo	*take revenge*
egkrateia (enkrateia)	*self-control*
epidueto	*"do not let set (the sun on your anger)"*
epistrepho	*turn back, turn around, repent*
eris	*strife*
eritheia	*dispute*
erithizo	*exasperate, embitter*
eros	*love (sexual)*
georgos	*one who tills the soil*
hairesis	*faction*
hamartanete	*"Do not sin!"*
hesuchios	*tranquil, peaceable*
homo	*same*
homologeo	*confess, say same words*
hupomone	*endurance patience, steadfastness*
kakia	*malice*
karpos	*fruit*
kathareo	*prune, clean*
krauge	*clamor*
logeo	*speak*
lupeo	*offend, cause deep sorrow, grieve*
machomai	*anger-fight*
makrothumia	*patience*
mathetes	*learner, follower, disciple*

meno	*live, abide, remain, persevere*
metamorphoo	*change, transform*
metanoeo	*repent, change one's mind*
noutheteo	*admonish, warn, exhort*
orge	*anger*
orgizethe	*"Be angry!"*
orgizo	*become enraged, exasperated*
parogizo	*provoke*
parorgimos	*wrath*
pharmakeia	*sorcery, use of drugs in idolatry*
philadelphia	*brotherly love*
phileo	*love (relationally)*
philos	*friend*
phobeo	*fear, reverence, respond to power, run*
pikria	*bitterness*
pistis	*faith, belief, firm confidence*
pistos	*faithfulness, trustworthiness*
pisteuo	*believe (verb)*
praus	*gentle*
prautes	*gentleness*
sterizo	*strengthen*
sterizo	*fix, make firm, strengthen*
storge	*familial love*
tekton	*carpenter, construction worker*
thumos	*jealousy*

Hebrew	**Meaning**
Adonai Eloheinu	*"Oh, Lord, Our God"*
aph	*anger visible in snorting and rapid breathing*
Azazel	*goat of removal, scapegoat*
bahal	*fearful, terrified*
baruch	*blessed*
chemah	*feverous anger, poisonous wrath*
ebrah	*explosive and overflowing fury*
emunah	*faithfulness*
etseb	*harsh, offensive person who causes pain*
hamah	*shout, brawl, uproar, growl, noisy*
ka'as	*frustration, grieving, disappointment*
kaphah	*subdues, soothes, pacifies*
luts	*mock, deride, spilling criticism, mouthy*
maskil	*a teaching psalm*
madown	*strife, contention, discord, disagreement*
medan	*discord, division based on false reports*

Melech ha Olam	*King of the Universe*
mashiach	*messiah*
mits (myts)	*pressing, squeezing, wringing*
naka	*wounded, broken-spirited person*
pasha	*rebellion, breaking away from authority*
qashah	*hardened, disappointed person, stubborn*
qatser	*quick-tempered , pursuing own way*
ra'ah	*shepherd*
Raca (Aramaic)	*"Empty-head, good-for-nothing"*
ragaz	*moved to anger, shaking and trembling*
rinnah	*shouting for joy, cheering*
riyh	*argumentative person*
ruwach	*quiet, settled, well-placed*
selah	*pause, stop*
shalom	*peace, wholeness*
shaqat	*tranquil, undisturbed*
tipharah	*glory*
Yahweh Shalom	*The God of Peace*
Yeshua	*Jesus*
Yeshua ha Mashiach	*Jesus, the Messiah*
Yom Kippur	*Day of Atonement*
za'am	*indignation, backbiting, criticism*
za'aph	*enraged like a wild animal, roaring*

Latin

Meaning

ad nauseum	*"to sickness," disgusting extent*
ad infinitum	*"to infinity," repeated without end*
Cydia pomonella	*the Codling Moth*
Durio zibethinus	*durian*
emotio	*move out, emote*
et cetera	*and so on and so on*
Punica granatum	*pomegranate*
Soli Deo Gloria	*"Glory to God alone"*
terra firma	*firm land, earth*

NOTES

For information regarding other
materials by Dr. Jim Cecy
or hosting a seminar
please contact:

JARON MINISTRIES
INTERNATIONAL, INC.

4710 N. Maple Avenue
Fresno CA 93726
(559) 227-7997
www.jaron.org